OPEN SCHOOLS/ HEALTHY SCHOOLS

OPEN SCHOOLS/ HEALTHY SCHOOLS

Measuring Organizational Climate

Wayne K. Hoy
C. John Tarter
Robert B. Kottkamp

SAGE PUBLICATIONS
The International Professional Publishers
Newbury Park   London   New Delhi

Distributed by Corwin Press, Inc., A Sage Publications Company.

Address inquiries and orders to:

> Corwin Press, Inc.
> P.O. Box 2526
> Newbury Park, CA 91319

> SAGE Publications Ltd.
> 6 Bonhill Street
> London EC2A 4PU
> United Kingdom

> SAGE Publications India Pvt. Ltd.
> M-32 Market
> Greater Kailash I
> New Delhi 110 048 India

Printed in the United States of America

Library of Congress Cataloging-in-Publication Data

Hoy, Wayne K.
    Open schools/healthy schools: measuring organizational
climate / Wayne K. Hoy, C. John Tarter, Robert B. Kottkamp.
        p.   cm.
    Includes bibliographical references and index.
    ISBN 0-8039-3784-9
    1. School management and organization—Evaluation.
2. School environment—Evaluation.   3. Educational surveys.
I. Tarter, Clemens John.   II. Kottkamp, Robert B.   III. Title.
LB2823.H69   1991
379.1'54—dc20   90-20086
                                                            CIP

FIRST PRINTING, 1991

Sage Production Editor: Michelle R. Starika

Contents

Preface   vii

1. **The Nature of the Workplace**   1
    The Work Environment   2
    Climate or Culture?   7
    Organizational Climate: A Personality Metaphor   9
    Organizational Climate: A Health Metaphor   19

2. **The Organizational Climate Description
    Questionnaire for Elementary Schools**   25
    A Revised School Climate Instrument: The OCDQ-RE   26
    Dimensions of Elementary School Climate   30
    A Test of the Revised Climate Instrument   34
    Summary and Discussion   42
    Implications   44

3. **The Organizational Climate Description
    Questionnaire for Secondary Schools**   46
    School Climate: A Personal View   47
    Rationale for a New Measure: OCDQ-RS   48
    Developing a New Measure: OCDQ-RS   48
    Dimensions of Secondary School Climate   52
    A Test of the Revised Climate Instrument   54
    A Further Test   59
    Summary and Discussion   60
    Implications   62

4. **The Organizational Health Inventory for
    Secondary Schools**   64
    Pilot Study   65
    In Search of a Theory: A Parsonian Perspective   67
    Organizational Health Inventory
        for Secondary Schools: OHI   70
    Dimensions of Secondary School Health   73
    A Test of the New Instrument: OHI   75

Summary and Discussion   82
Implications   83

5. **The Organizational Health Inventory for Elementary Schools**   85

Pilot Study I   86
Pilot Study II   89
Organizational Health Inventory for Elementary
   Schools: OHI-E   90
Dimensions of Elementary School Health   93
Summary and Discussion   103
Implications   105

6. **Research Results on School Health and Climate**   107

Faculty Trust and School Health: OHI   107
Faculty Trust and School Climate: OCDQ-RS   114
Teacher Commitment and School Health: OHI   121
Teacher Commitment and School Climate: OCDQ-RS   127
School Effectiveness, School Climate, and
   School Health: A Comparison of the OHI
   and the OCDQ-RS   130
Faculty Trust, Effectiveness, and
   School Climate: OCDQ-RE   142
Summary   148
Implications   149

7. **Using the Health and Climate Instruments: A Guide to Action**   154

The Organizational Climate Description Questionnaire
   for Elementary Schools: The OCDQ-RE   155
The OCDQ-RE Form   159
The Organizational Climate Description Questionnaire
   for Secondary Schools: The OCDQ-RS   171
The OCDQ-RS Form   173
The Organizational Health Inventory
   for Secondary Schools: OHI   181
The OHI Form   184
The Organizational Health Inventory
   for Elementary Schools: OHI-E   193
The OHI-E Form   196
A Conclusion and a Caution   204

References   208
Index   215
About the Authors   219

Preface

This book is the culmination of nearly a decade of research and development. Its purpose is twofold: to provide educational researchers with a set of reliable and valid measures to study the nature of the school workplace, and to provide practitioners with a set of tools to evaluate their school climate with an aim toward organizational improvement.

We use personality and health metaphors to explore the organizational climates of schools. The openness of a school is measured by two new instruments: the Organizational Climate Description Questionnaire for Elementary (OCDQ-RE) and for Secondary (OCDQ-RS) Schools. Similarly, school health is determined by two new inventories: the Organizational Health Inventory for Elementary (OHI-E) and for Secondary (OHI) Schools. The conceptual foundations for these instruments as well as their technical details are described for researchers and scholars interested in using the frameworks and instruments in their own work. In addition, a summary of basic research demonstrates the utility of the measures in studying school outcomes. For practitioners, who may be less interested in the technical properties, there are step-by-step directions for administering, scoring, and interpreting the measures. For graduate students, we have presented a rough outline of a research agenda that provides many doctoral students with research projects for years to come.

The book will be read differently by researchers and practitioners. Researchers will want to read carefully the first six chapters, which provide an overview of the frameworks, technical details of the instruments, and research findings, and then browse the last chapter, which provides copies of the instruments and scoring directions. Practitioners will be interested in the first chapter, an overview, and the last chapter, which provides both a summary of the conceptual bases for each instrument and the practical directions needed to use the tools in professional and organizational development. In fact, we believe that Chapter 7, the last chapter, is a practical guide for administrators; it contains all the information necessary for administrators and teachers to use the climate measures.

The research and development of these instruments has involved a large number of people. The impetus for the project came in a theory and research course in 1980 as graduate students in educational administration at Rutgers University read and discussed the conceptual and empirical work of Andrew Halpin and Matthew Miles. That discussion lead John Feldman and John Mulhern to team with Carol Mulhaire, Arthur Travlos, Robert Kottkamp, and Wayne Hoy to form a research group to study organizational climate. The group provided the initial thrust for the research reported in this book, but it was merely a beginning. Since then, other graduate students, including Sharon Clover, Carolyn Hartley, Thomas Podgurski, Louise Witkoskie, and Deborah Pavignano have made important contributions to our work. Madhu Golhar helped us solve a number of difficult computer problems. Professors James Bliss and C. John Tarter have labored diligently the past five years to expand and test the instruments. In a real sense, the work is a joint effort of all of these graduate students and professors.

We encourage all interested researchers and practitioners to use any of the instruments in this book. There is no fee; simply reproduce the instrument and use it in your research or organizational development. We ask only that you share your results with us so that we can refine the measures, develop more comprehensive norms, and add to the body of knowledge about school climate. Address all correspondence to Professor Wayne K. Hoy, Graduate School of Education, Rutgers University, New Brunswick, New Jersey 08903.

Finally, we would be remiss if we did not acknowledge the contributions of Anita Woolfolk, Frank Fahy, and Robert Rimmer, all of whom read sections of the book and made useful contributions. It is a better book because of their suggestions.

1 The Nature of the Workplace

> The day-by-day behavior of the immediate superior and of other significant people in the managerial organization communicates something about their assumptions concerning management which is of fundamental significance. . . . Many subtle behavioral manifestations of managerial attitude create what is often referred to as the "psychological climate."
>
> — Douglas McGregor
> *The Human Side of Enterprise*

The nature of the school workplace has long been of interest to scholars of educational organizations, but it is only recently that other educational researchers, reformers, and school practitioners have become fascinated with the topics as well. The notion of the feel of the workplace has been referred to and studied under a variety of labels including organizational character, milieu, atmosphere, organizational ideology, ecology, field, situation, informal organization, and—more recently—climate and culture. Teachers, administrators, and parents readily use such terms as school climate and school culture with ease, yet there is little shared conception of specific meaning for any of these terms.

Why the allure of these general, abstract, and ambiguous terms? First, they make intuitive sense. They seem to capture something real about organizations; schools do have distinctive identities and atmospheres. But more than that, the notion of climate has become a component of the school effectiveness and reform movement in education. School climate, for example, has been identified with Edmonds's (1979) model of effective schools in which he argues that strong administrative leadership, high performance expectations, a safe and orderly environment, an emphasis on basic skills, and a system of monitoring student progress constitute a school climate that promotes academic achievement. Thus positive school climate has become part of the effective school rhetoric and is advocated by educational practitioners and reformers as a specific means for improving student achievement.

Nonetheless, two nagging problems remain. First, there is no common understanding of the meaning of school climate. The rhetorical use of climate has obscured the need for clear definition. Second, there is little systematic empirical evidence linking school climate as a scientific construct with academic achievement (Purkey & Smith, 1983; Ralph & Fennessey, 1983; Rowan, Bossert, & Dwyer, 1983). Indeed, until school climate is carefully defined and its dimensions mapped and measured, little progress will be made in determining which aspects of climate are directly related to student achievement.

Notwithstanding its likely relationship to student achievement, the climate of a school is an important concept in its own right. The extent to which the school atmosphere promotes openness, colleagueship, professionalism, trust, loyalty, commitment, pride, academic excellence, and cooperation is critical in developing a healthy work environment for teachers and administrators. Thus we view the climate of a school as a potential means for making schools more productive as well as an important end in itself.

The Work Environment

There are a variety of ways to conceptualize the nature of the workplace. It should be clear from the preceding brief introduction that we view the concept of organizational climate as a useful perspective. The following chapters of this book are devoted to developing several different climate frameworks for analyzing and measuring important dimensions of the school workplace. To be sure, organizational climate is not the only way to view the atmosphere of school; in fact, the notion of organizational culture also has received widespread public notoriety (Deal & Kennedy, 1982; Ouchi, 1981; Pascale & Athos, 1981; Peters & Waterman, 1982) as well as serious attention among organizational theorists and researchers (Frost, Moore, Louis, Lundberg, & Martin, 1985; Kilmann, Saxton, Serpa, & Associates, 1985; Ouchi & Wilkins, 1985; Pettigrew, 1979; Schein, 1985). With the publication of two "best sellers," Ouchi's (1981) *Theory Z* and Peters and Waterman's (1982) analysis of America's most successful business corporations, the concept of organizational culture was propelled into contemporary thought as a model for examining effective organizations. Not surprisingly, organizational culture has become part of the language not only of the business world but also of educators and researchers. Because the use of climate and culture has become commonplace in the discussion and study of schools, each concept is defined and then the two compared.[1]

Organizational Climate

The concept of organizational climate originated in the late 1950s as social scientists studied variations in work environments. Although researchers interested in educational organizations (Halpin & Croft, 1963; Pace & Stern, 1958) made the initial efforts to define and measure dimensions of organizational climate, the usefulness of the concept soon was recognized by scholars of business organizations (Tagiuri, 1968). Climate initially was used as a general notion to express the enduring quality of organizational life. Tagiuri (1968, p. 23) observed that "a particular configuration of enduring characteristics of the ecology, milieu, social system and culture would constitute a climate, as much as a particular configuration of personal characteristics constitute a personality." Gilmer (1966, p. 57) specified organizational climate as "those characteristics that distinguish the organization from other organizations and that influence the behavior of people in the organization." Litwin and Stringer (1968, p. 1) suggested that perception is a critical ingredient of climate and defined it as "a set of measurable properties of the work environment, based on the collective perceptions of the people who live and work in the environment and demonstrated to influence their behavior." According to Gilmer (1966), the notion of psychological climates was introduced in the industrial psychology literature by Gellerman

(1959), but other writers (Forehand & Gilmer, 1964; Halpin & Croft, 1963; Tagiuri, 1968) also have noted that definitions of climate are quite similar to early descriptions of personality types. In fact, the climate of an organization may be roughly conceived as the "personality" of the organization; that is, climate is to organization as personality is to individual.

Organizational Culture

Organizational culture also has become a vehicle for understanding the basic meaning and character of institutional life. Concern for the culture of the workplace is not new. In the 1930s and 1940s, both Barnard (1938) and Mayo (1945) stressed the significance of norms, sentiments, values, and emergent interactions in the workplace as they described the nature and function of the informal organization. Similarly, Selznick (1957) emphasized the significance of viewing organizations as institutions rather than merely rational organizational structures. Institutions, observed Selznick (1957, p. 17), are "infused with value beyond the technical requirements at hand." The infusion of value produces a distinctive identity of the organization that pervades all aspects of organizational life and provides a social integration that goes well beyond formal coordination and command. This distinctive character binds the individual to the organization and generates in its members a sense of loyalty and commitment to the organization.

The notion of organizational culture also clearly is an attempt to capture the basic feel or sense of the organization, but it brings with it conceptual complexity and confusion. No intact definition of culture from anthropology or sociology readily lends itself for use as an organizational construct. Understandably, there are a variety of definitions of the term. For example, Ouchi (1981, p. 41) sees organizational culture as "systems, ceremonies, and myths that communicate the underlying values and beliefs of the organization to its employees." Lorsch (1985, p. 84), in contrast, defines culture as "the beliefs top managers in a company share about how they should manage themselves and other employees." To Mintzberg (1983, p. 152) culture is the organization's ideology, that is, "a system of beliefs about the organization, shared by its members, that distinguishes it from other organizations." Wilkins and Patterson (1985, p. 265) argue that "an organization's culture consists largely of what people believe about what works and what does not," while Martin (1985, p. 95) asserts that "culture is an expression of people's deepest needs, a means of endowing their experiences with meaning." Schwartz and Davis (1981, p. 33) define culture as "a pattern of beliefs and expectations shared by the organization's members, that produces norms that powerfully shape the behavior of individuals or groups in organizations." In contrast, Schein (1985, p. 6) argues that culture should be reserved for "the deeper level of *basic assumptions and beliefs* that are shared by members of an organization, that operate unconsciously, and that define in a basic 'taken-for-granted' fashion an organization's view of itself and its environment" (emphasis in original).

Although differences exist in conceptions, there is common ground for defining culture. *Organizational culture is a system of shared orientations that hold the unit together and give it a distinctive identity.* There is, however, some disagreement about what is shared. Are they norms, values, philosophies, beliefs, expectations, myths, ceremonies, or artifacts? One way to begin to untangle this problem of definition is to examine culture at different levels.

Culture can be manifest in norms, shared values, or basic assumptions, each occurring at a different level of abstraction (Kilmann et al., 1985; Schein, 1985; Hoy & Miskel, 1987). In its most abstract form (highest level of abstraction), culture is the collective manifestation of basic assumptions about the nature of relationships, human nature, truth, reality, and the environment (Dyer, 1985). For example, a tacit assumption about the nature of truth answers the question of whether truth is revealed by external authority figures or is determined by a process of personal investigation and testing. When a pattern of basic assumptions has been invented, discovered, or developed by the organization that is useful in defining itself, an organizational culture exists. Such assumptions are difficult to identify, however, because they are abstract, unconscious, and consequently hard to confront. Schein (1985) argues that an elaborate set of procedures is necessary to decipher the tacit assumptions of organizational members. The process is based on a combination of anthropological and clinical techniques, which involves a series of encounters and joint explorations between the investigator and motivated informants who live in the organization and embody its culture. The joint effort includes extensive data gathering that explores the history of the organization, critical events, organizational structure, myths, legends, artifacts, stories, and ceremonies. Questionnaires are rejected as devices to identify tacit assumptions; it is argued that, at best, such instruments produce only some of the espoused values of group members.

At a middle range of abstraction, culture is a set of shared values. Values are shared conceptions of the desirable. They are reflections of the more basic assumptions of culture that define what members should do in the organization to be successful. When participants are asked to explain why they behave the way they do, their answers often reflect the core values of the organization. Values define the character of the organization and give it identity and a sense of mission. Actions become infused with organizational values such as openness, trust, cooperation, intimacy, or teamwork. Stories, ceremonies, and rituals reinforce the core values. Much of the contemporary work on organizational culture is at this middle level of abstraction. For example, Ouchi's (1981) Theory Z describes a corporate culture where commitment, cooperation, teamwork, trust, loyalty, and egalitarianism are basic, and Peters and Waterman (1982) suggest that successful business organizations have cultures that value action, service, innovation, people, and quality.

In contrast to the abstract conception of culture as a set of tacit assumptions, or the middle range notion of culture as shared values, a more concrete perspective emerges when behavioral norms are used as the basic shared orientations of culture. Norms are typically unwritten and informal expectations that affect behavior. They are more overt than either core assumptions or shared values; consequently, they provide a more tangible means for helping people understand the cultural aspects of the organization. Further, norms can be changed more easily than either values or tacit assumptions. Norms are universal phenomena; they are essential and pervasive, but sometimes malleable. Kilmann et al. (1985, p. 361), moreover, suggest that with a little prodding and a few illustrations, group members quickly begin to enumerate norms; in fact, they revel in being able to articulate what beforehand was not formally stated and rarely discussed.

Prevailing norms map the "way things are" around the organization. For example, "Around here, it is all right to admit mistakes, as long as you don't make them again," or "We don't wash our dirty linen in public."

Each of the three views of culture has advantages as well as disadvantages. The more abstract formulations offer opportunities for rich and penetrating analyses of the workplace and seem to be preferred by theorists interested in understanding culture rather than managing it. Organizational participants, however, have difficulty openly identifying their tacit premises and discussing their basic assumptions of organizational life; in fact, they define such activities as merely academic (Kilmann et al., 1985). On the other hand, those definitions of culture that focus on behavioral norms are more useful to people who are interested in assessing and managing organizational cultures, albeit in a limited and, some would argue, superficial way.

Climate or Culture?

Which is a more useful framework for the study and analysis of the school workplace? It depends. Both concepts are attempts to identify significant properties of organizations; in fact, definitions of climate and culture often are blurred. A useful distinction is that culture consists of shared assumptions and ideologies, while climate is defined by shared perceptions of behavior (Ashforth, 1985). To be sure, the conceptual leap from shared assumptions (culture) to shared perceptions (climate) is not large, but the difference is real and seems meaningful. If the purpose of the analysis is to determine the underlying forces that motivate behavior in organizations or to focus on the language and symbolism of the organization, then a cultural approach seems preferable. But if the aim is to describe the actual behavior of organizational members with the purpose of managing and changing it, then a climate approach seems more desirable.

The two approaches come from different intellectual traditions. Scholars of climate use quantitative techniques and multivariate analyses to identify patterns of perceived behavior in organizations. They usually assume that organizations are rational instruments to accomplish purpose; thus they search for rational patterns. Their background and training are more likely to be in multivariate statistics and psychology or social psychology, rather than in ethnography and anthropology or sociology. Moreover, these researchers tend to be interested in climate as an independent variable, that is, how climate influences organizational outcomes. The goal of studying climate often is to determine effective strategies of change.

In contrast, scholars of organizational culture tend to use the qualitative and ethnographic techniques of anthropology and sociology to examine the character or atmosphere of organizations. Cultural analysis derives from two basic intellectual traditions: holistic studies in the tradition of Radcliffe-Brown (1952) and Malinowski (1961), which focus on the organization as a whole and how its cultural elements function to maintain a social structure; and semiotic studies in the tradition of Geertz (1973) and Goodenough (1971), which focus on language and symbolism. Some who study culture take a natural-systems view of organizations and conclude that the culture of an organization is a natural outgrowth of a particular time and place. As such, it is not responsive to attempts at manipulation and change (Ouchi & Wilkins, 1985).

In brief, researchers of climate usually deal with perceptions of behavior, use survey research techniques, employ multivariate statistics, have their intellectual roots in industrial and social psychology, assume a rational-systems perspective, examine climate as an independent variable, and are interested in using the knowledge to improve organizations. In contrast, scholars of culture typically focus on assumptions, values, and norms; use ethnographic techniques; eschew quantitative analysis; have their intellectual roots in anthropology and sociology; and assume a natural-systems perspective. There are, of course, exceptions to these patterns, but they do seem to be the dominant ones in the general literature on organizations as well as in specific work on educational organizations (Anderson, 1982; Miskel & Ogawa, 1988; Ouchi & Wilkins, 1985). Basic differences between organizational climate and culture are presented in Figure 1.1.

Organizational climate is the framework used to analyze the nature of schools in this book. Our concern is a pragmatic one. How can one examine the work and managerial atmospheres of schools systematically and efficiently? In our attempt to answer

	CLIMATE	CULTURE
DISCIPLINE:	Psychology & Social Psychology	Anthropology & Sociology
METHOD:	Survey research Multivariate Statistics	Ethnographic Techniques Linguistic Analysis
LEVEL OF ABSTRACTION:	Concrete	Abstract
CONTENT:	Perceptions of Behavior	Assumptions & Ideology

Figure 1.1. A Comparison of the Perspectives of Organizational Climate and Culture

this question we use the research techniques and multivariate statistical methods of industrial and social psychologists to discover patterns of teacher and administrator behaviors in schools. To that end, we provide several conceptualizations of school climate and reliable measures for each. Organizational climate is viewed using a personality metaphor, in which we analyze the openness of the organization, and using a health metaphor, in which we examine the general well-being of the interpersonal relationships in the organization.

Organizational Climate: A Personality Metaphor

Following the lead of industrial and social psychologists, organizational climate is a general term that refers to teachers' perceptions of their work environment; it is influenced by formal and informal relationships, personalities of participants, and leadership in the organization. Tagiuri's (1968) formulation of climate as a molar concept is composed of four descriptive dimensions—ecology, milieu, social system, and culture—that have been used to examine the literature on school climate (Anderson, 1982; Miskel & Ogawa, 1988). *Ecology* refers to the physical and material aspects of schools; *milieu* consists of the social aspects of particular individuals and groups in schools; *social system* deals with the patterns of relationships that exist between individuals and groups in organizations; and *culture* refers to belief systems, values, and cognitive structure. Most studies of school climate focus only on the social system or cultural dimensions (Anderson, 1982). Our analysis of climate is a social systems one.

Put simply, the organizational climate of a school is the set of internal characteristics that distinguishes one school from another and influences the behavior of its members. In more specific terms: *School climate is the relatively enduring quality of the school environment that is experienced by participants, affects their behavior, and is based on their collective perception of behavior in schools* (Hoy & Miskel, 1987; Tagiuri, 1968).

Organizational Climate of Schools

Undoubtedly the most well-known conceptualization and measurement of organizational climate in schools is the pioneering study of elementary schools by Halpin and Croft (1962, 1963). Their approach was to identify the critical aspects of teacher-teacher and teacher-principal interactions in schools. To that end they constructed the Organizational Climate Descriptive Questionnaire (OCDQ) that portrays the climate of an elementary school. School climate is construed as organizational "personality." Indeed, in conceptualizing the climates of schools along an open to closed continuum, Halpin and Croft were influenced by Milton Rokeach's (1960) analysis of personality types.

Given the fact that the early work on the OCDQ was the impetus for our analysis of school climate, we discuss in some detail the development of the original OCDQ to help the reader understand the basis of subsequent decisions in the refinement of the revised versions of the climate measures. The methods employed in constructing the questionnaires, the assumptions undergirding the approach, and some of the weaknesses and limitations are explained. Our discussion of the OCDQ is drawn heavily from Halpin and Croft's (1962) U.S. Office of Education research report.

An overview of the OCDQ. The OCDQ is an attempt to map and measure the domain of the climates of elementary schools along a continuum from open to closed. The instrument is composed of 64 Likert-type items that teachers and principals use to describe the interaction patterns in their schools. The items are short, simple, descriptive statements that measure eight dimensions of organizational life. Four of the dimensions or subtests refer to characteristics of the group and four pertain to the characteristics of the principal as leader. The eight dimensions are as follows:

CHARACTERISTICS OF THE GROUP

    (1) Disengagement

    (2) Hindrance

    (3) Esprit

    (4) Intimacy

BEHAVIOR OF LEADER

    (5) Aloofness

    (6) Production Emphasis

    (7) Thrust

    (8) Consideration

The names of the subtests merely suggest the behavior that each taps; subsequently each dimension is defined in detail.

    Profiles for schools on these eight dimensions were examined to determine if basic patterns existed. They did. Six configurations were identified and arrayed along a rough continuum. The open climate was portrayed as one low on disengagement, low on hindrance, high on esprit, average on intimacy, low on aloofness, low on production emphasis, high on thrust, and high on consideration; the closed climate had the opposite profile. Intermediary climates of autonomous, controlled, familiar, and paternal also were identified and described in terms of the eight dimensions and the relative degree of openness in the interaction patterns.

Research strategy. The development of the OCDQ was prompted by four factors: (1) schools differ markedly in their "feel"; (2) morale does not adequately capture this difference in feel among schools; (3) talented principals who take jobs in schools where improvement is necessary often are immobilized by a recalcitrant faculty; and (4) the notion of the "personality" of a school is intriguing in itself. Obviously, a climate profile should be helpful to administrators and teachers as they seek to improve the atmospheres of their schools.

The general approach used to conceptualize and measure the organizational climate of schools was empirical and statistical. Halpin and Croft developed an extensive set of descriptive items to modify important aspects of teacher and administrative behavior. A guiding assumption of the research was that a desirable organizational climate is one in which leadership acts emerge easily, from whatever source. If a school, or any organization for that matter, is to accomplish its tasks, leadership is essential; but leadership acts can be initiated by the formal leader or by the teachers. Thus items were written describing both behavior of the teachers interacting with each other as well as teacher-principal interactions. Teachers and administrators were asked to respond to Likert-type items that characterized behavior in their school; they were asked to indicate the extent to which each statement occurred in their schools. The following are typical examples of the items:

(1) The principal is in the building before teachers arrive.
(2) Teachers ask nonsensical questions at faculty meetings.
(3) The rules set by the principal are never questioned.
(4) Most of the teachers here accept the faults of their colleagues.
(5) Teachers talk about leaving the school.

The scale used for respondents to record school behavior was defined by the following four categories:

(1) Rarely occurs
(2) Sometimes occurs
(3) Often occurs
(4) Very frequently occurs

In constructing the items for the OCDQ, a basic two-pronged requirement was used. The researchers wanted items that would yield a reasonable amount of consensus within a given school, but ones that also would provide discrimination among schools. The ultimate test of the item was empirical; that is, items were subjected to numerous tests, refinements, and iterations. Answers to statements of the type used in the OCDQ are measures of individual perceptions, not fact. Teachers in a school may not—in fact, likely will not—agree completely with each other on the behavior patterns in the school. Items that survived the empirical tests were ones that had reasonable consensus. Of course, the question can be raised, "Is that really the behavior of the principal or group?" It is an unanswerable question. Halpin and Croft take the position that how the leader or group really behaves is less important than how its members perceive it. It is their perceptions of behavior that motivate action. Hence, the organizational climate of a school is the faculty's consensus in perception of school behavior. It is assumed that the consensus represents a dependable index of "what is out there" and is instrumental in influencing organizational behavior.

Using a series of empirical, conceptual, and statistical tests, the initial 1,000 descriptive statements in the item bank were drastically reduced until on the fourth iteration of the instrument, 64 items remained and comprised the final version of the OCDQ (Halpin & Croft, 1962). This version of the measure was administered to the entire professional staff of 71 elementary schools drawn from six different regions of the country. Factor analysis revealed that the 64 items could be grouped into eight factors or subtests. Four of the subtests referred to the characteristics of the faculty group and four described aspects of the principal-teacher interactions. These clusters of items were named and designated the eight critical dimensions of organizational climate. Examples of items in each of the subtests are given in Table 1.1, and definitions of the eight dimensions of the OCDQ are found in Table 1.2.

Taken together, these eight subtest scores map the climate profile of a given school. Before the school climate profiles are plotted, all the scores are standardized with a mean of 50 and a standard deviation of 10; hence, it is easy to see at a glance which scores are above and below the mean and by how much. Figure 1.2 represents the climate profiles of two contrasting schools in the

Table 1.1 The Dimensions of the OCDQ

Characteristics of Faculty Behavior

1. **Disengagement** refers to the teachers' tendency to not be "with it", that is, "to go through the motions" without commitment to the task at hand.

2. **Hindrance** refers to the teachers' feelings that the principal burdens them with routine duties, committee work, and other unnecessary busy work.

3. **Esprit** refers to morale growing out of a sense of both task accomplishment and the satisfaction of social needs.

4. **Intimacy** refers to the teachers' enjoyment of warm and friendly social relations with each other.

Characteristics of Principal Behavior

5. **Aloofness** refers to formal and impersonal principal behavior; the principal goes by the "book" and maintains social distance from subordinates.

6. **Production Emphasis** refers to close supervision. The principal is highly directive and not sensitive to faculty feedback.

7. **Thrust** refers to dynamic behavior in which the principal attempts to "move the organization" through the example the principal personally sets for teachers.

8. **Consideration** refers to warm, friendly behavior by the principal. The principal tries to be helpful and do a little something extra for the faculty.

Halpin and Croft study. One of the schools, the one plotted with the broken line, was relatively high in esprit, thrust, and consideration; low in hindrance, disengagement, production emphasis, and aloofness; and average in intimacy—a profile that was subsequently labeled an open school climate.

After the profiles were determined for each of the schools, Halpin and Croft used factor analytic techniques to identify six basic clusters of profiles; that is, the 71 elementary schools were grouped into six categories in which the schools in each set were similar. Thus six basic school climates were arrayed along a rough continuum from open to closed: open, autonomous, controlled, familiar, paternal, closed. For each of the six climate types, a prototypic profile was developed. Table 1.3 outlines the patterns of

Table 1.2 Sample Items for the OCDQ Subtests

Disengagement
-- Teachers ask nonsensical questions in faculty meetings.
-- Teachers talk about leaving the school system.

Hindrance
-- Routine duties interfere with the job of teaching.
-- Teachers have too many committee requirements.

Esprit
-- The morale of teachers is high.
-- Teachers in this school show much school spirit.

Intimacy
--Teachers invite other faculty members to visit them at home.
-- Teachers' closest friends are other faculty members at this school.

Aloofness
-- The rules set by the principal are never questioned.
-- Faculty meetings are mainly principal-report meetings.

Production Emphasis
-- The principal checks the subject-matter ability of teachers.
-- The principal corrects teachers' mistakes.

Thrust
--The principal sets an example by working hard.
-- The principal uses constructive criticism.

Consideration
-- The principal helps teachers solve personal problems.
-- The principal does personal favors for teachers.

these six prototypic profiles. Using the characteristics of the prototypes, it is possible to sketch a behavioral picture of each of the climate types. To illustrate, we developed composites for each of the two extremes—the open and closed climates.

The open and closed climate. The distinctive character of the *open climate* is its high degree of thrust and esprit and low disengagement. This combination suggests a climate in which both the principal and faculty are genuine and open in their interactions.

Table 1.3 Characteristics of Prototypic Profiles for Each Climate Type

Climate Dimension	Open	Autono-mous	Controlled	Familiar	Paternal	Closed
			Climate Type			
Disengagement	Low*	Low	Low	High	High	High*
Hindrance	Low	Low	High	Low	Low	High
Esprit	High*	High	High	Average	Low	Low*
Intimacy	Average	High	Low	High	Low	Average
Aloofness	Low	High	High	Low	Low	High
Production Emphasis	Low	Low	High	Low	High	High
Thrust	High*	Average	Average	Average	Average	Low*
Consideration	High	Average	Low	High	High	Low

*Salient characteristic of the open and closed climates

The principal leads by example (thrust), providing the proper blend of direction and support depending on the situation. Teachers work well together (esprit) and are committed to the task at hand (low disengagement). Given the "reality-centered" and considerate leadership of the principal as well as the commitment of the faculty, there is no need for burdensome paperwork (hindrance), close supervision (production emphasis), or impersonality and a plethora of rules and regulations (aloofness). Leadership develops easily and appropriately as it is needed. The open school climate is preoccupied with neither task achievement nor social needs, but both emerge freely. In brief, behavior of both the principal and faculty is authentic.

The *closed climate* is the antithesis of the open. Thrust and esprit are low and disengagement is high. The principal and teachers simply appear to go through the motions (disengagement), with the principal stressing routine trivia and unnecessary busywork (hindrance), rules and regulations (aloofness), and unconcern (low consideration). The teachers respond with minimal levels of morale (low esprit) and commitment (high disengagement). The principal's ineffective leadership is further seen in authoritarian and controlling behavior (production emphasis), formal declarations and impersonality (aloofness), as well as lack of consideration and unwillingness to provide a dynamic personal

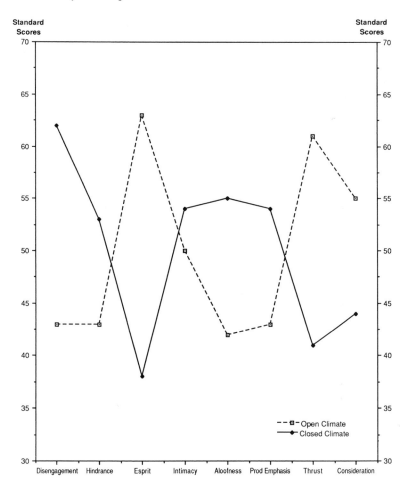

Figure 1.2. Comparison of an Open and Closed Organizational Climate

example. These misguided tactics, which are not taken seriously by the faculty, produce teacher frustration and apathy. They lead to an atmosphere of "game playing" in which the behavior of both the principal and teachers in the closed climate is not genuine; in fact, inauthenticity in teacher and principal behaviors pervades the school. The profiles of the prototypes for elementary schools with open and closed climates are graphically portrayed in Figure 1.2.

Criticisms, weaknesses, and limitations of the OCDQ. Since the inception of the OCDQ, there has been controversy over the usefulness of the six discrete climates identified by Halpin and Croft. For example, Robert J. Brown's (1964) attempted replication of the OCDQ findings with a sample of Minnesota elementary schools produced eight rather than six climate types; in fact, he argued that although the climate continuum from open to closed might be useful, it was not advisable to place schools into discrete climates. A number of other researchers (Andrews, 1965; Silver, 1983; Watkins, 1968) also have questioned the utility of the discrete climate types. Indeed Halpin and Croft were themselves circumspect about the clarity of the "middle climates" and described the placing of the six climate types along the open to closed continuum as a crude ranking.

An alternative to categorizing schools into discrete climates is to determine the relative openness or closedness of the climate. That is, an index of openness of school climate can be created by adding the esprit and thrust scores for each school and then subtracting from that sum the disengagement score; the higher the score, the more open the climate of the school (Hoy & Miskel, 1987). Appleberry and Hoy (1969) demonstrated the validity of the method, and others have used the method to examine the relationship between openness and other variables (Hoy, 1972a; Mullins, 1976; Schwandt, 1978).

The OCDQ also has been criticized for not being well suited for the study of urban schools or secondary schools (Carver & Sergiovanni, 1969; Halpin, 1966; Miskel & Ogawa, 1988). Not only is there a problem with the vagueness of the middle climate categories, but the OCDQ was designed to measure the climate of elementary schools, not secondary facilities. Secondary schools are different than elementary schools in a number of important ways, for example, size, specialization, and culture. Not surprisingly, urban schools and secondary schools invariably have closed climates when the OCDQ is used.

Paula Silver (1983) argued that the conceptual framework of the OCDQ lacks a clear logic, is cumbersome, and lacks parsimony. For example, although the hindrance subtest is described as a dimension of teacher behavior, it refers to administrative demands rather than interpersonal behavior of teachers. Other conceptual problems plague the instrument. Production emphasis is mislabeled; it measures close and autocratic control by the principal, not an emphasis on high production standards. Directive or controlling behavior is a more apt description of this aspect of principal behavior. Halpin and Croft (1962) themselves question the adequacy of the concept of consideration by suggesting that two or more facets of considerate behavior have been confounded within a single measure.

It is also strange to describe the climate of an organization and not deal with the prime participants—in this case, the students. Perhaps the OCDQ should more appropriately be called a measure of administrative or managerial climate. Clearly the focus is on teacher-teacher and teacher-administrator behaviors and not on teacher-student or student-student interactions.

The OCDQ has spawned hundreds of studies during the past three decades. Times and conditions have changed dramatically since the appearance of the OCDQ, yet there has been little effort to revise the instrument, notwithstanding the fact that many of the items no longer measure what they were intended to measure; that some of the subtests no longer are valid (e.g., aloofness); that the reliabilities of some of the subtests are low; and that time has rendered many of the items irrelevant to contemporary school organizations (Hayes, 1973; Hoy & Miskel, 1987). One purpose of this book is to describe in detail two new and simplified versions of the OCDQ; an elementary OCDQ-RE and a secondary OCDQ-RS are developed in the succeeding chapters.

Organizational Climate: A Health Metaphor

Another perspective for analyzing the nature of the workplace is organizational health. The health metaphor initially was used by Matthew Miles (1965) to examine the properties of schools. A healthy organization is one that not only survives in its environment, but continues to grow and prosper over the long term. An organization on any given day may be effective or ineffective, but healthy organizations avoid persistent ineffectiveness. Miles developed a configuration of healthy organization that consists of 10 important properties. The first three aspects reflect the task needs of a social system; the second set of properties describes its maintenance needs; and the final group of characteristics are growth and development needs.

The task needs are termed goal focus, communication adequacy, and optimal power equalization.

Healthy organizations have a *goal focus.* Participants understand the goals of the organization and accept them as realistic ends. Moreover, the goals also must be appropriate—that is, consistent with the demands of the environment; in fact, appropriateness may be the most critical feature. The salient question is always: Is this an appropriate goal given the range of other options?

Because organizations typically are much more complex than small groups, the communication of information is essential to the well-being of the system. *Communication adequacy* is critical in healthy organizations. Information needs to travel reasonably well. The system must be relatively distortion-free with members easily receiving the information they need to function efficiently. Such an efficient communication system enables the organization to sense internal strain and conflict and then promptly deal with them.

In healthy organizations there is *optimal power equalization.* That is, the distribution of power and influence is equitable. Subordinates exert influence upward and they perceive that their superiors can do likewise. The exertion of influence, however, rests on competence and knowledge rather than position, charisma, or other factors not related to the problem at hand. Collaboration rather than coercion imbues the healthy organization.

A second group of properties deals with the internal state of the organization, specifically with the maintenance needs of its members. These elements are resource utilization, cohesiveness, and morale.

Healthy organizations use their resources, especially their personnel, effectively (*resource utilization*). There is minimal internal strain; the people are neither overloaded nor idle. The fit between the personal needs of participants and the role demands of the organization is good. People in healthy organizations like their jobs and have a positive sense that they are learning and growing as they contribute to the organization.

Cohesiveness refers to a clear sense of identity participants have with the organization. Healthy organizations have members who are attracted to the organization, take pride in their membership, and wish to remain. They are influenced by the organization and exert their influence in a collaborative fashion. In brief, they are proud of the organization and glad they are part of it. *Morale* is a group concept. It is the sum of individual sentiments, centered around feelings of well-being and satisfaction as contrasted with feelings of discomfort and dissatisfaction. In healthy organizations the dominant personal response of organizational members is a sense of well-being.

Finally, there are four more properties of organizational health. Innovativeness, autonomy, adaptation, and problem-solving adequacy deal with the organization's needs for growth and change.

Healthy organizations invent new procedures when confronted with problems—procedures that enable them to move toward new objectives, produce new products, and diversify. Such systems grow, develop, and change rather than remain formalized and standardized. *Innovativeness* is the organization's ability to invent new procedures, move to new goals and objectives, and become more differentiated over time.

Autonomy describes the organization's relationship with its environment. Healthy organizations do not respond either passively or destructively to the environment. Rather, they demonstrate an ability to remain somewhat independent from negative forces in the environment; they use the environment constructively.

Adaptation is closely related to autonomy. Healthy organizations have effective contact with their surroundings. When environmental forces do not match organizational objectives, a problem-solving and restructuring strategy emerges to cope with the issue. In short, the organization has the ability to bring about corrective changes in itself.

All organizations, indeed all social systems, have problems and strains. Healthy organizations, just as healthy people, have troubles. *Problem-solving adequacy* describes the way organizations handle their difficulties. Argyris (1964) suggested that effective systems solve their problems with minimal difficulty and, once solved, they stay solved. In the process, problem-solving mechanisms are not weakened but strengthened.

Thus Miles (1965) postulated that healthy organizations are characterized by goal focus, communication adequacy, power equalization, resource utilization, cohesiveness, morale,

Table 1.4 Miles's Dimensions of Organizational Health

TASK NEEDS

Goal Focus - Goals are reasonably clear to the system members as well as accepted by them. The goals must also be realistic and appropriate-consistent with the demands of the environment.

Communication Adequacy - Communication is relatively distortion free; it produces a good and prompt sensing of internal strains. Members have the information that they need to function efficiently.

Optimal Power Equalization - The distribution of influence is relatively equitable. Subordinates can exert influence upward, and they perceive their superiors can do likewise.

MAINTENANCE NEEDS

Resource Utilization - Personnel is used effectively. The organization is neither overloaded nor idling. There is a good fit between individual needs and organizational demands.

Cohesiveness - Members are attracted to the organization and wish to remain. They are influenced by the organization and exert their own influence on the organization in a collaborative fashion.

Morale - The organization displays a general sense of well-being and group satisfaction.

GROWTH AND DEVELOPMENT NEEDS

Innovativeness - The organization invents new procedures, moves toward new goals, and becomes more differentiated over time.

Autonomy - The organization is not passive to the environment. It demonstrates some independence from outside forces.

Adaptation - The organization has the ability to bring about corrective changes in itself to grow and develop.

Problem-Solving Adequacy - Problems are solved with minimal energy, and problem-solving mechanisms are not weakened, but maintained or strengthened.

---

innovativeness, autonomy, adaptation, and effective problem solving. These 10 dimensions of a healthy organization are summarized in Table 1.4.

Organizational Health of Schools

One of the earliest published attempts to measure school health using Miles's conceptual framework was performed by Kimpston and Sonnabend (1975). Using the 10 critical dimensions of organizational health, they developed an Organizational Health Description Questionnaire (OHDQ). Likert items were written to measure each of the dimensions of health—five items for each dimension. A factor analysis of the instrument, however, was disappointing. Only five interpretable factors were identified and, of Miles's dimensions, only the autonomy and innovativeness factors were found in pure form. The other three factors were combinations of Miles's properties; for example, a factor called decision making contained optimal power equalization and problem-solving ability items, and school-community relations was a combination of communication adequacy and resource utilization. In fact, of the 50 items comprising the OHDQ, 30 did not load clearly on any of the five factors determined by the factor analysis and were discarded.

Clearly, there are some serious problems with this instrument. Only five of the dimensions were found as expected. The subtests measuring the two pure dimensions of health—autonomy and innovativeness—were unreliable. A reliability coefficient of .48 was reported for autonomy, and for innovativeness the error variance was greater than the individual variance. Indeed, except for the factor called interpersonal relations, a three-item variable composed of morale and cohesiveness items (reliability coefficient = .72), all of the subtests of the instrument had exceedingly low reliabilities. Moreover, no validity evidence is provided for any of the subtests. Miles (1975) himself, although applauding their effort, notes many of the same reservations about Kimpston and Sonnabend's (1975) organizational health questionnaire.

There have been other attempts to operationalize Miles's perspective on organizational health. Fairman and his colleagues (Childers & Fairman, 1985; Clark & Fairman, 1983) at the University of Arkansas have developed an Organizational Health Instrument that they use in in-service activities with schools. Unfortunately, their instrument seems to suffer from many of the same psychometric problems that have been described.

The literature points to a number of difficulties in the development of health inventories. First, the 10 characteristics proposed by Miles may not be mutually exclusive. Second, it is no easy feat to construct a measure of organizational health. Third, the appropriate unit of analysis for developing an organizational health instrument for schools is the organization, not the individual. Unfortunately, most developers of health instruments use the individual. Finally, factor analysis is no substitute for careful and extensive pilot work. A series of empirical tests and factor analyses is required to build a reliable and valid measure of organizational health. In Chapters 4 and 5, we turn our attention to that task.

Note

1. We have drawn heavily upon two sources (Hoy & Miskel, 1987; Hoy, 1990) for our analysis of school health and climate in this chapter.

2 The Organizational Climate Description Questionnaire for Elementary Schools

Anyone who visits more than a few schools notes quickly how schools differ from each other in their "feel." In one school the teachers and the principal are zestful and exude confidence. . . . In a second school the brooding discontent of the teachers is palpable; the principal tries to hide his incompetence and his lack of a sense of direction behind a cloak of authority, and yet he wears this cloak poorly because the attitude he displays to others vacillates randomly between the obsequious and the officious.

—Andrew W. Halpin
Theory and Research in Administration

Just as individuals have personalities, so too do schools. It is this "personality" of the school that Halpin (1966) described as the organizational climate of the school; that is, personality is to the individual what organizational climate is to the organization. Andrew Halpin's pioneering work mapping the domain of the organizational climate of schools served as the beginning point for the development of a new instrument to measure the climate of schools.

In the last chapter, we described Halpin's development of the Organizational Climate Description Questionnaire (OCDQ), an instrument that is nearly 30 years old and showing the signs of age. Questions about the reliability and validity of both items and subtests persist. Conceptual problems also abound: there is a lack of underlying logic to the framework; the meanings of some of the dimensions are vague; the climate continuum is ambiguous and likely not a single continuum; and the perspective excludes students. Finally, the unit of analysis in the development of the original OCDQ was the individual; the appropriate analytic unit is the school. In this chapter we detail the development of a new measure of school climate, the Organizational Climate Description Questionnaire for elementary schools (OCDQ-RE).[1]

A Revised School Climate Instrument: The OCDQ-RE

The development of the revised instrument involved a number of steps, each of which is described in some detail. First, the original items of the OCDQ were evaluated. Then new items were generated and assessed. Next, a pilot study was performed to deal with the unit-of-analysis issue, examine the conceptual validity of the items, reduce the number of items, and identify the factor structure of the revised OCDQ. Finally, the final version of the OCDQ-RE was field tested and the stability of its factor structure and its validity were assessed.

Item Generation

The first step in revising the OCDQ was to appraise the existing items in the OCDQ by examining Halpin and Croft's rotated item factor matrix for the original 64 items in their instrument. Factor loadings for all items within each subtest were scrutinized. Items with low factor loadings either were discarded or revised. Eventually 24 of the 64 items were discarded.

Next, it was decided to broaden the scope of the new instrument by writing items that focused on students and teacher-student interactions. In particular, items were written to measure the pupil control behavior of teachers and the academic press of the school. Pupil control is a basic problem faced by public schools

(Doyle, 1983; Hoy, 1968, 1969; Packard, 1988; Waller, 1932; and Willower, Eidell, & Hoy, 1967) and academic press has emerged from the school effectiveness literature as a critical ingredient of effective schools (Bossert, Dwyer, Rowan, & Lee, 1982; Edmonds, 1979; Purkey & Smith, 1983).

Items were developed by the researchers independently and jointly, but no items were included unless there was agreement on the following criteria:

(a) each item reflected a property of the school;
(b) the statement was clear and concise;
(c) the statement had content validity; and
(d) the statement had discriminatory potential.

Fourteen items were developed to measure the academic press of the school; 17 new items were generated to measure pupil control behavior; and new items were added to subtests with only a few items (subtests such as hindrance, intimacy, and consideration).

Special attention also was given to hindrance, production emphasis, and aloofness because of the lack of conceptual clarity of these dimensions. Although Halpin and Croft (1962) considered hindrance a teacher dimension, we viewed the concept as a characteristic of principal behavior because the concept reflects administrative demands rather than interpersonal behavior of teachers. Similarly, the concept of production emphasis seems poorly labeled. Items that described the principal's behavior as directing or controlling supplemented the remaining "production emphasis" items that focused on autocratic behavior. Aloofness probably was the weakest of the original OCDQ subtests and, in view of Hayes's (1973) evidence and conclusion that the items simply no longer measured aloofness, an entire new set of items was written.

In the tradition of the original OCDQ, all items were simple statements, and respondents were asked to indicate the extent that each statement characterized their school along a four-point scale as "rarely occurs," "sometimes occurs," "often occurs," or "very frequently occurs." Samples of the new items added to the item bank for the instrument included the following:

- The principal checks lesson plans.
- The principal treats teachers as equals.
- Teachers are burdened with busywork.
- Faculty meetings are useless.
- Teachers socialize with each other.
- Teachers help and support each other.
- Teachers are friendly with other teachers.
- Teachers praise pupils who do good work.
- The learning environment is orderly and serious.

The preliminary revised OCDQ now contained 131 potential, mostly untested items. Therefore, reduction of the number of items became an initial task as the factor structure of the revised instrument was explored. A pilot study was conducted toward this end.

Pilot Study

A pilot sample of 38 elementary schools was identified for exploration and refinement of the instrument. The sample included urban, suburban, and rural schools and represented a diverse subset of elementary schools. Only elementary schools with 10 or more teachers were included in the sample. Researchers collected data from four teachers selected at random in each of the schools. Since the unit of analysis was the school, individual data were aggregated at the school level for each item and the exploratory procedures were performed to reduce the number of items and determine the factor structure of the revised instrument.

The Unit-of-Analysis Problem: A Brief Digression. Sirotnik (1980) has identified three types of analyses that have been used in climate studies—total analysis, within-school analysis, and between-school analysis. Total analysis examines relationships among variables across individuals, ignoring possible relevant grouping factors. Within-school analysis also is an individual approach; however, in this case the group effect is removed from the individual scores before analysis. Finally, between-school analysis uses the group as the unit of analysis. When the property is viewed as fundamentally intrinsic to the group, as it is in school climate, then between-school analysis is the appropriate procedure.

Unfortunately, total analysis is most frequently used—or, more accurately, misused—in studies of organizational climate. Halpin and Croft (1962) used the total analysis approach to determine the eight basic dimensions of school climate. They factored an item-correlation matrix for the OCDQ based on 1,151 individuals, ignoring the fact that the individuals came from 71 different schools. The appropriate procedure would have been to aggregate the scores at the school level and then factor analyze the item matrix; then, of course, the size of the group would have been much smaller (n = 71 schools).

The correction of the flaw in the unit of analysis produced a major dilemma: the number of items of the original OCDQ (64) was almost as large as the sample (71). Although the minimum allowable ratio of cases to items (variables) is still a matter of debate, the number of cases should exceed the number of items; and in general, the ratio of cases to items should be as large as possible (Cattell, 1952; Rummel, 1970). In the present study, the preliminary instrument had 131 items with only 38 schools, nearly more than three times as many items as cases. Since it was not feasible to increase dramatically the size of the sample, the strategy was to use this small pilot sample simply to refine and to reduce substantially the length of the revised OCDQ so that subsequent analysis of the revised OCDQ could more closely meet the minimum criterion for the ratio of cases to items.

Factor Analysis

Three criteria were used to reduce the total number of items in the revised OCDQ. First, the criterion of simple structure was employed in all factor analyses; only items that loaded high on one factor and low on all the others were retained. Second, in addition to their mathematical contribution to the factor, items were evaluated for conceptual clarity and fit with primary items in the factor. Finally, items were eliminated if they reduced substantially the internal consistency of the subtest as measured by Cronbach's coefficient alpha.

A series of exploratory factor analyses of the pilot data was performed. School mean scores were generated for each item and the item-correlation matrices were factored. A 10-factor solution with a varimax rotation was performed, based on the expectation that there would be the eight original factors of the OCDQ and two new dimensions of academic press and pupil control. Immediately 56 items were eliminated because of their low factor loadings (< .3) across all factors. A subsequent factor analysis was conducted with the remaining 75 factors, and nine additional items were dropped. A third exploratory factor analysis then was performed with the remaining 66 items. Along with each factor analysis, reliability analyses were performed for each subtest to refine each dimension further.

In the process of performing the exploratory factor analyses, several conclusions were drawn that influenced the interpretation and further refinement of the new instrument. First, using the criterion of simple structure, there were fewer than 10 interpretable factors. The aloofness dimension never was sufficiently distinct in any of the factor solutions; hence, following Hayes's recommendation, the aloofness subtest was eliminated. Next, most of the items measuring consideration and thrust consistently loaded together on the same factor; consequently, only the nine items that most strongly clustered together were retained. Finally, the academic press items and pupil control items lost their conceptual identity as the analyses became more refined; that is, neither emerged as distinct factors. Instead, these items were interwoven into many dimensions of both principal and teacher behavior. Thus we reluctantly decided to remove academic press and pupil control items from the instrument. As a consequence, only 42 items remained in the pool of items for a revised OCDQ. After another series of iterations, a six-factor solution was selected as the best solution. The final set of items is summarized in Table 2.1.

Dimensions of Elementary School Climate

The six dimensions of school climate that finally emerged measured two general categories of behavior. Three of the dimensions described principal behavior and three depicted teacher behavior.

Those items on the original consideration and thrust subtests that came together to form one common factor all reflected cognitive

Table 2.1 Items in the Final Versions of the OCDQ-RE

1. The teachers accomplish their work with vim, vigor, and pleasure......................	RO	SO	O	VFO
2. Teachers' closest friends are other faculty members at this school........................	RO	SO	O	VFO
3. Faculty meetings are useless...	RO	SO	O	VFO
4. The principal goes out of his/her way to help teachers...	RO	SO	O	VFO
5. The principal rules with an iron fist..	RO	SO	O	VFO
6. Teachers leave school immediately after school is over...	RO	SO	O	VFO
7. Teachers invite faculty members to visit them at home...	RO	SO	O	VFO
8. There is a minority group of teachers who always oppose the majority................	RO	SO	O	VFO
9. The principal uses constructive criticism...	RO	SO	O	VFO
10. The principal checks the sign-in sheet every morning...	RO	SO	O	VFO
11. Routine duties interfere with the job of teaching..	RO	SO	O	VFO
12. Most of the teachers here accept the faults of their colleagues............................	RO	SO	O	VFO
13. Teachers know the family background of other faculty members.........................	RO	SO	O	VFO
14. Teachers exert group pressure on non-conforming faculty members..................	RO	SO	O	VFO
15. The principal explains his/her reasons for criticism to teachers.......................	RO	SO	O	VFO
16. The principal listens to and accepts teachers' suggestions..................................	RO	SO	O	VFO
17. The principal schedules the work for the teachers...	RO	SO	O	VFO
18. Teachers have too many committee requirements..	RO	SO	O	VFO
19. Teachers help and support each other..	RO	SO	O	VFO
20. Teachers have fun socializing together during school time..................................	RO	SO	O	VFO
21. Teachers ramble when they talk at faculty meetings..	RO	SO	O	VFO
22. The principal looks out for the personal welfare of teachers...............................	RO	SO	O	VFO
23. The principal treats teachers as equals..	RO	SO	O	VFO
24. The principal corrects teachers' mistakes...	RO	SO	O	VFO
25. Administrative paperwork is burdensome at this school......................................	RO	SO	O	VFO
26. Teachers are proud of their school..	RO	SO	O	VFO
27. Teachers have parties for each other...	RO	SO	O	VFO
28. The principal compliments teachers..	RO	SO	O	VFO
29. The principal is easy to understand..	RO	SO	O	VFO
30. The principal closely checks classroom (teacher) activities.................................	RO	SO	O	VFO
31. Clerical support reduces teachers' paperwork..	RO	SO	O	VFO
32. New teachers are readily accepted by colleagues..	RO	SO	O	VFO
33. Teachers socialize with each other on a regular basis..	RO	SO	O	VFO
34. The principal supervises teachers closely...	RO	SO	O	VFO
35. The principal checks lesson plans..	RO	SO	O	VFO
36. Teachers are burdened with busy work..	RO	SO	O	VFO
37. Teachers socialize together in small, select groups..	RO	SO	O	VFO
38. Teachers provide strong social support for colleagues...	RO	SO	O	VFO
39. The principal is autocratic..	RO	SO	O	VFO
40. Teachers respect the professional competence of their colleagues......................	RO	SO	O	VFO
41. The principal monitors everything teachers do...	RO	SO	O	VFO
42. The principal goes out of his/her way to show appreciation to teachers.............	RO	SO	O	VFO

SOURCE: Used with permission of Sharon Clover (1984)

and affective aspects of supportive principal behavior; hence, this factor was termed supportive leader behavior. The original and new "production emphasis" items also clustered to form a factor that we called directive leader behavior. Finally, the last dimension of leader behavior was a revised version of hindrance, which was more appropriately labeled restrictive leader behavior. The leader behavior of elementary principals thus was conceived in terms of supportive, directive, and restrictive behaviors.

The teacher dimensions identified in the factor analysis also were different from those of the original OCDQ. The original esprit subtest changed dramatically; in fact, only two of the original items remained. The new set of items described teachers as colleagues committed to each other, their work, and their school, a factor we called collegial teacher behavior. With minor revisions, two of the original OCDQ subtests, intimate teacher behavior and disengaged teacher behavior, remained. Thus the interaction patterns of elementary teachers were described in terms of collegial, intimate, and disengaged teacher behaviors. In brief, the six dimensions are summarized as follows.

Supportive principal behavior reflects a basic concern for teachers. The principal listens and is open to teacher suggestions. Praise is given genuinely and frequently, and criticism is handled constructively. The competence of the faculty is respected, and the principal exhibits both a personal and professional interest in teachers.

Directive principal behavior is rigid, close supervision. The principal maintains constant monitoring and control over all teacher and school activities, down to the smallest detail.

Restrictive principal behavior is behavior that hinders rather than facilitates teacher work. The principal burdens teachers with paperwork, committee requirements, routine duties, and other demands that interfere with their teaching responsibilities.

Collegial teacher behavior supports open and professional interactions among teachers. Teachers are proud of their school, enjoy working with their colleagues, and are enthusiastic, accepting, and mutually respectful of their colleagues.

Intimate teacher behavior is cohesive and strong social relations among teachers. Teachers know each other well, are close personal friends, socialize together regularly, and provide strong social support for each other.

Disengaged teacher behavior signifies a lack of meaning and focus to professional activities. Teachers simply are putting in time in nonproductive group efforts; they have no common goals. In fact, their behavior often is negative and critical of their colleagues and the school.

Each of these dimensions was measured by a subtest of the OCDQ-RE. Sample items of the subtests are provided in Table 2.2. The reliability scores for the scales were relatively high: supportive

Table 2.2   Sample Items for Each Subscale of the OCDQ-RE

SUPPORTIVE PRINCIPAL BEHAVIOR

The principal uses constructive criticism.
The principal compliments teachers.
The principal listens to and accepts teachers suggestions.

DIRECTIVE PRINCIPAL BEHAVIOR

The principal monitors everything teachers do.
The principal rules with an iron fist.
The principal checks lesson plans.

RESTRICTIVE PRINCIPAL BEHAVIOR

Teachers are burdened with busywork.
Routine duties interfere with the job of teaching.
Teachers have too many committee requirements.

COLLEGIAL TEACHER BEHAVIOR

Teachers help and support each other.
Teachers respect the professional competence of their colleagues.
Teachers accomplish their work with vim, vigor, and pleasure.

INTIMATE TEACHER BEHAVIOR

Teachers socialize with each other.
Teachers' closest friends are other faculty members at this school.
Teachers have parties for each other.

DISENGAGED TEACHER BEHAVIOR

Faculty meetings are useless.
There is a minority group of teachers who always oppose the majority.
Teachers ramble when they talk at faculty meetings.

(.94); directive (.88); restrictive (.81); collegial (.87); intimate (.83); and disengaged (.78).

A Test of the Revised Climate Instrument

There is little question that the OCDQ-RE is a new instrument. Although it builds upon the original OCDQ, it is more parsimonious; it has different dimensions, and one half of the items are new. The revised instrument, OCDQ-RE, was now ready for further analysis. The 42-item questionnaire was tested with a new sample of schools to demonstrate the stability of its factor structure, to confirm the validity and reliability of its subtests, and to explore its second-order factor structure.

Sample

Seventy elementary schools in New Jersey agreed to participate in the study. A separate, new, random sample of at least six teachers was drawn from each of the 38 pilot schools, and 32 new schools were added to the final sample. Although the school sample was not a random one, it represented a broad range of schools from urban, suburban, and rural areas, spanning the entire range of socioeconomic status. Extremely small schools were not included in the sample; in fact, only schools with 10 or more faculty members were considered candidates for the sample. Schools that participated came from 12 of the 21 counties in the state. Thirty-nine percent were located in the six counties having the least number of school districts; 37% of the schools came from the six counties with the largest number of districts; and 24% of the schools were gathered from the remaining nine middle counties.

Data typically were collected by a researcher in a faculty meeting, but in a few cases, the instrument was administered by a faculty member. In all cases the respondents were anonymous. Two-thirds of the faculty answered the revised OCDQ and the remaining one-third completed an instrument of similar length, which was not part of the OCDQ. Virtually all teachers answered the questionnaire; in total, 1,071 educators in 70 schools responded to the OCDQ-RE.

Factor Analysis

School mean scores were calculated for each item, and the item-correlation matrix from the 70 schools was factor analyzed. Once again, six factors with eigenvalues from 12.9 to 1.62 explaining 67.2% of the variance were retained. The six-factor solution, after varimax rotation, is summarized and presented in Table 2.3. The results strongly supported the factor structure uncovered in the pilot study. The items loaded on the appropriate subtest and generally loaded highly only on one factor. Moreover, the reliability scores for the subtests for the new data set remained high. The alpha coefficients were as follows:

	Number of items	Reliability (alpha)
Supportive	9	.95
Directive	9	.89
Restrictive	5	.80
Collegial	8	.90
Intimate	7	.85
Disengaged	4	.75
Total	**42**	

Finally, a comparison was made between the factor loadings on the six factors for the pilot data and for the final data set. The results were remarkably similar. The factor structures for both data sets were virtually identical.

The stability of the factor structure also supports the construct validity of the six measures of school climate. Factor analyses enable the researcher to study the constitutive meanings of constructs and thus, their construct validity (Kerlinger, 1986). In the current study, six hypothetical entities, dimensions of organizational climate, were constructed. The relations among the items (variables) were systematically related to each other as expected in the test of the factor structure of the OCDQ-RE.

Second-Order Factor Analysis

Thus far, the analysis of data has been concerned with identifying the items that formed the basic dimensions of climate. Now we turn our attention to an analysis of the six dimensions or subtests. To compute each school's scores on the six factors, items scores

Table 2.3 Six-Factor Varimax Solution for the 42 Items of the OCDQ-RE

SUBTEST	ITEM	I	II	III	IV	V	VI
	4	.82	-.07	.15	-.20	-.06	-.24
	9	.82	-.11	.24	.08	-.13	.13
	15	.82	-.28	.17	.09	-.17	.06
Supportive	22	.90	.10	.09	.09	.02	.02
Principal	28	.83	-.10	.07	.15	-.23	-.08
Behavior	16	.74	.08	.27	-.10	.00	-.15
	23	.73	.02	.06	.03	-.16	-.13
	29	.78	-.04	.26	.13	-.07	.10
	42	.84	-.07	.09	.13	-.07	-.22
	5	-.45	.68	-.18	-.19	.20	-.06
	10	-.09	.53	-.05	.08	.06	-.02
	17	-.38	.66	-.06	.08	-.02	.17
Directive	24	-.13	.64	-.19	-.11	.05	-.18
Principal	30	.18	.84	-.12	-.05	.12	-.13
Behavior	35	.04	.67	.03	.05	.02	.21
	39	-.58	.61	-.24	-.15	.11	-.14
	41	-.08	.81	-.01	-.16	.05	.23
	34	.04	.87	.01	-.09	.10	.02
	1	.13	.11	.62	.01	.19	.00
	*6	.03	-.25	.70	-.18	-.17	-.10
	12	.00	-.02	.64	.27	-.38	-.10
Collegial	19	.32	-.08	.64	.51	-.18	-.04
Teacher	26	.20	-.17	.76	.17	.03	-.24
Behavior	32	.26	-.10	.73	.32	-.09	.00
	*37	.28	-.05	.70	.32	-.25	.00
	40	.41	-.06	.46	.39	-.25	-.29

(continues)

were summed within each subtest, and subtest scores were computed for each school.

Halpin and Croft (1963) proposed the following useful standards for constructing a battery of subtests: first, each subtest should measure a relatively different type of behavior; second, the battery as a whole should tap enough common behavior to permit researchers to find a pattern of more general factors; and third, the general factors extracted should not be discordant with those already reported in the literature. The OCDQ-RE meets these criteria reasonably well. The subscales are relatively independent of each other; they explain 67% of the variance, and the dimen-

Table 2.3 (continued)

SUBTEST	ITEM	I	II	III	IV	V	VI
	2	.20	.17	.08	.62	-.04	.15
	7	.04	-.08	.08	.80	-.08	-.13
Intimate	13	-.04	-.22	.34	.58	.11	.21
Teacher	20	-.14	-.20	.21	.52	-.24	-.12
Behavior	27	.00	-.15	-.01	.82	-.03	-.21
	33	.05	.04	.10	.83	-.03	-.11
	38	.29	.00	.14	.72	-.16	-.29
	11	-.19	.39	.05	.10	.65	.26
Restrictive	18	-.17	-.02	-.06	.17	.78	.12
Principal	25	-.34	.20	-.47	.19	.52	.06
Behavior	*31	-.15	.28	-.26	-.14	.54	.09
	36	-.38	.19	.03	-.09	.58	.54
	3	-.39	.04	.11	-.30	.24	.49
Disengaged	8	.04	.11	-.42	.13	.03	.57
Teacher	14	-.10	.11	-.46	.14	-.24	.52
Behavior	21	-.07	.15	-.31	-.33	.18	.62
Eigenvalue		12.96	4.45	4.30	2.82	2.07	1.62
Cumulative Variance		.31	.41	.52	.58	.63	.67

*Score is reversed

Table 2.4 Correlations Between Subtest Scores of the OCDQ-RE

Subtest	S	D	R	C	I	D
Supportive (S)	(.95)*					
Directive (D)	−.30	(.89)				
Restrictive (R)	−.49	.44	(.80)			
Collegial (C)	.44	−.29	−.48	(.90)		
Intimate (I)	.28	−.20	−.28	.48	(.85)	
Disengaged (D)	−.31	.16	.41	−.63	−.45	(.75)

*Alpha coefficients of reliability are reported in parentheses.

sions are consistent with the leadership and early OCDQ literature. Although the scales are relatively independent, an examination of the correlations in Table 2.4 reveals that there are some moderate correlations between some of the pairs of subtests. Hence, a second-order factor analysis was performed on the

Table 2.5 Two-Factor Varimax Solution for the Six Dimensions of the OCDQ-RE

Subtest	I Teacher Openness	II Principal Closedness
Supportive	.33	−.65
Directive	.01	.83
Restrictive	−.34	.75
Collegial	.77	−.36
Intimate	.76	−.11
Disengaged	−.84	.15

subtest correlation matrix searching for a few general underlying variables.

A two-factor solution with a varimax rotation is given for the six scales in Table 2.5. Disengaged, intimate, and collegial teacher behavior load strongly only on Factor I while restrictive, supportive, and directive principal behavior load strongly only on Factor II. Factor I is characterized by teacher interactions that are meaningful and tolerant (low disengagement); friendly, warm, and social (high intimacy); and enthusiastic, accepting, and mutually respectful (high collegial behavior). In general, then, Factor I represents teacher interactions that are functionally flexible and open; accordingly, it was labeled "teacher openness." Factor II is defined by principal behavior that produces meaningless routines and burdensome duties for teachers (high restrictiveness); rigid, close, and constant control over teachers (high directiveness); and a lack of concern for and openness to teachers and their ideas (low supportiveness). In general, the second factor depicts principal behavior that is functionally rigid and closed; consequently, it was called "principal closedness." Thus both second-order factors are viewed along an open-closed continuum.

The theoretical underpinnings of the OCDQ-RE are consistent and clear. The instrument has two general factors—one a measure of the openness of teacher interactions and the other a measure of openness (or closedness) of principal leadership behavior. These two factors are relatively independent. That is, it is quite possible to have a school with an open principal and closed teacher relations or vice versa. Hence, four contrasting school climates are possible. First, both factors can be open, producing a

Table 2.6 Prototypic Profiles of Climate Types

	Climate Type			
Climate Dimension	Open	Engaged	Disengaged	Closed
Supportive	High	Low	High	Low
Directive	Low	High	Low	High
Restrictive	Low	High	Low	High
Collegial	High	High	Low	Low
Intimate	High	High	Low	Low
Disengaged	Low	Low	High	High

congruence of openness between the principal's and teachers' behavior. Second, both factors can be closed, producing a congruence of closedness. There also are two incongruent behavioral patterns. The principal's leadership behavior can be open with teachers, but the teachers' may be closed with each other; or the principal may be closed with teachers, while teachers are open with each other. Table 2.6 summarizes the patterns of four climate prototypes that are based on these two second-order factors. Using this information, a behavioral picture of each climate type can be sketched. The typology of school climates is illustrated in Figure 2.1.

Open climate. The distinctive characteristics of the open climate are cooperation, respect, and openness that exist within the faculty and between the faculty and principal. The principal listens and is receptive to teacher ideas, gives genuine and frequent praise, and respects the competence of faculty (high supportiveness). Principals also give their teachers freedom to perform without close scrutiny (low directiveness) and provide facilitating leadership devoid of bureaucratic trivia (low restrictiveness). Likewise, the faculty supports open and professional behavior (high collegial relations) among teachers. Teachers know each other well and typically are close personal friends (high intimacy). They cooperate and are committed to teaching and their job (low disengagement). In brief, the behavior of both the principal and teachers is genuine and open.

Engaged climate. The engaged climate is marked, on one hand, by ineffective attempts of the principal to lead, and on the other, by high professional performance of the teachers. The principal is

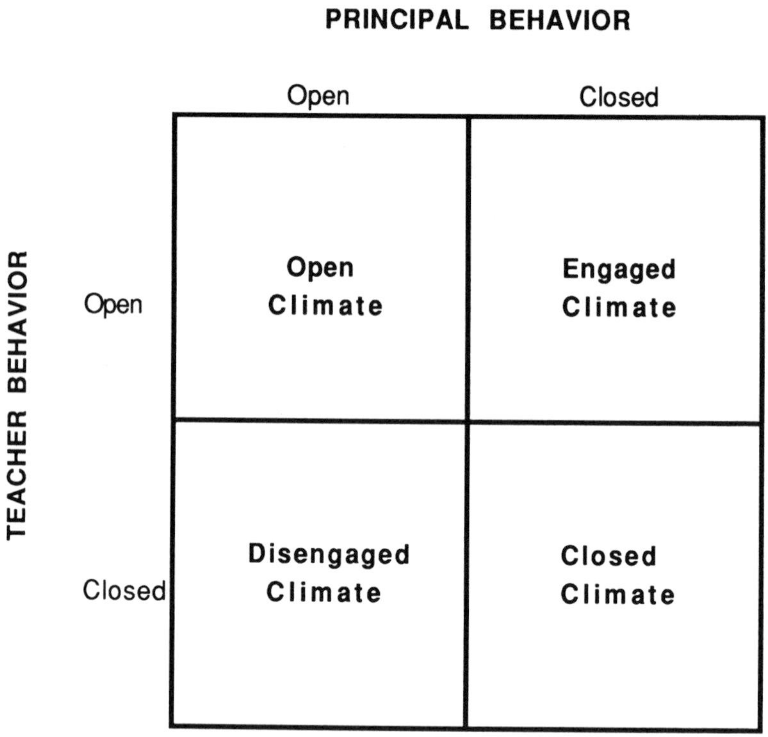

PRINCIPAL BEHAVIOR

	Open	Closed
Open	Open Climate	Engaged Climate
Closed	Disengaged Climate	Closed Climate

TEACHER BEHAVIOR

Figure 2.1. Typology of School Climates

rigid and authoritarian (high directiveness) and respects neither the professional expertise nor personal needs of the faculty (low supportiveness). In addition, the principal is seen as burdening faculty with unnecessary busy work (high restrictiveness). Surprisingly, however, the teachers simply ignore the principal's unsuccessful attempts to control, and conduct themselves as productive professionals. They respect and support each other, are proud of their school, and enjoy their work (high collegiality). They not only respect each other's professional competence but they like each other as friends (high intimacy). The teachers come together as a cooperative unit engaged and committed to the teaching-learning task (high engagement). In brief, the teachers are productive in spite of weak principal leadership; the faculty is cohesively committed, supportive, and engaged.

Disengaged climate. The disengaged climate stands in stark contrast to the engaged climate. The principal's leadership behavior is strong, supportive, and concerned. The principal listens to and is open to teachers' views (high supportiveness); gives teachers the freedom to act on the basis of their professional knowledge (low directiveness); and relieves teachers of most of the burdens of paperwork and bureaucratic trivia (low restrictiveness). Nevertheless, the faculty reacts badly; teachers are unwilling to accept responsibility. At best, the faculty simply ignores the initiatives of the principal; at worst, the faculty actively works to immobilize and sabotage the principal's leadership attempts. Teachers not only dislike the principal but also do not especially like each other as friends (low intimacy) or respect each other as colleagues (low collegiality). The faculty clearly is disengaged from their work. Although the principal is supportive, flexible, and noncontrolling (i.e., open), the faculty is divisive, intolerant, and uncommitted (i.e., closed).

Closed climate. The closed climate is the antithesis of the open. The principal and teachers simply go through the motions, with the principal stressing routine trivia and unnecessary busywork (high restrictiveness) and teachers responding minimally and exhibiting little commitment to the tasks at hand (high disengagement). The principal's leadership is seen as controlling and rigid (high directiveness) as well as unsympathetic and unresponsive (low supportiveness). These misguided tactics are accompanied not only by frustration and apathy, but also by suspicion and a lack of respect of teachers for their colleagues as well as the administration (low intimacy and noncollegiality). In sum, closed climates have principals who are nonsupportive, inflexible, hindering, and controlling, and a faculty that is divisive, apathetic, intolerant, and disingenuous.

Openness Indices

The three subtests of the OCDQ-RE that define principal openness are supportive, directive, and restrictive. An index of the degree of openness in principal-teacher relations can be computed by first standardizing the school scores on these dimensions, and then subtracting the sum of the directive and restrictive scores from the supportive score (Principal openness = $S - [D + R]$), where S, D, R are standard scores).

Likewise, the collegial, intimate, and disengaged subtests define the degree of openness in teacher behavior. Accordingly, a teacher openness index for the school can be computed by standardizing the school scores on these dimensions, and then subtracting the disengagement score from the sum of the collegial and intimate scores (Teacher openness = $[C + I] - D$, where C, I, D are standard scores).

The construct validity of each dimension of openness was supported by correlating each dimension with the original OCDQ index of openness (Hoy, 1972a). In the current sample, the index of teacher openness correlated positively with the original general school openness index ($r = .67$, $p < .01$) as did the index of principal openness ($r = .52$, $p < .01$).

Summary and Discussion

The Organizational Climate Description Questionnaire has been completely revised. The result, the OCDQ-RE, is a 42-item instrument with six subtests that describe the behavior of elementary teachers and principals. The revised instrument measures three aspects of principal leadership—supportive, directive, and restrictive. The aloofness dimension of the original OCDQ was eliminated; it simply could not be defined in the present study. Moreover, thrust and consideration merged to form one dimension of leadership, supportive behavior. Finally, hindrance was reformulated and measured as restrictive principal behavior. These three dimensions of principal behavior provided the components of a second-order construct, principal openness (or closedness); that is, principal-teacher interaction was conceived along a general continuum from open to closed. Open principal behavior is genuine. The principal creates an environment that supports teachers' efforts, encourages their participation and contributions, and frees teachers from routine busywork so they can concentrate on teaching, as contrasted with closed principal behavior that is rigid, close, critical, and controlling.

The OCDQ-RE also measures three dimensions of teacher interactions—collegial, intimate, and disengaged behavior. The esprit subtest of the original OCDQ was replaced by the concept of collegial teacher behavior. Collegial teachers not only take pleasure in their work and have pride in their school, but they work together and respect each other as competent professionals. Halpin and Croft's original intimacy and disengagement dimensions remain basic subtests of the OCDQ-RE, but both subtests were refined to improve their internal consistency. Like the subtests of principal behavior, the three elements of teacher behavior provided the elements of a second-order construct, teacher openness; that is, teacher-teacher interactions also are viewed along a general continuum of open to closed. Open teacher behavior is sincere, positive, and supportive; faculty relations are warm, close, and friendly; and teachers have mutual respect for each other and are tolerant of divergent teacher ideas and behavior. Closed behavior, in contrast, is ritualistic, divisive, apathetic, intolerant, and disingenuous. As we have seen, these two general dimensions of teacher openness and principal openness can be used to classify school climates into one of four types—an open, closed, engaged, or disengaged school climate (see Figure 2.1).

The properties of the six subtests of the OCDQ-RE are impressive. All of the scales have high reliability coefficients, much higher than those in the original OCDQ. The subtests are reasonably pure; that is, most items load high on one subtest and relatively low on the others when subjected to factor analysis. Moreover, the stability of the factor structures in two separate samples provided evidence of the construct validity of each subtest. Finally, the unit of analysis in all phases of the investigation was appropriately the school, not the individual. The six aspects of school climate are organizational properties, not individual ones.

One limitation of the OCDQ, however, was not overcome. The OCDQ-RE, like the original OCDQ, is restricted to social interactions among professional personnel. Initially, we attempted to include items in the new instrument that measured student-oriented behaviors, but unfortunately, the items did not fit into the conceptual perspective that eventually emerged. That is not to say that student variables are not related to the climate of schools. We believe they are. For example, those items that described student-student and teacher-student interactions were correlated with items in virtually all the subtests; and that was the rub. They did not form independent factors; hence, they were eliminated from the instrument. An academic press index was later constructed (Clover, 1984) that tapped the extent to which the school stressed academic performance and students respected others who were academically successful. Both openness in teacher-teacher relations ($r = .52$, $p < .01$) and openness in teacher-principal relations ($r = .43$, $p < .01$) were significantly correlated with academic press.

In sum, the OCDQ-RE is a parsimonious and reliable research tool ready for further use and testing. It is a contemporary set of measures that maps the domain of elementary schools. The six subtests of the OCDQ-RE can be grouped into two categories: characteristics of the principal's leadership and characteristics of faculty behavior. Each set of behaviors is defined by a more general construct of openness, but openness in principal behavior is relatively independent of openness in faculty behavior; hence, two continua of openness anchored our conceptualization of the climate of elementary schools and provided the basis for a four-celled typology of school climate: open, closed, engaged, and disengaged climates.

Implications

The OCDQ-RE has both theoretical and research implications. It seems reasonable to predict that openness in both teacher and principal behavior may be related to positive student outcomes, but it also seems likely that open principal behavior will not lead to effective student performance unless it is coupled with open teacher behavior. The key to successful principal leadership is to influence teachers. But open and supportive principal behavior does not guarantee an impact on teachers' behavior. In fact, a more directive and controlling pattern of principal behavior may be necessary with some faculties (e.g., disengaged climate) until the faculty matures and becomes more engaged (Hersey & Blanchard, 1982). It is likely that no *one* leadership style, not even an open one, is successful in all situations. Under what conditions does openness in leader behavior produce openness in teacher behavior? To what extent does openness in teacher behavior affect such student outcomes as self-concept, commitment to school, motivation, absenteeism, vandalism, and student achievement? The typology of school climates developed here provides a framework not only for the study of leadership, motivation, and school effectiveness but also of organizational communication, school structure, decision making, goal setting, and control processes. There is a host of important research questions to be addressed and the OCDQ-RE is a heuristic tool in the endeavor. The framework and measure also have more immediate and practical implications (see Chapter 7). Open and authentic interactions among teachers and between teachers and the principal should be goals in themselves. The school climate perspective and instrument provide vehicles for addressing the significant issue of improving the work environment. They give practitioners a set of tools to examine and diagnose difficulties in the school. The OCDQ-RE is easily administered to the faculty, simple to score, and provides a quick snapshot of the school atmosphere along some important dimensions. The instrument can serve not only as a basis for planning change strategies and school improvement programs but also as a device to assess the results of such efforts.

For example, the elementary school principal works closely with teachers in a relatively small and unspecialized setting. The lack of academic disciplines and the need for coordination of teaching and learning at this level forces the principal to build consensus and achieve the best decisions possible by attending simultaneously to the instructional aims of the school and the social needs of the faculty. The OCDQ-RE gives a reasonably reliable index of what might be wrong in a school functioning below par. The frustration that teachers may express on the frustration subtest or the disengagement of teachers can be indications to the alert administrator of where the school might be going without active intervention on the part of the principal. In this instance the OCDQ-RE can help both in diagnosis and prescription.

Note

1. A preliminary version of this work has been published by Hoy and Clover (1986).

3 The Organizational Climate Description Questionnaire for Secondary Schools

> We cannot rule out the possibility that . . . climate-profiles may actually constitute a better criterion of school effectiveness than many measures that already have entered the field of educational administration and now masquerade as criteria.
>
> —Andrew W. Halpin
> *Theory and Research in Administration*

A basic shortcoming of the OCDQ is that the instrument was developed for use in elementary schools. Secondary schools are more complex than elementary schools; they have greater specialization and division of labor, and more rules and regulations. Typically, they also are larger, often serving as a receiving school for a number of elementary schools. It should come as no surprise to learn that an instrument designed to measure the climate of one kind of school is not entirely satisfactory for another.

In the last chapter, we described the evolution of a revised OCDQ for elementary schools. We now turn to the secondary school—a context wholly neglected by Halpin and Croft (1963)—in an attempt to derive and test a climate measure for secondary schools, the Organizational Climate Description Questionnaire (OCDQ-RS).

School Climate: A Personal View

School climate may be known in at least two ways, experientially and conceptually. We begin this chapter on secondary school climate by reviewing the early teaching experience of several of the authors. After working in only a few schools, an awareness of the differences among them becomes apparent. Even a substitute teacher quickly learns that the school climate has a lot to do with how the day will go. Some schools are fun to work in; some decidedly are not.

The visible school—its age, architecture, physical condition, the types of open areas, the housing and commercial or industrial enterprises immediately surrounding the school, the people walking the sidewalks, the vehicles in the parking lot, the cleanliness and repair of the building—introduces the invisible school.

One of the authors recounts the following experience from a stint of substitute teaching:

I used to give a good look at the physical condition of the school and then the people inside the school. I was interested in how they dressed, moved about the building, talked to each other—those sorts of things. I got a preview of the people with whom I would be working that day. These were, of course, impressions formed without ever talking to anybody in the school. My guesses based on those impressions were often confirmed in my first personal encounters. In some schools an administrator greeted me and told me something about the assignment and the school; in others a department chairperson. I knew I was in for a hard day when "briefing the substitute" was left to a harried secretary at the beginning of the school day.

Here and there I could see teachers talking with one another, having a last cup of coffee, or, as was the case in some schools, simply isolated one from the other as little islands. Often the good feelings teachers seemed to have for one another were echoed in a pleasant classroom experience, but in those schools where the teachers didn't seem to get along with one another, the students usually were hellions. I knew the day would be a long one and I was seldom disappointed. Graduate school taught me conceptual labels for climate, but I had experienced it many times without knowing its name.

Rationale for a New Measure: OCDQ-RS

Halpin and Croft's (1963) broad conception of open and closed climate remains intellectually vital. As we have noted in Chapter 2, however, the original *measure* of climate, the OCDQ—as opposed to the *conception* of open and closed climates—is dated, flawed, and inappropriate for secondary schools.

Principals are important in all schools. Yet secondary teachers are less likely than elementary teachers to see the principal face-to-face on a daily basis. Rather, they usually work with assistant principals and department chairpersons. Secondary schools are staffed by teachers who consider themselves to be subject specialists and who are members of departments. Elementary schools, by way of comparison, generally are composed of teachers who are child-centered generalists concerned with the total development of the child.

These differences often were ignored by previous researchers (Carver & Sergiovanni, 1969; Kottkamp, Mulhern, & Hoy, 1987; Waldman, 1971). For these reasons and for the conceptual, psychometric, and methodological issues discussed in Chapters 1 and 2, we set about measuring the notion of climate as conceived by Halpin and Croft (1963) through an instrument formulated particularly for secondary schools.

Developing a New Measure: OCDQ-RS

The development of an OCDQ for secondary schools had several phases: (a) generating new items; (b) conducting a pilot study to reduce items and refine subtests; (c) conducting a second study to test stability of the factor structure; and (d) testing the reliability and validity of the new instrument.

Item Generation

Revising the OCDQ started with an attempt to create a parallel, valid, and reliable climate measure for high schools. Item revision, deletion, and development began with the conceptual framework established by Halpin and Croft. Old items were revised or eliminated for three reasons:

(a) they were not logically appropriate for the high school level;
(b) they were not conceptually consistent with the subtest in which they were placed; or
(c) they had poor measurement characteristics, for example, high factor loadings on more than one factor.

An example of item revision follows: "The principal stays after school to help teachers finish their work," was revised to "The principal is available after school to help teachers when assistance is needed." This modification represents an attempt to describe a situation more appropriate to a secondary school setting where many teachers are subject matter specialists. Rather than helping "to finish their work," a phrase that assumes the principal knows how to do the work, the new phrase "help when assistance is needed" is more open ended and carries less of an assumption that the principal may be helpful in the particular curricular dimension of the teacher's work. An initial aloofness item, "Teachers leave the grounds during the school day," was eliminated for conceptual reasons. The aloofness subscale measures principal behavior in maintaining social distance from faculty; the item does not tap teacher perceptions of principal behavior at all.

We eliminated or revised an item if it had one or more of the following measurement problems: it lowered the subscale reliability because of a low item total correlation; it had similar loadings on two or more subscales; or it had a higher factor loading on a subscale other than the one to which it was assigned.

Three researchers independently reviewed all OCDQ items for revision or elimination. Each individual also wrote revised or new items. We reached a consensus on a potential pool of items using the following criteria:

(a) each item reflected a property of the school;
(b) the statement was clear and concise;
(c) the statement had content validity; and
(d) the statement had discriminatory potential.

Of the eventual 100 items in the pilot form, 37 were original OCDQ items, 48 were modified or new items tapping the original ideas, and 15 were additional items created to describe the social interaction of teachers and students.

The response format for all items was a four-point Likert scale measuring frequency of the perceived behavior: "rarely occurs," "sometimes occurs," "often occurs," and "very frequently occurs." Samples of the new items added to the item bank included the following:

- Pupils are required to sit in assigned seats during assembly.
- New teachers are readily accepted by colleagues.
- Teachers revise their teaching methods when criticized by pupils.
- Teachers leave immediately after school is over.
- Classes are interrupted by the intercom.
- Teachers really enjoy working here.
- Teachers just "go through the motions" in this school.
- The principal supports teachers in front of parents.

The preliminary revised OCDQ now contained 100 potential, mostly untested items. Therefore, a factor analysis of the revised instrument was explored in a pilot study.

Pilot Study

In order to assess this preliminary instrument, we needed to administer the 100-item questionnaire to teachers and then factor analyze their responses. It is here that the unit-of-analysis problem (Knapp, 1977, 1982; Sirotnik, 1980) discussed in the last chapter came into play again. Remember that Halpin and Croft (1963) had incorrectly used a "total analysis" in reducing their larger set of items in the original OCDQ. They factor analyzed an item-correlation matrix based on 1,151 individuals, ignoring the fact that the individuals came from 71 different schools. The correct procedure would have been to aggregate the items at the school level and then factor analyze the matrix. School climate is a group variable; it is a property intrinsic to the group—not the individual. We assume that climate is a function of a set of relatively stable organizational properties rather than unique perceptions.

The correction of the flaw in the unit of analysis produces a major dilemma: the number of items on the original OCDQ (64) was almost as large as the sample (71). Although the minimum allowable ratio of cases to items (variables) is still a matter of debate, the number of cases should exceed the number of items; and in general, the ratio of cases to items should be as large as possible (Cattell, 1952; Rummel, 1970). In the present study, the preliminary instrument had 100 items. A ratio of two cases to each item would have required a sample of 200 schools, an unlikely prospect for either the pilot or final sample. Thus our strategy was to use a pilot sample to refine and to reduce substantially the length of the revised OCDQ so that subsequent analysis of the revised OCDQ could more closely meet the minimum criterion for the ratio of cases to items.

A pilot sample of 68 high schools was identified for exploration and refinement of the instrument. The sample represented most of the kinds of school districts found in New Jersey in terms of locale, size, socioeconomic status, and student composition. Data were collected at random from a small group of teachers in each school and then aggregated at the school level to produce school mean scores for each item in the questionnaire.

Because the proper unit of analysis for the perceptual climate measure in this study is the school, we aggregated item responses across subjects within each school; that is, 535 individual responses were reduced to 68 school scores. The items were worded to reflect group perceptions. Thus means were computed for each item within each school. These means then served as the data for computing subtest reliabilities and for constructing the item-level correlation matrix for the factor analyses.

We performed numerous iterations of the following three analytic procedures to reduce the 100 items and to refine the subtests of the instruments. First, we produced principal components factor analyses using the entire correlation matrix, rotating these analyses to both varimax orthogonal and promax oblique solutions and specifying the number-of-factors criterion from five to 12. Second, using the same factor analytic methods, we factor analyzed the items originally assigned to each of the subtests without setting a number-of-factors criterion. Third, we calculated an alpha reliability coefficient for each set of subtest items. These analyses produced both item-total correlation statistics and a statistic indicating how the alpha coefficient would be affected by the deletion of each item.

When these three empirical analyses were completed, we compared their results with each other and with the nine-dimension conceptual framework that was the origin of the items—the original eight OCDQ dimensions and a new dimension examining teacher-student interactions. Thus empirical results were compared with conceptual formulations. It was evident after the first set of analyses that the original eight-dimension conception underlying the OCDQ did not hold up in the empirical analyses of data collected at the secondary level, nor did the teacher-student interaction items load on a single factor. Aloofness items, for example, did not cluster into one factor but were spread across several. Items from the thrust and consideration scales for principal behavior collapsed into a single strong factor as did items from the teacher scales of hindrance and disengagement. It was clear from the exploratory analyses that conceptual reformulation was an issue in this study as much as the original conceptual formulation had been for Halpin and Croft. Operationally, we then made decisions about item deletion and repeated three types of empirical analysis on the reduced sets of items. Deletion decisions were based on an interaction between the evolving conceptual reformulation and the empirical factor loadings and item-total correlation statistics. We continued a process of item deletion (and, less frequently, item replacement) and reanalysis until we had a preliminary instrument with both conceptual meaning and reasonable measurement characteristics. In the end, the pilot analyses produced a 34-item questionnaire composed of five subtests. The final set of items is found in Table 3.1.

Dimensions of Secondary School Climate

The five dimensions of school climate that finally emerged fell into two categories: two of the dimensions described principal behavior; the other three focused on teacher behavior, in particular, teacher relationships with students, colleagues, and superiors.

Items on the original consideration and thrust subtests that came together to form one common factor were named supportive principal behavior. The original and new "production emphasis" items also clustered together and formed a factor called directive principal behavior. The aloofness items, however, simply did not hold up as an independent subtest and were eliminated. Thus the

Table 3.1   Items in the Final Version of the OCDQ-RS

1. The mannerisms of teachers at this school are annoying............................	RO	SO	O	VFO
2. Teachers have too many committee requirements..................................	RO	SO	O	VFO
3. Teachers spend time after school with students who have individual problems.....	RO	SO	O	VFO
4. Teachers are proud of their school..	RO	SO	O	VFO
5. The principal sets an example by working hard himself/herself.......................	RO	SO	O	VFO
6. The principal compliments teachers..	RO	SO	O	VFO
7. Teacher-principal conferences are dominated by the principal..........................	RO	SO	O	VFO
8. Routine duties interfere with the job of teaching................................	RO	SO	O	VFO
9. Teachers interrupt other faculty members who are talking in faculty meetings...	RO	SO	O	VFO
10. Student government has an influence on school policy............................	RO	SO	O	VFO
11. Teachers are friendly with students..	RO	SO	O	VFO
12. The principal rules with an iron fist...	RO	SO	O	VFO
13. The principal monitors everything teachers do...............................	RO	SO	O	VFO
14. Teachers' closest friends are other faculty members at this school..................	RO	SO	O	VFO
15. Administrative paper work is burdensome at this school................................	RO	SO	O	VFO
16. Teachers help and support each other..	RO	SO	O	VFO
17. Pupils solve their problems through logical reasoning.............................	RO	SO	O	VFO
18. The principal closely checks teacher activities.................................	RO	SO	O	VFO
19. The principal is autocratic..	RO	SO	O	VFO
20. The morale of teachers is high..	RO	SO	O	VFO
21. Teachers know the family background of other faculty members........................	RO	SO	O	VFO
22. Assigned non-teaching duties are excessive..	RO	SO	O	VFO
23. The principal goes out of his/her way to help teachers.............................	RO	SO	O	VFO
24. The principal explains his/her reason for criticism to teachers.......................	RO	SO	O	VFO
25. The principal is available after school to help teachers when assistance is needed...	RO	SO	O	VFO
26. Teachers invite other faculty members to visit them at home...........................	RO	SO	O	VFO
27. Teachers socialize with each other on a regular basis............................	RO	SO	O	VFO
28. Teachers really enjoy working here..	RO	SO	O	VFO
29. The principal uses constructive criticism....................................	RO	SO	O	VFO
30. The principal looks out for the personal welfare of the faculty.........................	RO	SO	O	VFO
31. The principal supervises teachers closely.......................................	RO	SO	O	VFO
32. The principal talks more than listens..	RO	SO	O	VFO
33. Pupils are trusted to work together without supervision................................	RO	SO	O	VFO
34. Teachers respect the personal competence of their colleagues........................	RO	SO	O	VFO

SOURCE: Used with permission of John A. Mulhern (1984)

leader behavior of secondary principals was conceived as supportive and directive behavior.

Items that directed teacher behavior clustered into three
groups. First, items that described humanistic pupil-teacher interactions joined with those that reflected high teacher morale to
form a strong common factor that was called engaged teacher
behavior. Next, because intimacy items formed a separate identi-
fiable factor, we retained the label, intimate teacher behavior, for
this subtest. Finally, certain disengagement and hindrance items
united on a common factor to form a pattern of teacher behavior
called frustrated. Hence, the patterns of teacher interaction were

described as engaged, intimate, and frustrated teacher behaviors. The five dimensions of climate are summarized as follows:

Supportive principal behavior is directed toward both the social needs and task achievement of the faculty. The principal is helpful, genuinely concerned with teachers, and attempts to motivate them by using constructive criticism and by setting an example through hard work.

Directive principal behavior is rigid and domineering control. The principal maintains close and constant monitoring of all teachers and school activities down to the smallest detail.

Engaged teacher behavior reflects a faculty in which teachers are proud of their school, enjoy working with each other, are supportive of their colleagues, and committed to the success of their students.

Frustrated teacher behavior depicts a faculty that feels itself burdened with routine duties, administrative paperwork, and excessive assignments unrelated to teaching.

Intimate teacher behavior reflects a strong and cohesive network of social relations among the faculty.

Each of these dimensions was measured by a subtest of the OCDQ-RS. Sample items for each subtest are found in Table 3.2. The reliability scores for each of these scales were relatively high: supportive (.94); directive (.79); engaged (.77); frustrated (.77); intimate (.73).

A Test of the Revised Climate Instrument

The revised instrument, OCDQ-RS, contained 34 items that mapped five dimensions of school climate—two at the administrative level and three at the teacher level. The OCDQ-RS is a new instrument. Although it builds upon and refines the original OCDQ, it is a secondary school measure; it is more parsimonious; it has different dimensions; and many of the items are new.

The OCDQ-RS was now ready for further analysis. The questionnaire was tested with a new sample of schools to demonstrate the stability of its factor structure, to confirm the validity and reliability of its subtests, and to explore its second-order factor structure.

Table 3.2 Sample Items for Each Subscale of the OCDQ-RS

SUPPORTIVE PRINCIPAL BEHAVIOR

The principal sets an example by working hard him/herself.
The principal uses constructive criticism.
The principal explains his/her reasons for criticisms to teachers.

DIRECTIVE PRINCIPAL BEHAVIOR

The principal rules with an iron fist.
The principal supervises teachers closely.
The principal monitors everything teachers do.

ENGAGED TEACHER BEHAVIOR

Teachers help and support each other.
Teachers are friendly with students.
Teachers spend time after school with students who have individual problems.

FRUSTRATED TEACHER BEHAVIOR

The mannerisms of teachers at this school are annoying.
Administrative paperwork is burdensome at this school.
Assigned non-teaching duties are excessive.

INTIMATE TEACHER BEHAVIOR

Teachers' closest friends are other faculty members at this school.
Teachers invite other faculty members to visit them at home.
Teachers socialize with each other on a regular basis.

Sample

Seventy-eight high schools in New Jersey participated in the study. A separate, new, random sample of teachers was drawn from each of the 68 pilot schools, and 10 new schools were added to the sample. Although participation was voluntary, we made an effort to obtain a reasonably representative sample of New Jersey secondary schools. Schools ranged in size from 250 to 2,000 students, represented 17 of the state's 22 counties, covered the entire spectrum of the 10 socioeconomic categories used by the state to classify schools, and were drawn from rural, suburban, and urban

Table 3.3 Five-Factor Varimax Solution for the 34 Items of the OCDQ-RS

Subtest	ITEM	I	II	III	IV	V
	5	.83	-.17	.16	-.15	.11
	6	.65	.36	.12	-.18	-.14
Supportive	23	.73	-.13	.12	-.30	.15
Principal	24	.69	.05	.19	-.11	.04
Behavior	25	.76	-.16	.00	-.04	-.01
	29	.81	-.16	.03	-.06	.01
	30	.74	.14	.06	-.12	-.08
	7	-.10	.72	-.15	.10	-.09
Directive	12	-.18	.63	-.17	.10	-.02
Principal	13	-.42	.64	-.10	.16	.13
Behavior	18	.42	.64	-.03	.10	-.01
	19	.04	.78	-.19	.19	.03
	31	-.40	.67	-.05	.22	.05
	32	.40	.75	.05	.16	-.06
	3	.24	.03	.44	-.51	.06
	4	.05	-.14	.63	.04	-.06
	10	.04	-.02	.54	.13	.10
	11	.10	-.20	.58	-.10	.39
Engaged	16	.17	-.04	.76	-.09	.19
Teacher	17	.20	.07	.75	-.30	.09
Behavior	20	.16	-.09	.67	-.42	.19
	28	.30	-.08	.43	-.20	.28
	33	-.01	-.09	.57	-.05	.09
	34	-.03	-.07	.60	-.11	-.02

(continues)

communities. The sample, however, was skewed slightly toward schools in the higher socioeconomic range.

This study was part of a larger study of high schools undertaken by the Rutgers Research Group on Organizational Behavior, in which nearly 5,000 teachers participated. In each school, four different questionnaires were distributed randomly to faculty members. One of these questionnaires contained the items used to develop the Organizational Climate Description Questionnaire for Secondary Schools (OCDQ-RS). Data were collected in faculty meetings and usable responses averaged over 90%.

Table 3.3   (continued)

Subtest	ITEM	I	II	III	IV	V
	1	-.06	.16	-.47	.43	-.06
Frustrated	2	-.20	.16	-.14	.82	.13
Teacher	8	-.09	.05	.07	.74	-.07
Behavior	9	.04	.11	-.16	.51	.20
	15	-.24	.31	-.05	.71	-.08
	22	-.20	.24	-.13	.70	-.03
	14	.13	.09	.21	.09	.58
Intimate	21	.05	.02	.11	.00	.80
Teacher	26	-.03	.01	.00	.00	.49
Behavior	27	-.14	-.17	.28	-.01	.61
Eigenvalue		8.61	4.44	3.77	2.46	1.94
Cumulative Variance		.25	.38	.49	.56	.63

Factor Analysis

School mean scores were calculated for each of the 34 items, and the item-correlation matrix for the 78 schools was factor analyzed. A five-factor solution with a varimax rotation was performed, and the five factors (unrotated) with eigenvalues of 8.61 to 1.94 explained 63.1% of the variance. The five-factor (rotated) solution is presented in Table 3.3.

The results strongly supported the factor structure uncovered in the pilot study. The items loaded on the appropriate subtest and generally loaded highly on only one factor. Moreover, the reliability scores for the subtests in the new data set remained high. The alpha coefficients were as follows:

	Number of items	Reliability (alpha)
Supportive	7	.91
Directive	7	.87
Engaged	10	.85
Frustrated	6	.85
Intimate	4	.71
Total	**34**	

Table 3.4 Intercorrelations and Two-Factor Varimax Solution of
Second-Order Analysis of Subtests

						Second-Order Factors	
Subtest	S	D	E	F	I	I	II
Supportive (S)	(.91)*					.56	.28
Directive (D)	−.09	(.87)				−.62	.27
Engaged (E)	.36	−.20	(.85)			.73	.33
Frustrated (F)	−.30	.41	−.51	(.85)		−.85	.09
Intimate (I)	.05	−.04	.16	.00	(.71)	.01	.89
Eigenvalue						1.99	1.03
Cumulative Variance						.40	.61

*Alpha coefficients of reliability are reported in the parentheses.

Finally, a comparison was made between the factor loadings on
the five factors for the pilot data and for the final data set. The
results were remarkably similar; in fact, the factor structures for
both data sets were virtually identical.

The stability of the factor structure also supports the construct
validity of the dimensions and the constitutive meanings of the
constructs. The relations among the items consistently held as
theoretically expected; that is, the items measuring each subtest
were systematically related to each other as expected in the final
analysis of the OCDQ-RS.

Second-Order Factor Analysis

Following the conceptual formulation of Halpin and Croft in
pursuit of an open-closed continuum, we then performed a second-
order factor analysis on the correlation matrix of the standardized
scores of the five subscales of the OCDQ-RS. The two-factor solution with a varimax rotation is given for the five subtests in Table
3.4. Supportive, directive, engaged, and frustrated behaviors load
strongly on Factor I, while intimate teacher behavior is the only
subtest to load strongly on Factor II. Factor I identifies schools
with energetic principals who lead by example, give teachers wide
latitude in professional decision making, are helpful and supportive, and work toward both the satisfaction of social needs and task
achievement by faculty. Teachers find the work environment facilitating, not frustrating, engage energetically in their teaching

task, and feel optimistic about both their colleagues and their students. This first factor constitutes precisely the *open-closed continuum* the researchers were seeking; hence Factor I was named openness.

The following combination of standardized scores on the subtests provides an openness index for secondary schools.

Openness Index = $(S + E) - (D + F)$

The second factor was defined by only one subtest; accordingly, Factor II was called intimacy.

A Further Test

Once constructed, the OCDQ-RS was tested further. Kottkamp and Mulhern (1987) studied the relationship between the four OCDQ-RS subtests comprising the openness index and expectancy motivation originally conceptualized by Vroom (1964) and operationalized for teachers by Miskel, DeFrain, and Wilcox (1980). Expectancy motivation contains three central constructs. *Valence* is the positive or negative value given by the individual to a reward or incentive potentially available through work in an organization. *Instrumentality* is the perceived probability a given incentive with a given valence will be received as a result of individual performance. *Expectancy* is the subjective probability that a given effort will result in a specified individual performance level. These three elements are combined to yield a score that represents the individual's motivational force (Miskel, DeFrain, and Wilcox, 1980).

It was hypothesized that openness of climate would be positively related to the force of motivation among teachers. The rationale was based on the assumption that where school climate is open—functionally flexible and meeting both task and social needs—teachers readily see the possibility of accomplishing their teaching goals. They see that applying effort toward goals results in achieving them, and they receive commonly desired classroom rewards: social need achievement with students, student task accomplishment, and a sense of personal development (Lortie, 1975).

The hypothesis was tested using the sample of 78 New Jersey high schools described above. In addition to the survey containing the OCDQ-RS items, another questionnaire containing motivation items was distributed to a different randomly selected subset of teachers within the same schools. This procedure strengthened the test by establishing methodological independence between the two measures. Expectancy motivation scores were averaged within each school so that the correlations between school climate and motivation were at the school level of analysis.

The correlation between the average expectancy motivation of teachers and climate openness was .32 ($p < .01$) and accounted for shared variance of about 10%. The confirmation of the climate-motivation hypothesis provides additional support for the validity of the OCDQ-RS.

We also have received numerous requests to use the OCDQ-RS within the United States and across the world (e.g., Australia, Austria, Barbados, Belgium, Canada, Czechoslovakia, Germany, Great Britain, India, Israel, the Netherlands, Portugal, Qatar, Republic of China, Republic of South Africa, and Spain). Most of these requests are from doctoral students. To date, the only completed study we have reviewed was done in India (Sebastian, Thom, & Muth, 1989). The current factor structure was not replicated in their work. Unfortunately, the sample ($N = 30$) was small; nonetheless, the study raises the question of whether the OCDQ-RS can be used cross-culturally or even translated into other languages with reasonable validity.

Summary and Discussion

The OCDQ-RS is a 34-item climate instrument with five dimensions describing the behavior of secondary teachers and principals. The instrument, unlike the original OCDQ, was designed for *secondary* schools. It measures two aspects of principal leadership—supportive and directive behavior, and three aspects of teacher interactions—engaged, frustrated, and intimate behavior. These five aspects of school interaction form two basic dimensions of school climate—openness and intimacy.

Open principal behavior is reflected in genuine relationships with teachers where the principal creates a supportive environment, encourages teacher participation and contribution, and frees teachers from routine busywork so they can concentrate on teaching. In contrast, closed principal behavior is rigid, close, and nonsupportive. Open teacher behavior is characterized by sincere, positive, and supportive relationships with students, administrators, and colleagues; teachers are committed to their school and the success of their students. They find the work environment facilitating rather than frustrating. In brief, openness refers to a school climate where both the teachers' and principal's behavior are authentic, energetic, goal-directed, and supportive, and in which satisfaction is derived both from task accomplishment and social-need gratification.

Intimacy is the second general dimension of secondary school climate. Intimate teacher behavior reflects a strong and cohesive network of social relationships among the faculty. Teachers know each other well, have close personal friends among the faculty, and regularly socialize together. The friendly social interactions that are the essence of this construct are limited, however, to social needs; in fact, task accomplishment is not germane to this dimension.

The conceptual foundations of OCDQ-RS are clear. Unlike the original OCDQ, the new measure has two general factors that are orthogonal. Open school climates may or may not have intimate teacher interactions. Intimacy is neither a sufficient nor a necessary condition for openness. In fact, schools with closed climates may be characterized by intimate teacher relations. In such schools, teachers are a cohesive group opposing an oppressive administration and concerned primarily with social matters. In contrast, some closed climates will not have intimate teacher interactions; relationships among teachers will be just as cold and destructive as they are with the administration.

Similarly, some open school climates will have intimate teacher relationships; others will not. In some schools, a friendly, cohesive, and social faculty will supplement the authentic, goal-directed, and supportive behavior of the faculty and administration. In others, however, close personal friendships and regular social activities typically will occur outside the social network of the school. The data are clear: openness and intimacy are independent aspects of school climate in secondary schools.

The properties of the five subtests of the OCDQ-RS are strong. All the scales have high reliability coefficients, higher than those of the original OCDQ. The subtests are reasonably pure; the factor matrices demonstrate that the items load high on one subtest and relatively low on the others. Moreover, the stability of the factor structures in two separate samples provides evidence of the construct validity of the subtests. Finally the unit of analysis in this study was the school, not the individual; hence the five aspects of school climate are organization properties, not individual ones.

Implications

The OCDQ-RE has both theoretical and research implications. It seems reasonable to predict that openness may be related to positive student outcomes. The subtest that is most different in the OCDQ-RS when contrasted with the original OCDQ is engagement. This scale taps not only teacher behavior with colleagues but also behavior and orientations toward students. Engagement seems most likely to be related directly to student achievement. In engaged schools, the faculty not only trust each other, but are committed to their students. Faculty members are friendly with students, dedicated to their achievement, and optimistic about their ability to succeed. Teacher engagement is a critical element of openness of secondary schools.

The key to successful principal leadership is to influence teachers. In secondary schools the principal who leads by example— that is, who does not ask teachers to do anything he or she would not do, and is supportive and helpful to teachers—will likely find voluntary compliance and cooperation among teachers. This does not mean the principal will not criticize; it means that when criticism comes it is constructive. Rigid and domineering administration rarely produces teacher engagement. In an atmosphere of close monitoring and suspicion, teachers will likely become alienated from their colleagues, frustrated in their tasks, and uncooperative. In brief, principal leadership is instrumental in developing an open organizational climate.

To what extent does climate openness affect such student outcome as self-concept, commitment to school, motivation, absenteeism, vandalism, and achievement? The framework for examining school climate developed here also provides for the study of leadership, motivation, and school effectiveness as well as organizational communication, school structure, decision making, goal setting, and control processes. The OCDQ-RS is a heuristic tool that can address important research questions.

The framework and measure also have more immediate and practical implications. An open school climate is a healthy climate (see Chapters 4, 5, and 6). Open and authentic interactions among teachers and between teachers and the principal should be goals in themselves. The school climate perspective and instrument provide vehicles for addressing the significant issue of improving the work environment. They give practitioners a set of tools to examine and diagnose difficulties and problems in the school.

Increasingly, the secondary school is seen as having unique challenges. Faculty are highly specialized, and the demands upon the school are broad. The principal in this setting may well be more of an institutional manager than is the case with the elementary principal. The OCDQ-RS is a tool for assessing the success of the principal and the commitment of teachers. Influence on the teaching staff can be wholly independent of the conflicts of disciplines and specialties that often plague secondary schools. The general goals of building openness or reducing arbitrary administrative decision making can guide school improvement. The OCDQ-RS seems useful in this regard. It is easily administered to the faculty, simple to score, and provides a quick snapshot of the school atmosphere along some important dimensions.

Note

1. A preliminary version of this work has been published by Kottkamp, Mulhern, and Hoy (1987).

4 The Organizational Health Inventory for Secondary Schools

A reasonably clear conception of organizational health would seem to be an important prerequisite to a wide range of activities involving organizations: research of any meaningful sort; attempts to improve the organization as a place to live, work, and learn; and—not the least—the day-to-day operation of any particular organization, such as your own school system.

—Matthew Miles
Planned Change and Organizational Health

The impetus for using the metaphor of health and well-being to examine the climate of schools came from Miles's (1969) seminal analysis of the organizational health of school systems. In Chapter 1 we delineated the conceptual perspective developed by Miles to assess the functioning of schools. In this chapter we describe the development and refinement of a measure of school health— the Organizational Health Inventory (OHI).

Pilot Study

Miles described a healthy organization as one that "not only survives in its environment, but continues to cope adequately over the long haul, and continuously develops and extends its surviving and coping abilities" (1969, p. 378). He argues that a continually ineffective organization would not be healthy. Although short-run operations on any given day may be effective or ineffective, health implies a summation of effective short-run coping. Miles's framework is a heuristic one for thinking about schools, but its utility as a basis for measuring the organizational health of schools is not well-established (Fairman, Holmes, Hardage, & Lucas, 1979; Kimpston & Sonnabend, 1975; Miles, 1969). Recall that Miles postulated 10 properties of healthy organizations, which are concerned with the task, maintenance, and growth needs of the system. These characteristics of health are cast within the framework of the organization as an open social system; this durable set of system properties is summarized in Table 4.1.

The initial step in the development of an instrument to measure organizational health was to operationalize the framework proposed by Miles, that is, to measure each of his 10 properties. To that end, short, descriptive items were written for each dimension as it might apply to a secondary school. The items then were assessed using the following criteria:

(a) each item reflected a property of the school;
(b) the statement was clear and concise;
(c) the statement had content validity; and
(d) the statement had discriminatory potential.

Item analysis initially was performed using an advanced doctoral seminar in organizational theory and research, and then a panel composed of two professors and two doctoral students used the criteria to eliminate and refine the items. The result was a tentative instrument composed of 113 items measuring the 10 dimensions of health proposed by Miles.

To test the instrument, a sample of 153 secondary school teachers responded to the preliminary scale. The sample of teachers represented a diverse set of secondary schools in New Jersey. Although participation was voluntary, virtually all teachers asked

Table 4.1   Miles's Dimensions of Organizational Health

TASK NEEDS

Goal Focus - Goals are reasonably clear to the system members as well as accepted by them. The goals must also be realistic and appropriate-consistent with the demands of the environment.

Communication Adequacy - Communication is relatively distortion free; it produces a good and prompt sensing of internal strains. Members have the information that they need to function   efficiently.

Optimal Power Equalization -   The distribution of influence is relatively equitable. Subordinates can exert influence upward, and they perceive their superiors can do likewise.

MAINTENANCE NEEDS

Resource Utilization - Personnel is used effectively.   The organization is neither overloaded nor idling.   There is a good fit between individual needs and organizational demands.

Cohesiveness - Members are attracted to the organization and wish to remain.   They are influenced by the organization and exert their own influence on the organization in a collaborative fashion.

Morale - The organization displays a general sense of well-being and group satisfaction.

GROWTH AND DEVELOPMENT NEEDS

Innovativeness-The organization invents new procedures, moves toward new goals, and becomes more differentiated over   time.

Autonomy - The organization is not passive to the environment.   It demonstrates some independence from outside forces.

Adaptation - The organization has the ability to bring about corrective changes in itself to grow and develop.

Problem-Solving Adequacy - Problems are solved with minimal energy, and problem-solving mechanisms are not weakened, but maintained or strengthened.

SOURCE: Adapted from Miles (1969)

to participate in the field testing agreed to help with the project. The responses were factor analyzed to refine, reduce, and classify the items. We expected the items to sort themselves into 10 categories.

A principal components factor analysis with varimax rotation was used, and the results were disappointing, to say the least. Only six factors were identified; five of the factors were variants of Miles's health properties. The first factor, which was composed of six items, we called morale. The second factor contained five cohesiveness items. The third factor, resource utilization, contained only four items. Five items defined a factor that we called optimal power utilization; all reflected the influence of the principal on the organization. The fifth factor was a combination of five items that emphasized academic tasks and accomplishments, which we labeled academic emphasis. Finally, the sixth factor, institutional integrity, represented a combination of five items representing autonomy and adaptation. Thus, only 29 of the 113 items were useful. When alpha coefficients of reliability were computed for each of the six scales, only four of them were reasonable. In brief, the following scales and their properties were developed in the pilot study:

	Number of items	Reliability (alpha)
Morale	6	.93
Cohesiveness	5	.89
Resource Utilization	4	.89
Optimal Power Utilization	5	.82
Academic Emphasis	4	.41
Institutional Integrity	5	.36
Total	**29**	

This attempt to operationalize Miles's notion of organizational health was no more successful than earlier attempts (Fairman et al., 1979; Kimpston & Sonnabend, 1975). Most of the items we wrote were not useful. Only four reliable scales were found from among the 10 dimensions. At this point, we concluded that Miles's framework was not useful for measuring school health. Nonetheless, we were intrigued with the idea of using the health metaphor to conceptualize the climate of a school. What was needed was a robust theory to guide our efforts.

In Search of a Theory: A Parsonian Perspective

After our unsuccessful attempt to operationalize Miles's dimensions of organizational health, we turned our attention to the theoretical analyses of Parsons, Bales, and Shils (1953) and Etzioni (1975) as well as the empirical literature on school effectiveness for a scheme to conceptualize and measure school health. All social systems must solve four basic problems if they are to survive, grow, and develop. Parsons and his colleagues (1953) refer to these as the imperative functions of adaptation, goal attainment, integration, and latency. In other words, schools must solve the problems of

(a) accommodating to their environment,

(b) setting and implementing goals,

(c) maintaining solidarity within the school, and

(d) creating and preserving a unique value system.

In brief, healthy schools effectively meet the instrumental needs of adaptation and goal achievement as well as the expressive needs of social and normative integration; that is, they must mobilize their resources to achieve their goals as well as infuse common values into the work group. Parsons (1967) also noted that schools have three distinct levels of control over these needs—the technical, managerial, and institutional.

The *technical level* of the school is concerned with the teaching-learning process. The primary function of the school is to produce educated students. Moreover, teachers and supervisors have primary responsibility for solving the problems associated with effective learning and teaching.

The *managerial level* controls the internal administrative function of the organization. Principals are the prime administrative officers of the school. They allocate resources and coordinate the work effort. They must find ways to develop teacher loyalty, trust, and commitment as well as to motivate teachers and to influence their own superiors.

The *institutional level* connects the school with its environment. Schools need legitimacy and support in the community. Both administrators and teachers need backing if they are to perform their respective functions in a harmonious fashion without undue pressure from individuals and groups from outside the school.

This broad Parsonian perspective provided the theoretical underpinnings for defining and operationalizing school health. Specifically, *a healthy school is one in which the technical, managerial, and institutional levels are in harmony and the school is meeting both its instrumental and expressive needs as it successfully copes with disruptive external forces and directs its energies toward its mission.*

In more specific terms, eight dimensions of school health were conceptualized using the Parsonian framework. Dimensions were selected to represent each of the basic needs of all social systems as well as the three levels of organizational control. At the institutional level, a dimension called institutional integrity was conceived as the ability of the school to remain relatively independent from its environment. Four managerial dimensions were conceptualized. Initiating structure and consideration of the principal were viewed as basic leadership dimensions, and resource support and influence with superiors were conceived as basic managerial activities. Finally, three critical aspects of the technical level were identified. Morale and cohesiveness were seen as key integrative properties of teacher life, and academic emphasis was conceptualized as a basic feature of effective schools that linked productive teacher and student interactions. These features of school health are summarized in Tables 4.2 and 4.3 to demonstrate their re lationship to the imperative functions and control systems described by Parsons.

Table 4.2 Imperative Functions and Health Dimensions

Health Dimension	Function	Activity
Institutional Integrity	Adaptation	Instrumental
Resource Support	Adaptation	Instrumental
Academic Emphasis	Goal Achievement	Instrumental
Initiating Structure	Goal Achievement	Instrumental
Principal Influence	Integration and Latency	Expressive
Consideration	Integration and Latency	Expressive
Morale	Integration and Latency	Expressive

Table 4.3 Health Dimensions and Hierarchical Level

Hierarchical Level	Health Dimension
Technical (produces teaching and learning)	Academic Emphasis Morale
Managerial (mediates and coordinates internal affairs)	Principal Influence Principal Consideration Principal Initiating Structure Resource Support
Institutional (connects the school with its environment)	Institutional Integrity

Organizational Health Inventory
for Secondary Schools: OHI

Using the Parsonian perspective just described, a measure of organizational health, the Organizational Health Inventory (OHI), was developed.[1] First, the items were generated and evaluated. Next, a pilot study was performed to refine and reduce the number of items and to identify the factor structure of the OHI. Then, the final version of the OHI was tested and the stability of its factor structure and its validity were evaluated.

Item Generation

Items were written to tap the technical, managerial, and institutional levels of the organization. At the technical level, we highlighted such issues as morale, cohesiveness, trust, enthusiasm, support, academic press, order, and achievement. The managerial level was described in terms of the behavior of the principal. In particular, interest centered on task- and achievement-oriented behavior, collegial and supportive behavior, ability to influence superiors, and ability to provide adequate resources for teachers. Institutional concern focused on the school's ability to cope successfully with outside forces. We had a bank of 29 items that were an outgrowth of our first pilot, most of which remained relevant.

New items were written by the researchers either independently or jointly, but no item was included unless there was consensus on its conceptual and content validity, clarity, and potential to discriminate. In all, 95 items were selected for testing in the pilot. Items were simple descriptive statements. Respondents were asked to indicate the extent to which each statement characterized their school along a four-point Likert scale as "rarely occurs," "sometimes occurs," "often occurs," or "very frequently occurs." Examples of items include the following:

- Teachers are protected from unreasonable community and parental demands.
- The principal gets what he or she asks from some superiors.
- The principal looks out for the professional welfare of faculty members.
- The principal lets faculty members know what is expected of them.

- Extra materials are available if requested.
- There is a feeling of trust and confidence among the staff.
- The school sets high standards for academic performance.
- Community demands are accepted even when they are not consistent with the educational program.

Pilot Study

This preliminary version of the OHI contained 95 potential, mostly untested items. Hence, an initial test of the utility of the items was conducted by exploring the factor structure of the instrument. A sample of 72 secondary schools was identified, which included urban, suburban, and rural schools and represented a diverse subset of secondary schools. Data were collected from a random sample of teachers in each school. However, because the unit of analysis was the school, the individual data were aggregated at the school level for each item, and exploratory procedures were performed to reduce the number of items and determine the factor structure of the instrument.

Three criteria were used to refine the OHI. First, the criterion of simple structure was employed in all factor analyses; only items that loaded high on one factor and weak on all others were retained. Next, in addition to their mathematical contribution to the factor (high factor loadings), items were evaluated for conceptual clarity and fit; that is, items were retained only if they clearly were related to the concept being measured. Finally, items were eliminated if they reduced substantially the internal consistency of the subtests as measured by Cronbach's coefficient alpha. School mean scores were generated for each item, and the item-correlation matrices were factored.

Using the criteria specified above, a series of exploratory factor analyses of the pilot data was performed and the number of items was reduced by one half. Ultimately, using a principal components factor analysis with a varimax rotation, a seven-factor solution was selected as the best solution. Instead of the eight-factor solution that was expected, only seven factors were identified. The morale and cohesiveness items merged to produce one strong morale dimension. Forty-four items remained in the refined OHI, which defined seven dimensions of school health. The final set of items is summarized in Table 4.4.

Table 4.4 Items in the Final Version of the OHI

1. Teachers are protected from unreasonable community and parental demands........	RO SO O VFO
2. The principal gets what he or she asks for from superiors.................................	RO SO O VFO
3. The principal is friendly and approachable..	RO SO O VFO
4. The principal asks that faculty members follow standard rules and regulations....	RO SO O VFO
5. Extra materials are available if requested...	RO SO O VFO
6. Teachers do favors for each other..	RO SO O VFO
7. The students in this school can achieve the goals that have been set for them........	RO SO O VFO
8. The school is vulnerable to outside pressures...	RO SO O VFO
9. The principal is able to influence the actions of his or her superiors...................	RO SO O VFO
10. The principal treats all faculty members as his or her equal...............................	RO SO O VFO
11. The principal makes his or her attitudes clear to the school................................	RO SO O VFO
12. Teachers are provided with adequate materials for their classrooms...................	RO SO O VFO
13. Teachers in this school like each other..	RO SO O VFO
14. The school sets high standards for academic performance.................................	RO SO O VFO
15. Community demands are accepted even when they are not consistent with the educational program...	RO SO O VFO
16. The principal is able to work well with the superintendent.................................	RO SO O VFO
17. The principal puts suggestions made by the faculty into operation......................	RO SO O VFO
18. The principal lets faculty know what is expected of them...................................	RO SO O VFO
19. Teachers receive necessary classroom supplies...	RO SO O VFO
20. Teachers are indifferent to each other...	RO SO O VFO
21. Students respect others who get good grades...	RO SO O VFO
22. Teachers feel pressure from the community...	RO SO O VFO
23. The principal's recommendations are given serious consideration by his or her superiors...	RO SO O VFO
24. The principal is willing to make changes...	RO SO O VFO
25. The principal maintains definite standards of performance.................................	RO SO O VFO
26. Supplementary materials are available for classroom use...................................	RO SO O VFO
27. Teachers exhibit friendliness to each other...	RO SO O VFO
28. Students seek extra work so they can get good grades..	RO SO O VFO
29. Select citizen groups are influential with the board..	RO SO O VFO
30. The principal is impeded by the superiors...	RO SO O VFO
31. The principal looks out for the personal welfare of faculty members..................	RO SO O VFO
32. The principal schedules the work to be done...	RO SO O VFO
33. Teachers have access to needed instructional materials......................................	RO SO O VFO
34. Teachers in this school are cool and aloof to each other.....................................	RO SO O VFO
35. Teachers in this school believe that their students have the ability to achieve academically...	RO SO O VFO
36. The school is open to the whims of the public...	RO SO O VFO
37. The morale of the teachers is high..	RO SO O VFO
38. Academic achievement is recognized and acknowledged by the school...................	RO SO O VFO
39. A few vocal parents can change school policy...	RO SO O VFO
40. There is a feeling of trust and confidence among the staff.................................	RO SO O VFO
41. Students try hard to improve on previous work...	RO SO O VFO
42. Teachers accomplish their jobs with enthusiasm..	RO SO O VFO
43. The learning environment is orderly and serious..	RO SO O VFO
44. Teachers identify with the school...	RO SO O VFO

SOURCE: Used with permission of John A. Feldman (1985)

Dimensions of Secondary School Health

Thus the pilot study led to the specification and measure of seven dimensions of organizational health—institutional integrity, principal influence, consideration, initiating structure, resource support, morale, and academic emphasis. These critical aspects of organizational life meet the instrumental and expressive needs of the school social system, and they fall into Parsons's three levels of responsibility and control within the school.

Institutional integrity is the school's ability to cope with its environment in a way that maintains the educational integrity of its programs. Teachers are protected from unreasonable community and parental demands.

Principal influence is the principal's ability to influence the actions of superiors. Being able to persuade superiors, to get additional consideration, and to proceed unimpeded by the hierarchy are important aspects of school administration.

Consideration is principal behavior that is friendly, supportive, open, and collegial; it represents a genuine concern on the part of the principal for the welfare of the teachers.

Initiating structure is principal behavior that is both task- and achievement-oriented. Work expectations, standards of performance, and procedures are articulated clearly by the principal.

Resource support refers to a school where adequate classroom supplies and instructional materials are available and extra materials are readily supplied if requested.

Morale is a collective sense of friendliness, openness, enthusiasm, and trust among faculty members. Teachers like each other, like their jobs, and help each other, and they are proud of their school and feel a sense of accomplishment in their jobs.

Academic emphasis is the extent to which the school is driven by a quest for academic excellence. High but achievable academic goals are set for students; the learning environment is orderly and serious; teachers believe in their students' ability to achieve; and students work hard and respect those who do well academically.

Thus institutional integrity serves as an indicator of health at the institutional level. Principal influence, consideration, initiating structure, and resource support provide measures of the health of the managerial system; morale and academic emphasis are the indices of health at the technical level. Each of these

Table 4.5   Sample Items for Health Subtests

INSTITUTIONAL INTEGRITY

Teachers are protected from unreasonable community and parental demands.
The school is vulnerable to outside pressure.*

PRINCIPAL INFLUENCE

The principal is able to influence the actions of superiors.
The principal is impeded by superiors.*

CONSIDERATION

The principal is friendly and approachable.
The principal looks out for the personal welfare of faculty members.

INITIATING STRUCTURE

The principal lets faculty know what is expected of them.
The principal schedules work to be done.

RESOURCE SUPPORT

Teachers receive necessary classroom supplies.
Extra materials are available if requested.

MORALE

Teachers identify with the school.
Teachers are indifferent to each other.*

ACADEMIC EMPHASIS

The school sets high standards for academic performance.
The learning environment is orderly and serious.

---

*Score is reversed

dimensions of organizational health is measured by a subtest of
the OHI. Sample items for each subtest are provided in Table 4.5.

A Test of the New Instrument: OHI

Having completed the data reduction and conceptualization of the OHI in the pilot study, the 44-item instrument was ready to be tested with a new data set in order to demonstrate the stability of the factor structure, confirm the validity and reliability of the subtests, and explore the second-order factor structure.

Sample

Seventy-eight secondary schools in New Jersey agreed to participate in the study. A separate, new, random sample of at least five teachers was drawn from each of the 72 pilot schools and from six additional schools that were added to the sample. Although the school sample was not a random one, it was a diverse one representing a broad range of districts and spanning the entire range of socioeconomic status. Schools that participated came from 17 of the 21 counties in the state. If any group of schools was underrepresented it was the urban one; only 7.5% of the schools were from urban districts.

Typically, data were collected by a researcher at a regular faculty meeting, but in a few schools, a faculty member collected the anonymous questionnaires. The faculty selected at random responded to the OHI and the others responded to a battery of other instruments, which was not part of the OHI development. In total, 1,131 educators in 78 secondary schools participated in the study.

Factor Analysis

School mean scores were calculated for each item, and the item-correlation matrix from the 78 schools was factor analyzed. Seven factors with eigenvalues from 14.28 to 1.35 explaining 74% of the variance were retained. The seven-factor solution, after the varimax rotation, is summarized and presented in Table 4.6.

The results support strongly the factor structure discovered in the pilot study. The items loaded on the appropriate subtest, and the reliability scores for each subtest were high; the alpha coefficients were as follows: institutional integrity (.91); principal influence (.87); consideration (.90); initiating structure (.89); resource support (.95); morale (.92); and academic emphasis (.93). The

Table 4.6 Seven-Factor Varimax Solution for the 44 Items of the OHI

SUBTEST	ITEM	I	II	III	IV	V	VI	VII
	7	.66	.28	.09	.30	.20	.12	.05
	14	.83	.16	.07	.17	.09	.25	.13
	21	.82	.16	-.07	.06	.12	-.09	.16
Academic	28	.75	-.07	.09	.14	.17	-.01	.05
Emphasis	35	.84	.11	.11	.16	.14	.12	.02
	38	.74	.12	-.14	.01	.08	.32	.02
	41	.85	.17	-.01	.06	.03	.11	.11
	43	.68	.29	-.22	.32	.07	.31	.10
	6	.07	.80	-.03	.20	.02	.07	-.07
	13	.20	.87	-.12	-.01	-.02	.03	.03
	20	.12	.79	-.17	-.09	-.07	.08	-.07
	27	.16	.83	-.16	.09	.03	-.02	.07
Morale	34	-.04	.72	-.15	.08	.10	.04	-.04
	37	.08	.52	-.27	.26	.42	.23	.17
	42	.46	.61	-.11	.16	.09	.07	.17
	40	.15	.69	-.26	-.02	.42	.09	.19
	44	.26	.66	-.28	.29	.24	.15	-.09
	1	-.20	-.20	.70	-.22	-.12	-.23	-.20
	8	-.12	-.10	.85	.06	-.01	+.05	-.19
Institutional	15	.00	-.14	.81	-.12	-.11	-.17	.06
Integrity	22	.28	-.19	.78	-.04	-.01	.09	-.04
	29	.09	-.24	.70	.02	-.22	.11	-.20
	36	-.10	-.09	.75	-.08	-.18	-.24	.07
	39	-.04	-.18	.82	-.01	-.15	-.13	-.16

(continues)

pattern of factor loadings in the pilot study was virtually identical to the pattern in the final test.

The stability of the factor structure of the OHI also supports the construct validity of the seven dimensions of school health. Factor analysis enables the researchers to study the constitutive meanings of constructs and, thus, their construct validity (Kerlinger, 1986). In the present investigation, seven hypothetical entities—dimensions of organizational health—were constructed. The relations among the items consistently held up as theoretically expected; that is, the items (variables) measuring each dimension systematically were related as predicted.

Table 4.6 (continued)

SUBTEST	ITEM	I	II	III	IV	V	VI	VII
	5	.07	.04	-.06	.86	.20	.01	.15
	12	.23	.14	-.05	.88	.04	.11	.04
Resource	19	.17	.17	-.08	.88	.05	.12	.14
Support	26	.16	.15	.03	.88	.02	-.01	.10
	33	.17	.21	-.21	.84	.10	.04	.19
	3	.08	.07	-.14	-.01	.91	-.02	.03
	10	.08	.22	-.18	-.07	.80	-.06	.10
Consideration	17	.10	.07	-.08	.12	.77	.25	.04
	24	.27	.04	-.11	.27	.74	.18	-.01
	31	.25	.13	-.09	.18	.74	.30	-.02
	4	-.02	.13	-.07	.03	-.10	.79	-.02
	11	.27	.10	-.17	.03	.24	.78	.16
Initiating	18	.23	.13	-.17	.01	.23	.80	.18
Structure	25	.43	.09	-.23	-.02	.28	.64	.26
	32	.10	-.06	.04	.15	.15	.70	.25
	2	.31	.02	-.03	.21	.04	.27	.66
	9	.26	.12	-.19	.23	.12	.50	.55
Principal	16	.10	-.02	-.04	.10	.09	.13	.83
Influence	23	.30	.11	-.16	.36	.16	.42	.55
	30	.01	.07	-.22	.39	-.08	.15	.60
Eigenvalue		14.280	5.056	3.808	3.454	2.711	2.037	1.375
Cumulative Variance		.32	.44	.52	.60	.67	.71	.74

Second-Order Factor Analysis

Next, we examined the underlying structure of the seven dimensions of the OHI. Is there a more general set of factors that defines the health of a school? To answer this question, subtest scores for each school were computed and a correlation matrix among the subtests was derived. Because many of the correlations were moderate (see Table 4.7), it was appropriate to perform a second-order factor analysis on the subtest correlations.

One strong general factor emerged that accounted for 45% of the variance; in fact, this factor was the only one to meet Kaiser's (1960) criterion of an eigenvalue greater than one. Likewise, a scree test (Rummel, 1970) yielded the same second-order factor. All of the dimensions of organizational health had strong factor

Table 4.7 Correlations Among the Seven Subtests of the OHI

Subtest	AE	M	II	RS	C	IS	PI
Academic Emphasis (AE)	(.93)*						
Morale (M)	.45	(.92)					
Institutional Integrity (II)	.11	.46	(.91)				
Resource Support (RS)	.40	.37	.18	(.95)			
Consideration (C)	.36	.42	.32	.25	(.90)		
Initiating Structure (IS)	.47	.34	.31	.23	.39	(.89)	
Principal Influence (PI)	.44	.30	.37	.47	.28	.58	(.87)

*Alpha coefficients of reliability for the subtests are displayed in the parentheses

loadings on this general factor: institutional integrity (.563); principal influence (.747); consideration (.633); initiating structure (.722); resource support (.607); morale (.707); and academic emphasis (.703). The factor identified schools that were relatively strong on all seven dimensions. Accordingly, the factor was called school health. An index of the health of a school can be determined simply by adding the standard scores on the seven subtests; the higher the score, the healthier the school dynamics. It is possible to sketch a description of the prototype for each of the poles of the continuum—that is, for very healthy and unhealthy schools.

Healthy school. A healthy school is protected from unreasonable community and parental pressures. The board successfully resists all narrow efforts of vested interest groups to influence policy (high institutional integrity). The principal of a healthy school is a dynamic leader, integrating both task-oriented and relations-oriented leader behavior. Such behavior is supportive of teachers and yet provides high standards for performance (high consideration and initiating structure). Moreover, the principal has influence with her or his superiors, which is demonstrated by the ability to get what is needed for the effective operation of the school (high influence). Teachers in a healthy school are committed to teaching and learning. They set high but achievable goals for students, maintain high standards of performance, and promote a serious and orderly learning environment. Furthermore, students work hard on their school work, are highly motivated, and respect other students who achieve academically (high academic emphasis). Classroom supplies, instructional materials, and supplementary materials always are available (high resource support). Finally, in healthy schools, teachers like each other, trust each other, are enthusiastic about their work, and identify positively with the school. They are proud of their school (high morale).

Unhealthy school. The unhealthy school is vulnerable to destructive outside forces. Teachers and administrators are bombarded by unreasonable parental demands, and the school is buffeted by the whims of the public (low institutional integrity). The school is without an effective principal. The principal provides little direction or structure (low initiating structure), exhibits little encouragement and support for teachers (low consideration), and has little clout with superiors (low influence). Teachers feel good about neither their colleagues nor their jobs. They act aloof, suspicious, and defensive (low morale). Instructional materials, supplies, and supplementary materials are not available when needed (low resource support). Finally, there is little press for academic excellence. Neither teachers nor students take academic life seriously; in fact, academically oriented students are ridiculed by their peers and viewed by their teachers as threats (low academic emphasis).

Prototypic profiles for healthy and unhealthy schools are depicted in Figure 4.1. A score of 500 is average on each of the health dimensions; standard deviation is 100. Schools with scores above 550 are relatively high on the dimensions, and scores below 450 are relatively low. Most secondary schools that we have examined using the OHI fall between the two prototypes in Figure 4.1.

Health Index

The seven subtests developed to measure the critical dimensions of school life are highly reliable scales that have reasonable construct validity. Moreover, given the emergence of one strong second-order factor (healthiness), it is possible to create a general index of health for each school. The seven aspects of health fit together to form a general indicator of health. Simply by summing the standard scores of all the subtests a health index is computed—the higher the score, the healthier the organizational

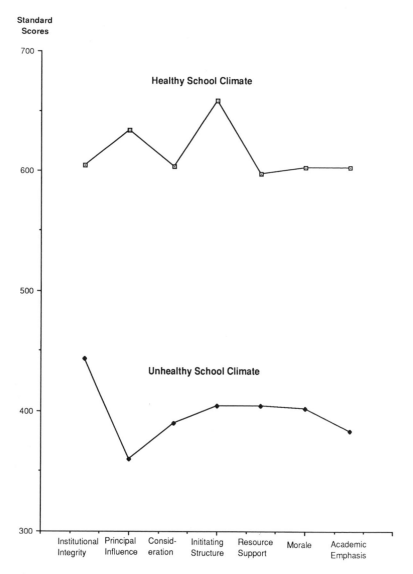

Figure 4.1. Contrasting Health Profiles

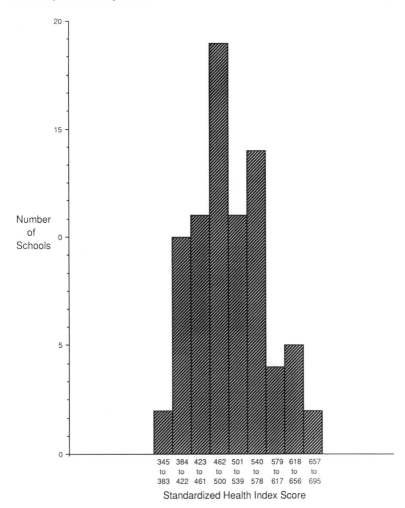

Figure 4.2. Distribution of School Health Scores

dynamics in a school. We standardized the scores using a mean of 500 and a standard deviation of 100. In the present study, the schools arrayed themselves along a continuum from healthy to unhealthy; health index scores ranged from 360 to 670, with a mean of 500. The distribution of health scores is depicted in Figure 4.2.

Summary and Discussion

The Organizational Health Inventory (OHI) is a new, 44-item instrument that maps the organizational health of secondary schools along seven dimensions. At the technical level, the faculty morale and the academic press of the school are seen as critical ingredients of good school health. At the managerial level, the leadership and support of the principal in terms of consideration, initiating structure, influence with superiors, and resource support are key elements. Finally, healthy schools have institutional integrity; they cope with disruptive external forces and direct their energies toward the educational mission.

The OHI has considerable research potential as well as practical utility. Our preliminary research findings are encouraging and provide further support for the validity of the instrument. As one would expect, the healthier the organizational dynamics of a school, the greater the degree of faculty trust in the principal, trust in colleagues, and trust in the organization itself (Tarter & Hoy, 1988). Indeed, trust has been identified as a basic characteristic of effective organizational cultures (Ouchi, 1981; Peters & Waterman, 1982). As Ouchi (1981) noted, "productivity and trust go hand in hand." Healthy school climates also have more open organizational climates; teacher interactions with each other and the principal are open and authentic. Likewise, trust and authenticity go together (Hoy & Kupersmith, 1985). In brief, healthy school climates are characterized by many of the same attributes stressed in the effective schools literature: an orderly and serious environment; visible rewards for academic achievement; influential principals who blend their behavior to fit the situation; openness in behavior; and a cohesive work unit based upon mutual trust.

Much remains to be demonstrated by subsequent study, but we suspect that a school's health is likely to be related to less student alienation, lower dropout rates, greater student and faculty motivation, and higher student achievement. Clearly, there are many important school variables that likely are related to school health, including absenteeism, the number of merit scholars, and the comprehensiveness of extracurricular and athletic programs. Healthy schools also should have principals who are more resourceful, confident, secure, and change-oriented than those found in less healthy schools. Moreover, principals of healthy schools should have more dedicated, loyal, and satisfied teachers who are resourceful, secure, and innovative. Healthy organizational climates also provide atmospheres conducive to the improvement of instruction through cooperative and diagnostic supervision; in fact, healthy organizational dynamics are necessary conditions for an effective program of supervision.

Implications

What implications does this research have for students of administration? The OHI is a parsimonious and reliable research tool ready for further testing. The instrument is one of the few measures that has been designed for use in secondary schools. The health inventory provides measures of seven important attributes of student-teacher, teacher-teacher, teacher-principal, and principal-superior relationships, which fit together in a way that yields a global index of the state of organizational health.

The instrument and its conceptual underpinnings provide a framework for the study of leadership, motivation, decision making, structure, communication, and school effectiveness, as well as a perspective for evaluating school improvement programs. Although the OHI was developed for use in secondary schools, the framework seems sound for work in elementary schools, but it should be tested and evaluated in a variety of other samples, including elementary ones (see Chapter 5). Clearly the OHI is a heuristic instrument both for researchers and practitioners.

What implications does this research have for administrators? For those administrators who seriously are interested in change and improving school effectiveness, the OHI offers a simple diagnostic tool. Improvement of instruction, curriculum development, and critical inquiry into the teaching-learning process are likely only in schools with a healthy organizational climate. Healthy climates can be facilitated by enlightened and secure administrators who are willing to evaluate systematically the state of health of their schools. The OHI can be used to provide baseline data on seven critical dimensions as well as a general index of organizational health. Principals and superintendents not only can determine the health of their schools, they can compare their own perceptions of the working atmosphere with the perceptions of their teachers. Discrepancies often are at the heart of many school problems.

The position taken here is that improvement in the state of organizational health should be the prime target of change efforts in schools because only when the systems' dynamics are open and healthy will more specific change strategies be effective. Successful innovation requires self-study, security, and commitment of the professional staff. Change is a systematic process that demands not only modifying individual attitudes but also developing new relationships among members in group settings. Focusing efforts on groups and relationships, and increasing the flow of information about the organization to participants, often alters existing norms that regulate interpersonal transactions in groups.

We agree with Miles (1969) that the state of organizational health will likely tell us more than anything else about the probable success of most change efforts: "Economy of effort would suggest that we should look at the state of an organization's health as such, and try to improve it—in preference to struggling with a series of more or less inspired short-run change efforts as ends in themselves" (p. 388). This is not to say that schools must be in a perfect state of health before any meaningful change can occur, but rather that the basic innovation should be one of organizational development itself.

Note

1. A preliminary version of this research has been published by Hoy and Feldman (1987).

5 The Organizational Health Inventory for Elementary Schools

Teachers stand ready to award deference and loyalty to principals who make their authority available to teachers; that authority can help them achieve working conditions which favor classroom achievement and its rewards.

—Dan Lortie
Schoolteacher: A Sociological Study

Given the success of the health metaphor in conceptualizing and measuring the climate of secondary schools, we turn our attention to elementary schools. Other research (Fieldler, 1972; Kottkamp, Mulhern, & Hoy, 1987; Herriott & Firestone, 1984) has demonstrated that elementary schools are substantially different than secondary schools in structure, complexity, and climate; thus we expected to find that an OHI for the elementary school would differ in several important aspects from the typical OHI for a secondary school. This expectation was borne out in the analyses.

We first describe findings from several pilot studies and then consolidate those results in a larger developmental study of an elementary version of the Organizational Health Inventory. Analyses of school health in pilot studies of elementary schools showed the collapse of some secondary health dimensions into larger factors. With respect to leadership, both consideration and initiating structure combined to form a factor we call collegial leadership. What had been resource support and principal influence combined to form a factor we call resource influence, an element of principal behavior that describes the principal's efforts to influence superiors so that teachers have the materials they feel they need to carry out their tasks.

Pilot Study I

In the first pilot (Podgurski, 1990), the secondary version of the OHI was reviewed to make it a more appropriate measure of the health of the elementary school. Old items were modified or deleted and new items were created depending upon how well the item was judged to discriminate in describing some element of life in the elementary school. The new items were consistent with the original criteria used in the development of the OHI. Namely, each item reflected a property of the school, the statement was clear and concise, the statement had content validity, and the statement had discriminatory potential. This preliminary elementary version, which now had 65 items, was given to a sample of 131 elementary teachers. Sample items of the OHI can be found in Table 5.1.

The sample of teachers was one of opportunity: Teachers taking graduate courses in two institutions, and some of their colleagues in the field, were asked to respond to the instrument. The sample represented a wide variety of elementary schools. This pilot study was used as a coarse screen to reduce and refine the items to be used in the development of an initial version of the OHI. The scores of individual teachers were used to represent the typical response expected for teachers in their schools. Thus the 131 teachers in this sample provide climate scores for 131 schools.

Factor analysis of the data from this sample identified eight factors. Academic emphasis separated into two subtests—teachers' academic orientation and students' academic orientation. These were the weakest of the health dimensions, and neither scale had a reliability coefficient above .60; however, the two subtests combined had an alpha coefficient of .69. On balance, the

Table 5.1 Sample Items for Health Subtests

INSTITUTIONAL INTEGRITY

A few vocal parents can change school policy.*
Select citizen groups are influential with the board.*

PRINCIPAL INFLUENCE

The principal's recommendations are given serious consideration by his or her superiors.
The principal gets caught in the middle between teachers and superiors.*

CONSIDERATION

The principal treats teachers as equals.
The principal goes out of his/her way to show appreciation to teachers.

INITIATING STRUCTURE

The principal maintains definite standards of performance.
The principal corrects teachers' mistakes.

RESOURCE SUPPORT

Teachers are provided with adequate materials for their classrooms.
Supplementary materials are available for classroom use.

MORALE

Teachers exhibit friendliness to each other.
Teachers accomplish their jobs with enthusiasm.

ACADEMIC EMPHASIS

Students try hard to improve on previous work.
Students are cooperative during classroom instruction.

---

*Score is reversed

seven factors were defined by a set of 40 items and each factor had a sufficient reliability score to proceed to the next step of development: resource support = .92; institutional integrity = .85; consideration = .88; morale = .91; initiating structure = .78; principal influence = .77; academic emphasis = .69. Because of the conceptual

Table 5.2 Preliminary Organizational Health Inventory for Elementary
Schools (OHI-E)

(AE) 1. Students respect others who get good grades.
(II) 2. Select citizen groups are influential with the board.
(AE) 3. Teachers set high standards for their classroom performance.
(C) 4. The principal goes out of his or her way to show appreciation to teachers.
(AE) 5. Students receive recognition for academic achievement.**
(IS) 6. The principal conducts meaningful evaluations.
(RS) 7. Supplementary materials are available for classroom use.
(II) 8. The school is open to the whims of the public.
(C) 9. The principal treats faculty members as his or her equal.
(AE) 10. Students are cooperative during classroom instruction.
(PI) 11. The principal is impeded by superiors.
(AE) 12. Academic achievement is recognized and acknowledged by the school.**
(AE) 13. Students try hard to improve on previous work.
(IS) 14. The principal corrects teacher's mistakes.**
(AE) 15. The school sets high standards for academic performance.
(AE) 16. Teachers show commitment to their students.
(IS) 17. The principal lets faculty know what is expected of them.
(RS) 18. Teachers receive necessary classroom supplies.
(II) 19. Teachers feel pressure from the community.
(AE) 20. The school encourages teachers to strive for excellence.
(M) 21. There is a feeling of trust and confidence among the staff.
(IS) 22. The principal maintains definite standards of performance.
(AE) 23. Students neglect to complete homework.
(M) 24. Teachers are indifferent to each other.
(C) 25. The principal discusses classroom issues with teachers.
(AE) 26. The learning environment is orderly and serious.
(II) 27. The school is vulnerable to outside pressure.
(M) 28. Teachers express pride in this school.
(M) 29. Teachers exhibit friendliness to each other.
(AE) 30. Students are not prepared to participate in classroom lessons.**
(RS) 31. Extra materials are available if requested.
(C) 32. The principal accepts questions without appearing to snub or quash the teacher.
(M) 33. Teachers identify with the school.
(II) 34. Community demands are accepted even when they are not consistent with the
educational programs.

(continues)

ambiguity of the academic emphasis dimension and its low reliability, seven new items were developed to measure academic
emphasis of elementary schools. Two new items also were added
to bolster the morale and consideration subtests. The final 49

Table 5.2 (continued)

(AE) 35. Teachers in this school believe that their students have the ability to achieve
         academically.
(C) 36. The principal looks out for the personal welfare of faculty members.
(I I) 37. A few vocal parents can change school policy.
(RS) 38. Teachers have access to needed instructional materials.**
(P I) 39. The principal gets caught in the middle between teachers and superiors.
(I I) 40. Teachers are protected from unreasonable community and parental demands.**
(M) 41. Teachers in this school like each other.
(RS) 42. Teachers are provided with adequate materials for their classrooms.
(P I) 43. The principal is able to influence the actions of his or her superiors.
(P I) 44. The principal gets what he or she asks for from superiors.
(P I) 45. The principal's recommendations are given serious consideration by his or her
         superiors.
(M) 46. Teachers accomplish their jobs with enthusiasm.
(C) 47. The principal explores all sides of topics and admits that other opinions exist.
(AE) 48. Students seek extra work so they can get good grades.
(C) 49. The principal is friendly and approachable.

NOTE: II = Institutional Integrity   RS = Resource Support   IS = Initiating Structure
M = Morale   C = Consideration   AE = Academic Emphasis   PI = Principal Influence
**Items deleted in pilot study II

SOURCE: Used with permission of Thomas P. Podgurski (1990)

items that composed the OHI in its initial elementary version are
given in Table 5.2.

Pilot Study II

The 49-item version of the OHI-E was given to a sample of 598
educators from 41 elementary schools representing middle class,
suburban, and rural communities in a further test of the instrument's factor stability (Podgurski, 1990). The unit of analysis
for this phase of the investigation was the school; therefore, the
individual responses from each school were averaged to represent
school properties, the dimensions of organizational health.

The most striking result of the survey was that the original
seven-factor description of organizational health at the secondary
level appeared to consolidate into six factors at the elementary
level. Initiating structure and consideration merged into a factor
called integrated leadership. Apparently, elementary principals
who are task oriented also are considerate and supportive in

working with teachers. Six of the 49 items (see Table 5.2), however, were conceptually vague or did not load strongly on one and only one factor. Thus only 43 of the 49 items were useful.[1] When alpha coefficients of reliability were computed, the following scales and their properties were established:

	Number of items	Reliability (alpha)
Institutional Integrity	6	.87
Integrated Leadership	10	.95
Principal Influence	5	.85
Resource Support	4	.89
Morale	11	.93
Academic Emphasis	7	.90
Total	**43**	

Organizational Health Inventory for Elementary Schools: OHI-E

A final test of the OHI-E was performed by combining the 41 schools of the second pilot with an additional 37 schools. This additional analysis was done for three reasons: first, to check the factor stability of the instrument; second, to check the reliability of the subtests; and third, to provide a broader sample of schools representing a variety of social and economic levels as well as regions within the state. Then the findings were examined within the Parsonian framework that drove the concept of organizational health.

A Test of the Revised OHI-E

Our goal remained to develop a parsimonious instrument using the criterion of simple structure; only items that loaded high on one factor and relatively low on all others were retained. Items were evaluated for conceptual clarity and fit; that is, items were retained only if they were judged to be valid measures of the subtest. The ultimate test of what items remained in the inventory was based on both conceptual fit and empirical results.

Sample

Seventy-eight elementary schools provided the sample for this analysis. Given that the health measures are organizational prop-

Table 5.3   Five-Factor Varimax Solution for the 43 Items of the OHI-E

SUBTEST	ITEM	I	II	III	IV	V
	29	.82	.22	.07	.03	.06
	28	.81	.21	.26	-.03	.15
	41	.81	.36	.01	.06	.01
	24	.79	.15	.07	.23	-.12
	46	.77	.06	.20	.11	.03
Affiliation	33	.71	.31	.22	.17	.23
	16	.69	.07	.13	-.04	.16
	21	.68	.48	.17	.09	-.02
	26	.62	.23	.05	-.01	.31
	**15	.57	.11	.25	-.14	.46
	**35	.54	.12	.22	.12	.44
	**3	.54	.17	.19	.02	.35
	**20	.52	.25	.30	-.27	.36
	9	.11	.85	-.01	.17	.12
	47	.17	.85	.17	.01	.22
	4	.12	.83	.16	.09	.19
	49	.28	.79	-.01	.18	.04
Collegial	32	.21	.79	.16	.24	.01
Leadership	36	.29	.74	.24	.07	.11
	25	.16	.68	.26	-.08	.25
	6	.06	.68	.42	.01	.14
	17	.29	.66	.21	-.16	.18
	22	.35	.62	.36	-.09	.14
	31	.24	.13	.77	.07	-.03
	7	.09	.02	.75	.17	.18
	18	.21	.07	.73	.07	-.04
Resource	44	.11	.25	.66	-.02	.16
Influence	42	.31	.25	.65	.11	.11
	43	-.04	.31	.63	-.03	.12
	45	.20	.35	.57	.09	.18

(continues)

erties and not individual ones, school means were generated for each item of the OHI-E by averaging the scores of the respondents in each school on each item. Thus each school had an aggregated response for each item; the school was the unit of analysis. The responding teachers had a mean of 14.5 years of experience and an average age of 42; most were tenured (80%) and women (83%). Typically, they taught classes of about 20-28 students.

Table 5.3 (continued)

SUBTEST	ITEM	I	II	III	IV	V
	2 7	.07	.17	.16	.83	.09
	1 9	-.09	-.05	.01	.79	-.12
Institutional	3 7	.15	.21	.13	.79	.10
Integrity	8	.20	.10	-.08	.77	.06
	3 4	.08	.05	.12	.73	.09
	2	-.09	-.05	.02	.71	-.11
	1	.31	.17	.12	.17	.68
	1 3	.30	.15	.20	.17	.64
	4 8	.26	.23	.09	.05	.63
Academic	2 3	.37	.14	-.05	.22	.53
Emphasis	1 0	.41	-.01	-.01	.01	.43
	** 3 9	-.19	.11	-.01	-.11	.35
	** 1 1	-.05	.06	.10	-.11	.28
Eigenvalue		14.586	4.269	3.874	2.669	2.261
Cumulative Varianced		.35	.45	.54	.61	.66

**Items deleted

Factor Analysis

School means were calculated for each item and the item-correlation matrix from the 78 schools was factor analyzed. Factor analysis of this combined data set revealed five factors that explained about 66% of the variance—that is, the original seven factors of the OHI collapsed into five factors in this investigation of elementary schools. The construction of the five factors was guided by the factor eigenvalues (an index of contribution of each factor), the reliability score of each factor, and the conceptual appropriateness of each item on the dimension. The five-factor solution, after varimax rotation, is summarized and presented in Table 5.3. Note that six of the 43 items have been deleted from the dimensions because they load high on two aspects of health or are conceptually misplaced.

Four of the six health dimensions of the second pilot were replicated in the final analysis: teacher affiliation, collegial leadership, institutional integrity, and academic emphasis. Initiating structure and consideration merged in this analysis, as they did in the pilot, to form collegial leadership. Unlike the pilot, however, principal influence and resource support came together to define resource influence. One aspect of health we have named teacher affiliation rather than morale because these items represented not only the morale of the school but a strong identification with the school, the job, and one's students and colleagues. Principal influence and resource support were not identified as distinct subtests of the OHI-E. As we have seen, these two dimensions become one factor, which we have labeled resource influence. The number of items and reliability coefficients for each subtest are summarized below:

	Number of items	Reliability (alpha)
Teacher Affiliation	9	.94
Collegial Leadership	10	.95
Resource Influence	7	.89
Institutional Integrity	6	.90
Academic Emphasis	5	.87
Total	**37**	

Sample items for each subtest of the final OHI-E are given in Table 5.4.

Dimensions of Elementary School Health

Teacher affiliation emerged as the strongest factor underlying organizational health, just as morale had been on previous analyses. Teacher affiliation represents not only friendliness among teachers and between students and teachers, but a commitment to the seriousness of the teaching-learning enterprise. Such items as "Teachers show commitment to their students" and "The learning environment is orderly and serious" measure the notion of affiliation as a normative identification with the people and goals of the organization. Drawing on the Parsonian framework and the items on the subtest, teacher affiliation is a concept logically linked to the maintenance of the organization and defined as commitment and identification with the mission of the school. Highly affiliated teachers enjoy the social satisfaction of the work environment and work out discord and restore harmony to the organization. They find ways to accommodate to the routine, accomplishing "their jobs with enthusiasm," and maintaining a productive membership in the school.

Table 5.4   Sample Items for the Final Version of the OHI-E

INSTITUTIONAL INTEGRITY

The school is open to the whims of the public.*
Select citizen groups are influential with the board.*

COLLEGIAL LEADERSHIP

The principal discusses classroom issues with teachers.
The principal treats teachers as equals.

RESOURCE INFLUENCE

The principal gets what he or she asks for from superiors.
Supplementary materials are available for classroom use.

TEACHER AFFILIATION

Teachers exhibit friendliness to each other.
Teachers identify with the school.

ACADEMIC EMPHASIS

Students try hard to improve on previous work.
Students are cooperative during classroom instruction.

---

*Score is reversed

As was the case in the previous analyses, *institutional integrity* emerged as an important factor. This factor measures the degree to which the school is able to continue its mission unhindered by one of the groups it most immediately serves, the local constituency. Educators make professional decisions and, often enough, the consequences of these decisions are monitored, but—and this may seem paradoxical in a time when parent involvement is solicited—the local community should not assume an importance that limits other professional considerations. When teachers see the school as resisting the pressure of vocal parents or public whim, teachers are likely to feel that the educational mission of the school will go forward without unwarranted parochial concern.

Collegial leadership, the second factor, combines the initiating structure and consideration subtests to form a single factor that joins the setting and monitoring of tasks with support and concern for teachers as a social group. The principal treats people as equals, shows appreciation of teachers, and generally looks out for the welfare of the school staff. Teachers know that the principal expects them to maintain some standard of performance. The integration of initiating structure and consideration—a point to be taken up at length later—should be seen as a comment on the structural characteristics of the elementary school. These schools are, as a rule, small and not highly specialized. The leader elicits a consensus on goals and, given the support of the group, does not need formal means of control. The principal in the elementary setting is much more likely to be an instructional leader instead of the institutional manager who might be found in a large and specialized high school.

Resource influence represents the combining of two subtests, resource support and principal leadership, to form a factor that describes the success of the principal in influencing superiors for the maintenance and supply of classroom materials. Elementary schools are busy places; children use substantial amounts of consumable items, and the absence of these items is quickly noted by the teaching staff. Districts are sometimes slow to buy manipulatives, paper, paints, and other materials necessary for elementary instruction. Thus the principal who is able to get materials the teachers need is viewed with favor by the staff and contributes to the health of the school.

It is not surprising that the subtests of principal influence and resource support should combine in an elementary school. Principal influence describes the principal's skill in influencing superiors, in having recommendations receive serious consideration, and obtaining what is asked for. The influence of the principal combines with the object of the influence, that is, obtaining the materials of the job.

Academic emphasis emerges as the teachers' view of how much the students care about their own schoolwork. The health of the school should be high where students try hard to improve on previous work, complete homework, and are cooperative during classroom instruction. Teachers who perceive their students' concern for learning will likely act in a way that fosters that concern.

Table 5.5 Dimensions of Organizational Health of Elementary Schools (OHI)

INSTITUTIONAL LEVEL

Institutional Integrity describes a school that has integrity in its educational program. The school is not vulnerable to narrow, vested interests of community groups; indeed, teachers are protected from unreasonable community and parental demands. The school is able to cope successfully with destructive outside forces.

MANAGERIAL LEVEL

Collegial Leadership refers to behavior by the principal that is friendly, supportive, open, and guided by norms of equality. At the same time, however, the principal sets the tone for high performance by letting people know what is expected of them.

Resource Influence describes principal's ability to affect the action of superiors to the benefit of teachers. Teachers are given adequate classroom supplies, and extra instructional materials and supplies are easily obtained.

TECHNICAL LEVEL

Teacher Affiliation refers to a sense of friendliness and strong affiliation with the school. Teachers feel good about each other and, at the same time, have a sense of accomplishment from their jobs. They are committed to both their students and their colleagues. They find ways to accommodate to the routine, accomplishing their jobs with enthusiasm.

Academic Emphasis refers to the school's press for achievement. The expectation of high achievement is met by students who work hard, are cooperative, seek extra work, and respect other students who get good grades.

Table 5.5 presents a concise definition for each of the five dimensions of school health for elementary schools.

School Health and the Parsonian Framework

The OHI-E is an instrument that combines two Parsonian views of organization, the familiar four-function perspective and the less familiar levels of responsibility. It is important in this

Table 5.6 Imperative Functions and Health Dimensions

Health Dimension	Function	Activity
INSTITUTIONAL LEVEL		
Institutional Integrity	Adaptation	Instrumental
MANAGERIAL LEVEL		
Collegial Leadership	Goal Achievement	Instrumental
	Integration and Latency	Expressive
Resource Influence	Adaptation	Instrumental
	Integration and Latency	Expressive
TECHNICAL LEVEL		
Academic Emphasis	Goal Achievement	Instrumental
Teacher Affiliation	Integration and Latency	Expressive

analysis that the differences between secondary schools and elementary schools be considered in terms of both functions and levels.

The original OHI—that is, the instrument that initially tested the practicality of looking at schools in terms of four functions—had instrumental and expressive functions of the organization that were manifested in seven factors (see Chapter 4). However, when items describing life in the elementary school were factored, the seven factors of the high school studies were reduced to five as two of the subtests combined with two others. Table 5.6 presents the five factors and their relationships to organizational levels and functions. See Table 4.2 in Chapter 4 for a comparison with the high school.

Recall that the underlying argument of the imperative functions is that adaptation and goal achievement (two functions combined in instrumental activity) and integration and latency (two functions combined in expressive activity) are functions necessary if the school, or any other kind of organization, is to continue to exist. Organizations that do not adapt or achieve goals lose a rationale for existing; organizations that cannot integrate their members or provide mechanisms to foster integration simply find that their members leave. One would expect to find similar functions in schools generally, but, insofar as schools differ from one another, the factors that describe those functions vary. The functions themselves, of course, do not.

Institutional integrity is as important to the elementary school as it is to the high school. Organizations contain officials and specialists who make decisions about what to do based on their position and their expertise. Often, decision makers seek information from their environment, but they cannot be overwhelmed by outside forces that are hostile to the mission of the organization. Indeed, institutional integrity did emerge as an important factor both in the high school and the elementary school.

Initiating structure and consideration developed into a single factor we have termed collegial leadership. Herriott and Firestone (1984), in their study of centralized decision making and goal consensus in the schools, found that elementary schools are more centralized in their decision making than are high schools. Moreover, the elementary schools elicit a greater goal consensus than would be found in high schools. The successful elementary school principal, for example, is likely to let people know what is expected of them and schedule the activities of the school. The need for consensus, however, apparently requires a principal who is approachable and concerned about the welfare of the faculty as a whole.

These findings are not surprising. Elementary schools tend to be smaller than high schools; they have fewer students, and consequently, fewer staff people. Relations among staff in general and between the administrator and faculty tend to be less formal. In relatively small schools there is less need for the formal coordination than in large schools (Mintzberg, 1979).

Not only are the elementary schools less formal than the secondary schools, they are less specialized as well. The departmental structure and diversity of subject specialists in the high school stand in sharp contrast to the elementary school's relatively narrow focus. This is not to say that the work of the elementary teacher is not complex or that young children do not pose challenges of their own; rather, it is to point out that the subject specialization and departmentalization that characterize high schools typically is absent. In its place is a curriculum limited by the emerging abilities of young children. A consequence of low specialization is that professionals in the school learn the variety of tasks in the school that contribute to goal consensus.

The principal in the elementary school can be an instructional leader for the faculty, but the secondary principal needs to be more of a manager who administers the work of specialists. The administrator in a K-6, for example, is close to the technical level and probably shares in the subject expertise of the faculty. The informal authority arising from shared expertise is joined to the formal authority that goes with the office. Therefore, leaders in the elementary school appear to combine the concern for structure with a concern for the social relations of the work group.

Centralized decision making in the elementary school underscores the grade-to-grade articulation that attempts to connect curriculum through the grades. Contrast this concern with the lack of articulation between, let us say, the science department and the English department in a high school. Neither relies on the other to prepare its students for a sequential course of study. Centralized decision making in the elementary school provides the structure that gives direction to the consensus in the school setting. The leader in a healthy elementary school, then, must combine structure and consideration or the joining of instrumental and expressive activities of leadership.

A second combination of factors occurred in the joining of resource support and principal influence. Probably as a consequence of low specialization, the principal's influence with superiors primarily is one of gathering the supplies necessary for instruction. The demands for consumable supplies seem to be a constant across the elementary school, while the kind of supplies necessary for high school teaching vary greatly. In elementary schools, principals who administer healthy schools exert their good offices with superiors to get teachers those things they need to do the job. In this combination, the principal carries out the instrumental activities that aid in goal achievement of the organization.

Teacher affiliation is a measure of the social satisfaction teachers find in working at the school. Here, there is not a substantial difference between elementary and secondary. The measure taps the feeling of affiliation teachers have for the school and for each other. These feelings of solidarity integrate teachers into the social fabric of the school and should be seen as the expressive dimension of school life.

Academic emphasis is the instrumental aim of the school; starkly, it is the formal goal. Schools with strong academic emphasis are not simply bleak factories; on the contrary, students cooperate with the teacher and with each other. They respect those

Table 5.7 Correlations Among the Five Subtests of the OHI-E

Subtest	TA	II	CL	RI	AE
Teacher Affiliation (TA)	(.94)*				
Institutional Integrity (II)	.15	(.90)			
Collegial Leadership (CL)	.64	.17	(.95)		
Resource Influence (RI)	.48	.17	.50	(.89)	
Academic Emphasis (AE)	.67	.17	.45	.40	(.87)

*Alpha coefficients of reliability for the subtests are displayed in the parentheses.

students who do well academically; they are willing to improve, do extra work, and complete homework assignments.

Second-Order Factor Analysis

As we did in our analysis of secondary school health, we now address the question of whether a more general set of factors explains the health of elementary schools. To answer this question, subtest scores for each school were computed and a correlation matrix among the subtests was derived. Given the moderate correlations between the individual subtests, it was appropriate to perform a second-order factor analysis of the matrix (see Table 5.7).

Again, one strong factor emerged that accounted for 53% of the variance; in fact, this factor was the only one to meet Kaiser's (1960) criterion of an eigenvalue greater than one. All five dimensions of organizational health loaded on a single factor: teacher affiliation (.881); institutional integrity (.220); integrated leadership (.731); resource influence (.601); and academic emphasis (.695). With the possible exception of institutional integrity, the dimensions of organizational health measure a more general property that we call school health. An index of the health of the school can be determined simply by adding the standard scores of the five subtests; the higher the score, the healthier the school.

Healthy school. The healthy elementary school is a pleasant place. It is protected from unwarranted intrusion (high institutional integrity). Teachers like the school, the students, and each other (high teacher affiliation). They see the students as diligent in their learning (high academic emphasis). They see the principal as their ally in the improvement of instruction; the principal is approachable, supportive, and considerate, yet establishes high standards of teacher performance (high collegial leadership). Teachers rely upon the principal to foster a structure in which learning can take place and, at the same time, to be a leader sensitive to the social and emotional needs of the group. The principal has influence with organizational superiors and is seen by the teachers as someone who can deliver, in particular, the teaching resources they need (high resource influence). The healthy school has no need to coerce cooperation; it is freely given by professionals who are in basic agreement about the task at hand.

Unhealthy school. An unhealthy school, by way of contrast, is a rather sad place. The school is an arena for various pressure groups to work out their own agendas (low institutional integrity). The principal is inactive and ineffective in moving the school toward its goals or in building a sense of community among the teachers (low collegial leadership). The principal has no influence with superiors, and teachers see themselves on the short end of supplies (low resource influence). They feel they do not have what they need to teach. The teachers do not like one another, the school, or the youngsters (low teacher affiliation). They see the students as academically unworthy; in the view of the teachers, these children do not work hard, do not do their homework, are hard to work with in class, and are not serious about learning (low academic emphasis).

In all likelihood, the unhealthy school is not capable of adapting to the environment because there is no central leadership. The school is turned into a political arena as it loses its institutional integrity. The principal abdicates, in effect, and goals are compromised. The teachers lose a sense of integration with the school and its mission and see the students as unwilling learners. Were the schools not "domesticated organizations," that is, organizations so necessary to the society that they are not permitted to fail, the school would cease to exist (Carlson, 1964).

Prototypic profiles for healthy and unhealthy schools are depicted in Figure 5.1. A score of 500 is average on each of the health dimensions with a standard deviation of 100. Schools with scores above 550 are relatively high on the dimensions, while scores

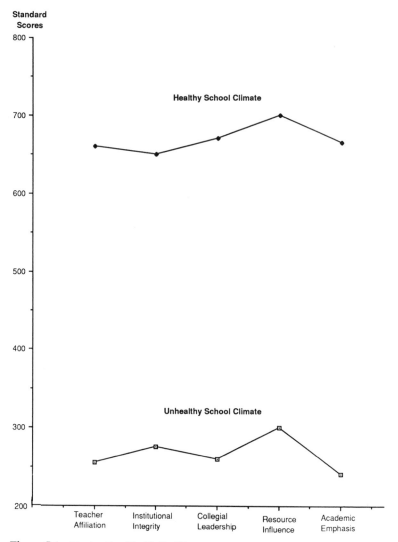

Figure 5.1. Contrasting Health Profiles

below 450 are relatively low. The majority of elementary schools in the current sample fall between the two prototypes in Figure 5.1.

Health Index

The five subtests developed to measure the critical dimensions of elementary school life are highly reliable scales that appear to have reasonable construct validity. Moreover, given the emergence of one second-order factor, which we have called health, it is possible to create a crude index of the health for each school. The five aspects of health fit together to form a general indicator of health. Simply by averaging the standard scores of all the subtests, the health index is created—the higher the score, the healthier the organizational dynamics. In the current study, the schools arrayed themselves along the health continuum (see Figure 5.2); health index scores ranged from 260 to 687, with a mean of 500.

Summary and Discussion

The Organizational Health Inventory (OHI-E) for elementary schools is a new, 37-item instrument that maps the organizational health of elementary schools. At the technical level, teacher affiliation and academic emphasis are the critical elements of health. Healthy schools are characterized by teachers who enjoy working with colleagues and with students. At the managerial level, collegial leadership and resource influence are the important factors that explain health. Successful leaders in this analysis are ones who combine the initiation of structure with consideration, and who can influence superiors sufficiently to provide the teachers with the things they need to teach. At the institutional level, institutional integrity, the ability to be relatively independent of the parochial concerns of the environment, appears to be a major factor in a healthy school.

One must be careful, however, not to promise too much from an instrument that has not been tested widely. Of the four instruments that appear in this book, the OHI-E is the newest and, therefore, has not been used extensively. We suspect that the instrument is the equal of the other climate instruments and will become a useful tool for practitioners and researchers, but ultimately its utility is an empirical question.

Some of the empirical issues that should be addressed concern the relationship of a healthy school climate to such antecedent

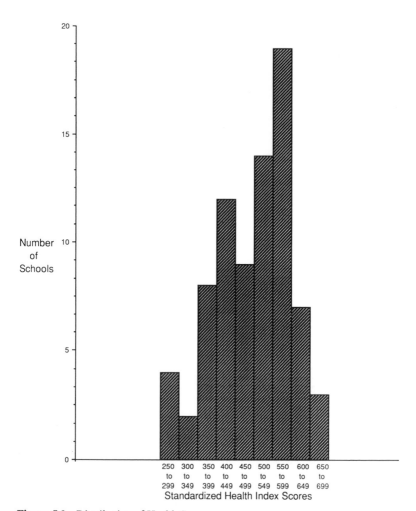

Figure 5.2. Distribution of Health Scores

variables as the school community, professionalism of teachers, instructional organization, teacher efficacy, school-based management and empowerment, organizational structure, and teacher participation in decision making.

For example, we would hypothesize that the greater the teacher participation in decision making, the healthier the climate of the school (Conway, 1976); simple organizational structures will have healthier climates than machine bureaucracies (Mintzberg, 1979; 1989); the greater the sense of teacher efficacy, the healthier the school climate (Ashton, 1985; Ashton & Webb, 1986); the greater the empowerment of the teachers, the healthier the school climate (Lieberman & Rosenholtz, 1987); the greater the sense of teacher professionalism, the healthier the climate (Corwin, 1965; Lanier & Little, 1985; Little, 1982); the greater the organized parental involvement, the healthier the climate or, alternately, the more random the parental involvement, the less healthy the climate (Tangri & Moles, 1987). This short list merely is illustrative of the heuristic nature of the instrument. There are a myriad of important research questions to be studied by researchers and practitioners.

Perhaps more important are the consequences of a healthy climate, that is, the conception of health as an independent variable capable of predicting such important school outcomes as academic achievement, self-esteem of students, student alienation and commitment, vandalism, teacher absenteeism, teacher satisfaction and commitment, school status in the community, openness in communication, and positive student orientation to school and education. It seems likely that healthy school climates also provide the setting for cooperative supervisory relationships that, in turn, lead to instructional improvement. Again, the list is not intended to be an exhaustive example of the research possibilities of the instrument.

Implications

The practical implications of the OHI-E lie in its use as an organizing framework, a diagnostic tool, and a guide to action. Many practitioners informally classify what happens in schools as behavior related to getting the job done or to how people feel about doing the job. The school health framework is a classification that allows the administrator to look at school behavior in terms of the level (i.e., technical, managerial, or institutional) or the nature of the activity, whether it is instrumental or expressive. In other words, the framework itself provides a conceptual guide for analysis.

The instrument can be used in a more formal way. The overall score of the OHI and the individual subtests may be analyzed in order to describe the school. In the current sample we found schools with wide variation in their health profiles (see Figure 5.1). There is little question that a great many unhealthy school climates exist; our data suggest that many schools fit the profile of the unhealthy school. The OHI not only can identify those schools, it also can pinpoint those aspects of school health that are undesirable and most in need of immediate amelioration. For example, scores on teacher affiliation varied widely from school to school. The usefulness of this empirical measure of the solidarity of the staff is two-fold. It describes teachers' perceptions of their relationship with each other in a more systematic way than personal impressions of administrators. And it places this information within the broader framework of teacher-teacher and teacher-administrator interactions, that is, it is only one element of school health. For a more salient analysis, all the elements of the OHI should be considered.

The instrument can be used for in-service and professional development activities for teachers and administrators. The profile of school climate is a snapshot of the school at a given point in time. The picture does not explain causes for the current state of affairs; it simply describes what exists. Teachers and administrators who find the profile of their school undesirable must undertake the difficult task of diagnosing the causes of the poor health and then develop strategies for improvement. Successive administrations of the OHI can yield a rough measure of the success of the strategies that are employed to improve the school. Some might be tempted to use the OHI as a tool for summative evaluation. We caution against this use because it probably would diminish the usefulness of the measure in self-improvement and organizational development activities.

Note

1. In our reanalysis of the Podgurski (1990) data, we found one additional academic emphasis item that he did not include in his final version. We included the item, "Students neglect to complete homework," as an academic emphasis measure because of its high loading and conceptual fit.

6 Research Results on School Health and Climate

> Results of educational research cannot be used by themselves to guide educational decisions; our values and laws must also be involved. But only research can provide the kind of objective information needed to intelligently make educational decisions.
>
> —Robert E. Slavin
> *Research Methods in Education: A Practical Guide*

Although the instruments developed in this book are of recent vintage, a body of knowledge linking school health and climate to other important school variables is emerging. In this chapter recent research using the instruments is summarized and analyzed. Three dependent variables—faculty trust, teacher commitment, and school effectiveness—provided the criteria to test the usefulness of the measures. We conclude by drawing some tentative implications for practitioners and researchers.

Faculty Trust and School Health: OHI

The organizational health of high schools should correlate with the trust that faculty members have in the principal and in one another. Health and trust both are significant features of life in schools. Healthy schools satisfy the Parsonian requirement that goals be achieved and members integrated into the organization. Trust logically seems a key element in both the instrumental and expressive activities of the organization.

The concept of trust is complex, and most discussions of the term occur at the global level. The empirical investigation of trust, however, requires the specification of its dimensions. After a careful review of the literature, Hoy and Kupersmith (1985) used the work of Rotter (1967) and Golembiewski and McConkie (1975) to conceptualize trust. Trust is associated with a general confidence and overall optimism in occurrent events. In more specific terms, trust is a generalized expectancy held by the work group that the word, action, and written or oral statement of another individual, group, or organization can be relied upon (Hoy & Kupersmith, 1985). The focus of this definition implies that trust can be viewed in relation to a variety of reference groups—student, colleague, principal, or the school organization. One would trust a person, not simply in the sense of consistency of action, but in the sense of reliance to act in one's best interest. The present analysis considers the following two specific aspects of trust:

(1) Faculty trust in the principal—The faculty has confidence that the principal will keep his or her word and will act in the best interests of the teachers.

(2) Faculty trust in colleagues—The faculty believes that teachers can depend on one another in a difficult situation; teachers can rely on the integrity of their colleagues.

Although the concepts of health and trust are not identical, they are complementary. Thus it was assumed that the seven elements of health should predict faculty trust in the principal and in colleagues. It was also expected that different patterns of organizational properties would predict each aspect of faculty trust. Six hypotheses guided the empirical phase of this study:

(H.1.) Each aspect of the school's health is positively related to faculty trust in the principal.

(H.2.) The greater the general state of school health, the greater the faculty trust in the principal.

(H.3.) Institutional integrity, principal influence, initiating structure, consideration, and resource support are the best predictors of faculty trust in the principal.

(H.4.) Each aspect of the school's health is positively related to faculty trust in colleagues.

(H.5.) The greater the general state of school health, the greater the faculty trust in colleagues.

(H.6.) Institutional integrity, morale, and academic emphasis are the best predictors of faculty trust in colleagues.

The two trust scales used in this study were developed by Hoy and Kupersmith (1985). Each is composed of seven Likert-type items. Subjects respond along a six-point scale from "strongly agree" to "strongly disagree." Examples of items for trust in the principal are "The teachers in this school have faith in the integrity of the principal" and "The principal takes unfair advantage of teachers in this school (score reversed)." Examples of items for trust in colleagues include "Even in difficult situations teachers in this school can depend on each other" and "Teachers in this school are suspicious of each other (score reversed)."

The alpha coefficients of reliability for the scales were .89 for faculty trust in the principal and .92 for faculty trust in colleagues. Construct and predictive validity of the scales were supported in a factor analytic study by Hoy and Kupersmith (1985).

The hypotheses were tested using a sample of 75 high schools in New Jersey. Although the sample was not a random one, it represented a broad range of districts and spanned the entire socioeconomic range. Typically, data were collected by a researcher at a regular faculty meeting, but in a few cases a faculty member collected the questionnaires. All respondents were anonymous.

Because the unit of analysis was the school, separate random sets of faculty members were drawn from each school; that is, a random set of teachers responded to the OHI and a separate set of teachers in the same school responded to the trust scales. Thus the measurement of the independent and dependent variables was methodologically independent. Data for each school were used to perform the statistical analyses and to test the hypotheses. A total of 1,083 educators participated in the study (see Tarter & Hoy, 1988).

In order to test the hypotheses, correlation coefficients first were computed for each aspect of health with each dimension of trust; next, correlation coefficients were calculated between a general index of school health and each dimension of trust; and, finally, multiple regression analyses were performed to determine the best set of predictors for trust in the principal and trust in colleagues.

Faculty Trust in the Principal

As predicted, institutional integrity ($r = .36$, $p < .01$); consideration ($r = .52$, $p < .01$); initiating structure ($r = .26$, $p < .05$); and morale ($r = .24$, $p < .05$) were positively related to trust in the principal. Moreover, the greater the general state of school health, the higher the level of faculty trust in the principal ($r = .40$, $p < .01$). Surprisingly, principal influence ($r = .22$, n.s.); resource support ($r = .09$, n.s.); and academic emphasis ($r = .14$, n.s.) were not associated with faculty trust in the principal.

In order to identify the best set of health variables to predict the two dimensions of trust, two stepwise regression analyses were performed; one for each aspect of trust. A forward selection procedure was used in which the best single predictor is found, then the best additional predictor is identified, and then the next best, and so on.

Consideration and institutional integrity best predicted faculty trust in the principal; only these two variables had independent significant effects on trust in the principal. Together they had a multiple R of .56 with trust, which explained 31% of the trust variance. Principal influence, initiating structure, and resource support did not have independent effects on trust.

Faculty Trust in Colleagues

As hypothesized, institutional integrity ($r = .25$, $p < .05$); principal influence ($r = .34$, $p < .05$); consideration ($r = .29$, $p < .05$); morale ($r = .50$, $p < .01$); and academic emphasis $r = .30$, $p < .05$) were significantly correlated with faculty trust in colleagues. Only initiating structure ($r = .22$, n.s.) and resource support ($r = .11$, n.s.) were unrelated to trust in colleagues. Furthermore, the

Table 6.1 Regression Analyses for School Health and Faculty Trust

Health Variables	Faculty Trust in Principal			Faculty Trust in Colleagues		
	r			r		
Institutional Integrity	.36*			.25*		
Principal Influence	.22			.34*		
Consideration	.52**			.29*		
Initiating Structure	.26*			.22		
Resource Support	.09			.11		
Morale	.24*			.50**		
Academic Emphasis	.14			.30*		
School Health	.40**			.45**		

Regression Variables	Partial r	R	R^2	Partial r	R	R^2
STEP 1						
Consideration	.42**	.52**	.27**			
STEP 2						
Institutional Integrity	.22*	.56*	.31*			
STEP 1						
Morale				.44**	.50**	.25**
STEP 2						
Principal Influence				.22*	.55*	.30*

*$p < .05$; **$p < .01$

greater the general state of school health, the higher the level of faculty trust in colleagues ($r = .45$, $p < .01$).

Morale and principal influence best predicted faculty trust in colleagues. Together these two variables explained 30% of the variance in faculty trust in colleagues ($R = .55$, $p < .05$). None of the other variables in school health had significant independent effects on trust in colleagues. All the data are summarized in Table 6.1.

Discussion

The results supported several of the general assumptions undergirding the study. Thus it was not surprising that most of the aspects of organizational health were related in predictable ways to faculty trust in principals and trust in colleagues; and, as expected, different patterns of the health variables were found to predict each aspect of trust.

The significant correlations between organizational health and feelings of trust both toward colleagues and the principal give persuasive demonstration that reliability in the word of one's colleague or superior is consistent with healthy organizational dynamics in schools, findings that support the construct validity of the Organizational Health Inventory.

The trust measures are quite distinct from elements of the health index, as can be seen both in the moderate correlations and in the variability of the correlations. If the measures were not distinct, the correlations would be uniformly higher. Trust and health, though clearly related, are different concepts and operate in different ways within the school.

There was one element of school health that was not related to either aspect of trust. Apparently, the availability of classroom supplies, instructional materials, and extra materials is not related to trust. Although resource support likely is important in nurturing healthy organizational dynamics in schools, it may not be a significant factor in developing trust among colleagues and with administrators in secondary schools. Teacher professionals simply may expect adequate resources to do the job, and when they do not get them they may become disgruntled, but not distrustful.

Consideration and institutional integrity were the major predictors of the faculty's trust in the principal. The principal who is friendly, supportive, open, and collegial in interactions with teachers is able to command their respect and trust, and trust is further enhanced by protecting teachers from unreasonable community and parental demands. Teachers perceive such principals as acting in their best interests and as leaders who keep their promises independently of their ability to affect the actions of superiors, garner resources, or press for academic achievement. The major explanation for the establishment of a climate of trust in the principal seems to arise from behavior of the principal that is caring, collegial, supportive, and protective.

In some contrast to trust in the principal, morale and principal influence best predicted faculty trust in colleagues. The fact that morale was the best single predictor of faculty trust in colleagues was not surprising. Morale—the teachers' liking of one another and working with enthusiasm—taps many of the same interactions as trust in colleagues, that is, those feelings on the part of the faculty that they can rely upon one another and that they look out for each other. It seems likely that both morale and trust in colleagues are salient measures of the vitality of organizational life, and that this explains the strong relationship.

The principal's behavior also is instrumental in developing an atmosphere of trust. Principals who are persuasive, work effectively with their superiors, and who demonstrate an independence in thought and action promote mutual trust among the faculty. Although academic emphasis, institutional integrity, and consideration are related to trust in colleagues, it is morale and principal influence that combine to provide the best explanation of faculty trust in colleagues.

The correlational analysis shows the important role that the principal plays in developing a climate of trust in schools. What kind of principal is successful in this regard? The principal who integrates a press for the task and a consideration for teachers, who influences superiors without "selling out" the teachers, and who protects teachers from unwarranted outside interference seems likely to promote trust. We suspect that effective principals not only are intellectual leaders in their schools but also colleagues who serve and support their teachers.

Health and trust are related. The healthy school is protected from unreasonable parental pressures. The principal provides dynamic leadership—leadership that is both task-oriented and relations-oriented. Such behavior is supportive of teachers, yet provides direction and maintains high standards of performance. The principal, as well, has influence with his or her superiors while retaining the ability to exercise independence. Teachers in a healthy school are committed to teaching and learning. They set high, but achievable, goals for students; they maintain high standards for student performance; and the learning environment is orderly and serious. Students work hard on academic matters, are highly motivated, and respect other students who achieve academically. Classroom supplies are sufficient. Teachers like each other, are enthusiastic about their work, and are proud of their school. Finally, an integrative theme of trust runs through the interactions of the healthy school. Teachers come to trust each other and the principal.

Faculty Trust and School Climate: OCDQ-RS

Just as we expected the OHI to predict trust, we anticipated that the OCDQ-RS would also be related to faculty trust. Openness in interpersonal relations should promote a sense of confidence and trust in others. Parsons (1951; Parsons, Bales, & Shils, 1953) argued that every social system must solve four basic fundamental problems; it must fulfill the two instrumental needs of adaptation and goal attainment and the two expressive needs of integration and pattern-maintenance. Supportive principal behavior and engaged teacher behavior address fundamental expressive concerns, while directive principal behavior and frustrated teacher behavior speak to instrumental needs. Openness in organizations describes the degree to which these functional imperatives are satisfied. A closed climate, in comparison, hinders the solution of the functional needs of the school.

Although the concepts of organizational climate and trust are not identical, they are complementary, and one would logically expect them to be related. Trust is an intrinsic element of pattern-maintenance (Parsons, 1961). Thus it is reasonable to expect that those elements of organizational climate that are inherently expressive in character will likely be associated with trust. Similarly, those instrumental elements of the organization that hinder expressive development should be negatively related to trust. In particular, we hypothesize that:

(H.1.) The more supportive the leadership behavior of the principal, the greater the degree of faculty trust in the principal.

(H.2.) The less directive the leadership behavior of the principal, the greater the degree of faculty trust in the principal.

(H.3.) The more engaged the teacher behavior in a school, the greater the degree of faculty trust in colleagues.

(H.4.) The less frustrated the teacher behavior in a school, the greater the degree of faculty trust in colleagues.

The general openness of climate is a reflection of harmony in the instrumental and expressive activities in school life. Consequently, in the current research it was expected that openness in climate would be positively related to aspects of faculty trust. In particular, it was hypothesized that:

(H.5.) The more open the organizational climate of a secondary school, the greater the degree of faculty trust in the principal.

(H.6.) The more open the organizational climate of a secondary school, the greater the degree of faculty trust in colleagues.

It also was expected that different patterns of organizational climate would predict each of the two aspects of faculty trust. Thus it was assumed that faculty trust in the principal would be directly related to the leadership behavior of the principal and that faculty trust in colleagues would be related to the open and supportive interactions among teacher colleagues. Although the discussion implies that climate promotes trust, it is also likely that trust facilitates the development of openness. The relationship is one of mutual dependence (Homans, 1950).

The hypotheses were tested using a diverse sample of 72 high schools in New Jersey (see Tarter, Bliss, & Hoy, 1989, for elaboration). Once again the school was the unit of analysis; that is, all data were aggregated at the school level. Random sets of teachers in each school responded to the instruments while their colleagues were busy responding to another battery of measures. We used school mean scores to test the hypotheses.

Faculty Trust and School Climate

The first two hypotheses argued that the openness of the school climate would be positively correlated with teachers' trust in the principal and in one another. Both were supported; openness was significantly correlated with trust in the principal ($r = .44, p < .01$) and trust in colleagues ($r = .35, p < .01$).

Hypothesis 3 proposed that the more the principal set an example of hard work and was genuinely helpful to the teachers—that is, the more the principal engaged in supportive behavior—the greater the likelihood that the teachers would trust the principal. The zero-order correlation of .50 ($p < .01$) supported the hypothesis.

Table 6.2 Product-Moment Correlations Between Measures of
Organizational Climate and Measures of Faculty Trust (N = 72)

Measures of Organizational Climate	Measures of Trust	
	Trust in Principal	Trust in Teachers
Openness	.44**	.35**
Principal Behavior		
Supportive	.50**	.18
Directive	−.22*	−.08
Teacher Behavior		
Engaged	.29**	.44**
Frustrated	−.23*	−.29**

*p < .05; **p < .01

Hypothesis 4 predicted that rigid and domineering principal behavior—that is, directive leadership—would be negatively correlated with trust in the principal. When teachers are not given the freedom to make professional judgments and are watched closely, they tend to be distrustful of the principal. Indeed, the data bear this out; directive behavior has a significant, negative relationship to faculty trust in the principal (r = −.22, p < .05). Neither aspect of the principal's behavior was significantly related to faculty trust in each other.

Hypothesis 5 examined the relationship between engaged teacher behavior and faculty trust in colleagues. Schools in which teachers were engaged had higher levels of trust in colleagues (r = .44, p < .01).

Hypothesis 6 considered the relationship between frustrated teacher behavior and faculty trust in colleagues. As expected, schools where teachers perceived a general pattern of interference both from administrators and other teachers were schools of lower levels of faculty trust in fellow teachers (r = .29, p < .05). The results of hypothesis testing are summarized in Table 6.2.

Although there were no predictions about either the relationships between teacher behavior and trust in the principal or about principal behavior and trust in colleagues, the correlations also are reported in Table 6.2. Principal behavior was not significantly related to trust in teachers, but engaged and frustrated teacher behaviors both were significantly related to trust in the principal (r = .29, p < .05; r = −.23, p < .05, respectively).

Faculty trust in colleagues was significantly correlated with faculty trust in the principal ($r = .43$, $p < .05$). Although there is some relationship between faculty trust in colleagues and principal, the two aspects of trust are different from each other and from the measures of climate.

One of the problems facing educational researchers is determining the effect of one variable independent of other variables. The relationships between variables such as directive principal behavior and teacher trust in the principal may be a consequence of their relationships with a third variable, such as supportive principal behavior. Thus partial correlation and multiple regression analyses were used to determine the unique and combined contributions of the independent variables. The correlations that test the possible interrelationships among the aspects of organizational climate are summarized in Table 6.3.

The first relationship concerns two aspects of principal behavior—supportive and directive—and their relationships with

Table 6.3 Coefficients of Partial Correlation (One Variable Controlled) and Beta Weights Indicating Relative Importance of Measures of Organizational Climate Predicting Faculty Trust ($N = 72$)

| | Measures of Trust | | | |
| | Trust in Principal (Y) | | Trust in Teachers (Z) | |
Measures of Organizational Climate	Coefficients of partial correlation	Beta weights	Coefficients of partial correlation	Beta weights
Section A				
Principal Behavior				
1. Supportive	.49**	.48**	.17	.18
2. Directive	−.19	−.16	−.06	−.06
Multiple correlation	.53**		.19	
Section B				
Teacher Behavior				
3. Engaged	.20*	.23*	.35**	.40**
4. Frustrated	−.09	−.10	−.06	−.07
Multiple correlation	.30**		.44**	

*$p < .05$; **$p < .01$
NOTE: Beta weights are in standard measure

faculty trust in the principal and in colleagues. Section A of Table 6.3 shows the effect of supportive behavior on trust in the principal ($r_{y1.2} = .49$, $p < .01$) and on trust in colleagues ($r_{z1.2} = .17$, $p < .05$), while controlling for directive behavior, remains nearly the same as the zero-order correlation. The beta weights show similar relationships. Neither dimension of principal behavior has an independent, significant effect on trust in fellow teachers. The combined effect of both aspects of leader behavior on trust in the principal was $R = .53$ ($p < .01$); however, leadership had no significant influence on trust in colleagues. Faculty trust in the principal seems to depend on behavior of the principal, whereas faculty trust in colleagues is uninfluenced by the behavior of the principal. Perhaps, by nurturing open, authentic relationships among teachers, the principal can indirectly contribute to the growth of trust among teaching colleagues, but such conjecture remains untested.

Section B of Table 6.3 concerns two aspects of teacher behavior—engaged and frustrated—as they are related to the two dimensions of trust. Only engaged teacher behavior has an independent influence on trust in principal ($r_{y3.4} = .20$, $p < .05$) and on trust in colleagues ($r_{z3.4} = .35$, $p < .01$). In both cases, the partial correlations are substantially lower than the zero-order correlations. Moreover, frustrated teacher behavior does not have an independent significant effect on trust in principal ($r_{y4.3} = -.09$, ns) and trust in colleagues ($r_{z4.3} = -.07$, ns). Again, the beta weights show similar relationships. Clearly, engaged teacher behavior is more strongly related to trust than is frustrated teacher behavior. The reason for the reduction in the partial correlations is because of the moderate inverse correlation ($r = -.52$, $p < .01$) between engaged and frustrated behavior. Together the teacher behavior variables are significantly related to both trust in the principal ($R = .30$, $p < .01$) and trust in colleagues ($R = .44$, $p < .01$). Unlike the leadership characteristics, the teacher variables when combined are related to both measures of trust. Apparently, the interaction patterns of teachers have a more pervasive influence on trust relationships than the leadership behavior of the principal. It may be that teachers develop trust among themselves; principals can only build trust between the principal and the teachers; they cannot make teachers trust one another.

Table 6.4 Coefficients of Partial Correlation (Three Variables Controlled) and Beta Weights Indicating Relative Importance of Measures of Organizational Climate Predicting Faculty Trust ($N = 72$)

Measures of Organizational Climate	Measures of Trust			
	Trust in Principal (Y)		Trust in Teachers (Z)	
	Coefficients of partial correlation	Beta weights	Coefficients of partial correlation	Beta weights
Principal Behavior				
1. Supportive	.44**	.46**	.01	.01
2. Directive	−.16	−.15	.06	.06
Teacher Behavior				
3. Engaged	.10	.10	.34**	.40**
4. Frustrated	.03	.03	−.09	−.09
Multiple correlation	.53**		.44**	

$*p < .05; **p < .01$
NOTE: Beta weights are in standard measure

Having examined the relative importance of aspects of teacher-teacher and principal-teacher interactions separately, we now turn to the question of which of these individual climate characteristics is the most important in predicting each aspect of trust. Table 6.4 shows that the supportive leadership of the principal ($r_{y1.234} = .44$, $p < .01$) is the only variable that has a substantial and independent effect on faculty trust in the principal. However, only engaged teacher behavior has an independent, significant effect on faculty trust in colleagues ($r_{z3.124} = .34$, $p < .01$). The beta weights show similar relationships. The supportive leadership style of the principal is most directly related to faculty trust in the principal, and engaged teacher behavior is most closely associated with an atmosphere of trust among colleagues.

Discussion

The results of this study are consistent with the theoretical foundations on which it was built. Elements of organizational climate that are inherently expressive are associated with trust, and instrumental elements that hinder expressive development tend to be negatively related to trust. Openness in the climate of a school and trust in interpersonal relationships complement each other. The measures of trust are distinct from the dimensions of openness in climate as is demonstrated in both the moderate correlations and the variability of the correlations.

As we predicted, different dimensions of the climate of a school are associated with different aspects of faculty trust. Leadership behavior of the principal, rather than the interrelationships of the teachers, predicts trust in the administration. Interrelationships among teachers, not the leadership of the principal, facilitate trust in colleagues. The relationships can be specified even further. Supportive behavior is most strongly related to trust in the principal. Principals who are helpful and genuinely concerned about the professional and personal welfare of their teachers are likely to have the trust of their teachers. Engaged teacher behavior may elicit trust in colleagues through shared sentiments of pride in school, commitment to students, and concern for colleagues, and conversely, trust is likely to promote engaged teacher behavior.

The finding that trust in the principal is related to the supportive behavior of the principal is consonant with earlier findings that suggest consideration and institutional integrity nurture teacher trust in the principal. Principals who are friendly, open, and collegial with teachers are able to command respect and trust, and trust is enhanced further by protecting teachers from unreasonable outside demands (Tarter & Hoy, 1988).

Teachers who are engaged in their work also trust their colleagues. It is the teachers who initiate collegiality. One would think that the principal would be a major figure in the creation of such feelings among the faculty, but the data do not demonstrate this. One is struck by the importance of the teacher group in developing a climate of trust.

The finding that teachers trust in one another, independently of the actions of the principal, lends empirical support to the broad synthesis of supervision offered by Hoy and Forsyth (1986). Combining the results of this study with the Hoy and Forsyth model suggests that teachers and principals often operate on different levels. The current debate over the roles of "instructional leader" and "institutional manager" obscures both the leadership and managerial characteristics of each role; that is, no principal is totally an instructional leader, nor is any completely a manager. The principal cannot be ignorant of the instructional process. The primary role of the principal, however, is to improve instruction indirectly through the development of an open, healthy, and trustful climate. See Hoy and Forsyth (1986) for a detailed explanation of the model and process.

Teachers are professionals actively engaged in the technical task of teaching; they are the experts on teaching and learning. Principals are professionals actively engaged in the managerial task of nurturing the climate of the organization. Principals provide the intellectual milieu in which effective teaching takes place, and teachers themselves critically analyze and improve their teaching, but principals must do even more.

We have suggested that administrators and teachers operate on different levels. If this is true, future studies will show weak and negative relationships between faculty trust in the principal and principal behaviors that intrude upon teachers' work. In all likelihood, the principal's insistence upon using certain instructional methods in the classroom or even an advocacy of some particular model will have a negative effect on faculty trust in the principal.

The multiple regression analyses indicated a negative but nonsignificant relationship between directive principal behavior and faculty trust. Further studies are needed to clarify the effect of directiveness in various areas of principal-teacher interaction. One study, for example, could compare the effects of directive behavior in two different domains—"Does strict monitoring of faculty absences and punctuality by the principal affect trust to the same extent as insistence on particular methods of instruction?"

Teacher Commitment and School Health: OHI

Organizational commitment is the strength of identification and involvement with the organization (Steers, 1977). It can be characterized by a belief in and acceptance of the organization's goals and values, a willingness to exert substantial effort on behalf of the organization, and a desire to maintain membership in the organization (Porter, Steers, Mowday, & Boulian, 1974). Commitment in this study is defined in terms of attitude. When "the identity of a person [is linked] to the organization" (Sheldon, 1971, p. 143) or when "the goals of the organization and those of the individual become increasingly integrated or congruent" (Hall, Schneider, & Nygren, 1970, p. 176), attitudinal commitment exists. Attitudinal commitment is a state in which individuals identify with their organization and its goals and desire to maintain membership in order to accomplish these goals (Mowday, Steers, & Porter, 1979). March and Simon (1958) argue that such commitment commonly is a function of an exchange in which the inducements offered by the organization are sufficient to prompt not merely participation, but commitment to the organization. Commitment in this sense is not simply loyalty or compliance but rather a wholehearted support of organizational ventures and values.

The Organizational Commitment Questionnaire (OCQ) is a Likert scale that measures the degree of involvement of participants in organizations. The measure is a revised form of the organizational commitment questionnaire developed by Porter, Steers, Mowday, and Boulian (1974). The OCQ measures three aspects of commitment to the organization: (a) acceptance of the goals and values of the organization, (b) willingness to exert extra effort on behalf of the organization, and (c) desire to remain in the organization. The original OCQ contained 15 Likert response items. Mowday, Steers, and Porter (1979) analyzed 2,563 employees in nine occupations and demonstrated the internal consistency, test-retest, and factorial reliability of the instrument as well as its predictive, convergent, and discriminant validity. The study at hand uses a nine-item version that Mowday and his colleagues used with four occupational groups. Alpha coefficients for the four groups ranged from .84 to .90. In the present sample the alpha was .91.

The teachers responded to each item along a five-point scale ranging from "strongly agree" to "strongly disagree." Examples of items include the following: "I find my values and the school's values are very similar"; "I am willing to put in a great deal of effort beyond that normally expected in order to help this school be successful"; and "For me this is the best of all possible schools for which to work."

We assumed that together the elements of organizational health contribute to the inducement pattern that schools offer teachers. Although elements on each level of the organization contribute to the inducement pattern, it is likely that they do not contribute equally. Theoretically, the greater the inducement pattern, the more committed teachers will be to the school. It is expected that the leadership of the principal will play a critical role in the generation of teacher commitment as well as the general interaction patterns of the faculty. It seems reasonable to postulate that schools that protect their teachers from unwarranted interference; schools that are led by principals who provide structure, resources, consideration, and useful influence; and schools that are places where teachers like each other and hold high expectations for themselves and their students will be settings that elicit teacher commitment. Using the same sample (see above), the following three hypotheses were tested (Tarter, Hoy, & Kottkamp, 1990):

(H.1.) Overall health of the schools is positively related to the teachers' organizational commitment.

(H.2.) Each element of school health is positively related to the teachers' organizational commitment.

(H.3.) Together the elements of organizational health will make contributions to a linear composite that is significantly related to the teachers' organizational commitment.

Hypothesis 1, which predicted a positive correlation between a general index of school health and organizational commitment, was supported. A correlation of .55 ($p < .01$) indicates a moderately strong relationship between the variables.

Hypothesis 2, which predicted positive correlations between each of the seven elements of the health inventory and teacher commitment to the school, also was supported. Each zero-order correlation was statistically significant, ranging from $r = .28$ ($p < .01$) for institutional integrity with commitment to $r = .44$ ($p < .01$) for academic emphasis with commitment. See Table 6.5 for all of the coefficients of correlation.

Hypothesis 3, the regression hypothesis, predicted that the elements of health would form a significant linear composite for explaining teachers' commitment to the school. The statistical analysis supports this hypothesis. The regression equation for teachers' commitment to the school was statistically significant

Table 6.5 Summary of Zero-Order Correlations and Regression Analysis for Organizational Commitment and Elements of School Health

Independent Variables	r	beta	t	R^2
Institutional Integrity	.28**	.071	.58	
Principal Influence	.44**	.292	2.10*	
Consideration	.36**	.147	1.24	
Initiating Structure	.30**	−.089	−.67	
Resource Allocation	.31**	−.011	−.09	
Morale	.40**	.151	1.17	
Academic Emphasis	.44**	.248	1.90[a]	
Total Equation	R = .58**		F = 4.73**	.34
Health	.55**			

*p < .05; **p < .01; ap = .06

($F = 4.7$, $p < .01$) and .34 of the variance of commitment to school ($R = .58$) was explained. Only the variable principal influence made a significant and unique contribution to the school commitment equation: principal influence, $r = .44$, beta = .29, $t = 2.1$ ($p < .05$). Academic emphasis also made a substantial contribution to school commitment: academic emphasis, $r = .44$, beta = .25, $t = 1.9$ ($p = .06$). All the data for the regression equation are summarized in Table 6.5.

Discussion

The results of this study are consistent with the theory that workers will be committed to an organization that not only survives in its environment but continues to develop and direct its energies toward the accomplishment of its mission (Miles, 1969). Such an organization is led by a leader who integrates task and concern for people and, at the same time, has clout with superiors. It is an organization that is characterized by a press for excellence and high morale. In a word, healthy organizations seem to breed high *commitment*—but how?

Teaching is an activity that is readily subject to criticism. The goals of schools are abstract and ambiguous, and there is no consensus on the appropriate measures of effectiveness. Everyone believes oneself to be an expert on matters of the classroom.

Virtually all individuals have experience of one kind or another in the classroom; it is easy to criticize. Teachers like to be—and perhaps need to be—protected from the vagaries of unfounded and ill-considered complaint. It is not surprising that institutional integrity is associated with the commitment of teachers to their school.

There is little doubt that the leadership of the principal also is important in developing teacher commitment to the school. The finding that initiating structure and consideration are positively associated with organizational commitment of teachers is consistent with many of the leadership findings in schools (Halpin, 1966; Bass, 1981). Apparently resource support contributes to teacher commitment. Perhaps the most provocative finding, however, is the significance of the principal's influence in generating teacher commitment. It combines with all the other health variables to explain the development of organizational commitment, but alone it makes a significant and unique contribution to the explanation of commitment.

To paraphrase Pelz (1952), give the workers the right tools to do the job and they will. The administrator's influence conditions the effects of his or her leadership behavior. For instance, administrative behaviors of "siding with employees" or establishing "social closeness to employees" will raise employee satisfaction only if the administrator has enough influence to make these behaviors pay off in terms of actual benefits (Pelz, 1952). Similarly, Hoy and Reese (1977) found that a principal's influence conditioned the consequences of leadership behavior. Nonauthoritarian principals had more loyal teachers than authoritarian ones *only when* their influence was high. Principals who are perceived as unable or unwilling to influence their superiors are at a distinct disadvantage in influencing their subordinates. This is indicative of an important theoretical difference between the function of the administrator who develops and maintains a setting and the function of the teacher who must work within the classroom, but who has little control over the school in which the classroom is embedded. The principal who can improve the classroom setting by influencing the larger social system earns the commitment of the teachers. The mark of teacher commitment is doing extra work, sharing the goals of the school, and developing pride in the school.

Morale—those feelings of affiliation and genuine liking for one's coworkers—is a manifestation of a school that meets its goals and maintains feelings of solidarity among its teachers. Teachers like to work in such schools and enjoy working with others who share their opinion. Thus commitment of teachers to their school is likely an integral part of developing high teacher morale.

If there is one thing that teachers agree upon, it is that a major goal of the school is student learning. When there is a strong emphasis on learning, there is a strong press for academic excellence. Such schools set high standards, create an orderly learning environment, and nurture a climate where outstanding academic performance is rewarded both by teachers and students. The findings of this study suggest that the press for high academic standards facilitates the development of teacher commitment.

Theoretically, the data suggest that school health is useful in explaining an important organizational characteristic. Healthy organizational dynamics represent a fair exchange between the organization and its participants. A fair exchange provides an inducement for employees to develop a commitment to the organization. As Barnard (1938) notes, "the vitality of organizations lies in the willingness of individuals to contribute forces to the cooperative system" (p. 82). We suspect that organizational commitment is an index of the balance between satisfactions obtained and sacrifices required. When organizational commitment is high, satisfactions that are secured by individual contributors are greater than the personal sacrifices asked of the worker. Low commitment indicates that members of the organization feel that the return for their contributions to the organization is not adequate.

Organizational commitment to the school is an important concept in the analysis of school life. It goes beyond the standard notions of satisfaction, loyalty, and esprit de corps. The principal plays a key role in mediating the relationships between teachers, parents, and students, and in developing a climate of commitment.

The pivotal importance of the principal's leadership in creating this identification with the organization is emphasized by the findings of this study. Too many principals have only the power of their office. In a real sense, they merely are officers, not leaders. This narrow range of authority, the power of the office, can be used to ensure meeting minimum requirements for the operation of the school, but it is not sufficient to encourage teachers to exert extra effort, to accept added responsibility, or to innovate. Nor is it sufficient to promote organizational commitment. Principals need to support the task of teaching and the needs of their teachers, but, above all, they need to develop strong influence within the hierarchical structure of the school system. Structuring activities, demonstrating consideration, and procuring resources simply may not be enough to develop a favorable response to the school organization *unless* the principal has influence with superiors. The message to the principal is clear: the principal must be an energetic and effective actor not only within the school but also within the school system. The principal cannot be a stranger to the teachers—something we have always known—or to the influential stakeholders of the system.

Teacher Commitment and School Climate: OCDQ-RS

School climate also seems to have a natural affinity with organizational commitment. To be sure, a teacher accepts certain wages and working conditions in the formal agreement with the school. However, the identification with the organization that arises from what essentially is a calculated involvement does not seem as intense as the attitudes captured by commitment. Exerting extra effort, for example, implies that the organization is giving something to the teacher beyond the bare contract.

The quality of the work climate may enter into the exchange between teacher and school. Characteristics of supportive principal behavior, for example, "The principal uses constructive criticism" or "The principal sets an example by working hard him- or herself" seem more likely to elicit commitment than directive principal behavior (e.g., "The principal rules with an iron fist"). Similarly, where teachers support one another and are proud of their school (teacher engagement), one would expect to find a committed staff. Conversely, where teachers feel the paperwork is burdensome and the mannerisms of their colleagues annoying (teacher frustration), one would not expect to find a high level of commitment. Finally, where teachers socialize with each other on a regular basis, invite one another to their homes, and find close friends among their colleagues (teacher intimacy), one would expect to find high commitment. Therefore, the following was hypothesized:

(H.1.) Each element of school climate is related to the teachers' organizational commitment.

Two factors, in a second-order factor analysis of the subtests, have emerged from the OCDQ-RS development. It was found that four of the measures—principal support, principal control, teacher engagement, and teacher frustration—were linked by a single underlying concept that was labeled openness; the subtest teacher intimacy was not related to these four.
It seemed logical to hypothesize the following:

(H.2.) Openness in school climate is positively correlated to teachers' organizational commitment.

A regression hypothesis was proposed to test what unique relationship a subtest might have for commitment, while controlling for the effect of the other subtests. It seemed reasonable to assume that the combination of subtests would explain a significant portion of the commitment variance, but regression would allow for identification of the unique contributions hitherto unidentified. Thus the following was hypothesized:

(H.3.) Together the elements of school climate make contributions to a linear composite that is significantly related to teachers' organizational commitment.

Teacher Commitment and School Climate

The first hypothesis, that each element of climate would be related to commitment, was borne out in the main (see Table 6.6.). Principal support and teacher engagement were significantly correlated in the proper direction as were principal control and teacher frustration. Although teacher intimacy was not related significantly to commitment, this lack of association of intimacy with commitment was not entirely unanticipated. Recall that intimacy is not part of the openness construct.

Table 6.6 Summary of Zero-Order Correlations and Regression Analysis for Organizational Commitment and Elements of School Climate

Independent Variables	r	beta	t	R^2
Principal Support	.29**	.126	1.08	
Principal Control	−.22**	−.075	−.64	
Teacher Engagement	.45**	.303	2.21*	
Teacher Frustration	−.36**	−.125	−.91	
Teacher Intimacy	.13	.046	.42	
Total Equation	**R = .46****		**F = 4.17****	**R^2 = .24****
Openness	.46**			

*$p < .05$; **$p < .01$

In the second hypothesis openness was predicted to be related to commitment, and it was ($r = .46$, $p < .01$); the more open the climate of the school, the more committed the teachers.

Finally, the third hypothesis, which tested the regressed teacher commitment on all dimensions of climate, was supported. The subtests explained 24% of the variance of commitment, which was statistically significant. Only teacher engagement, however, made a unique and statistically significant contribution to commitment.

Discussion

This investigation also supports the usefulness of the measure. Climate appears to give an empirical explanation for commitment. The finding that only teacher engagement makes a unique contribution to commitment is theoretically intriguing. Commitment is a relationship primarily to the organization, and teacher engagement (described as behavior that supports teachers and students in the official goals of the organization) also is an organizational affiliation. Contrast engagement with intimacy, a measure of the teachers' social relationships independent of the purpose of the work, and the organizational nature of engagement and its logical tie to commitment seem clear.

Although principal support, principal control, and teacher frustration were not individually significant in the regression equation, the simple correlations of these subtests with commitment suggest that their importance to teacher engagement may be indirect. That is to say, behavior of the principal in supporting teachers and giving them some latitude in determining the way the work is to be done lowers teacher frustration and, together, these three subtests indicate a necessary condition of teacher engagement.

School Effectiveness, School Climate, and School Health: A Comparison of the OHI and the OCDQ-RS

The purpose of this analysis is to test the predictive utility of the two frameworks and their measures as well as to synthesize the empirical findings. The OCDQ-RS is a refinement of the OCDQ, a starkly empirical measure developed through the factor analysis of teacher-teacher and teacher-principal interaction in schools. As we noted earlier, the OCDQ has been plagued by conceptual vagueness and psychometric problems. The OCDQ-RS addresses the psychometric issues, but the lack of a theoretical underpinning remains and may well limit its usefulness. In contrast, the OHI is an instrument built on the foundations of Parsonian social systems theory. Both of these climate instruments should predict organizational outcomes, the OCDQ-RS because it has a long history of predictive use (Anderson, 1982; Miskel & Ogawa, 1988) and the OHI because it is so closely tied to a theoretical base intrinsically involved in organizational function.

Both instruments in their own right identify important organizational attributes. Interestingly, however, neither of the instruments was designed to be a measure of effectiveness—the ultimate question of organizational analysis (Hall, 1972). Although the concept of organizational effectiveness is an enigma, most would agree that academic achievement of students is one of the criteria of school effectiveness. Even here, however, critics maintain that test scores represent a narrow spectrum of the aims and purposes of schooling. In Parsonian terms, achievement is one important instrumental outcome of the school; thus student achievement is one of the dependent variables of this study.

Inherent in the Parsonian emphasis on the integration of members into the organization is the idea that effective organizations will have members who share in the values of the organization, are willing to exert extra effort in their roles, and desire to continue their membership in the organization; commitment is central to organizational life (DeCotiis & Summers, 1987). In the absence of these characteristics, members will in all likelihood drift away from the organization. Therefore, teacher commitment to the school and faculty trust serve as expressive outcomes of the organization. To be sure, organizational commitment and faculty trust are teacher outcome variables, while academic achievement is a student one. Nonetheless, all are important and serve as the criteria for testing the predictive utility of the competing climate frameworks.

The OHI, based upon Parsonian social systems theory, is built on a stronger conceptual foundation than is the OCDQ-RS. Since the theoretical underpinnings of the OCDQ-RS are neither as clear nor as strong as the OHI, it is reasonable to hypothesize that the OHI will be a better predictor of the outcome variables than the OCDQ-RS.

Data for the comparative analysis of the two frameworks were gathered using a sample of 872 teachers in 58 secondary schools in an Eastern industrial state (see Hoy, Tarter, & Bliss, 1990, for elaboration). Although the school sample was not a random one, it was a diverse one representing a broad range of districts and spanning the range of socioeconomic status. Typically data were collected by researchers at regular faculty meetings. Since the appropriate unit of analysis was the school, separate random sets of faculty members were drawn from each school to respond to the Organizational Health Inventory (OHI), the Organizational Climate Description Questionnaire (OCDQ-RS), and the Organizational Commitment Questionnaire (OCQ) and Trust Scales. Student academic achievement was measured by the High School Proficiency Test (HSPT), a statewide test of verbal and quantitative skills.

The High School Proficiency Test (HSPT) is a statewide examination to analyze academic performance in reading, writing, and mathematics. Our analysis used the reading and mathematics scores. Because these scores were correlated at .93, we used a composite index of the two tests for the measure of academic achievement. The state has reported reliabilities of .94 for the reading measure and .95 for mathematics. The reading examination consisted of 87 items that tapped literal comprehension, inferential comprehension, critical comprehension, and study skills. The mathematics section consisted of 39 items that measured such standard arithmetic topics as fractions, decimals, percentages, geometry, algebra, and problem solving (New Jersey Department of Education, 1984).

Socioeconomic status for the school was measured by the use of state district factor groups (DFG). DFG is a composite index of socioeconomic status (SES) based on a factor composed of the following variables: educational level of adults in the district; the occupations of adults in the district; the percentage of people who have lived in the district for the past 10 years; the number of people per housing unit; the percentage of urban population in the district; average family income; and the rate of unemployment and poverty. Districts are arrayed along a continuum from 1 to 10; the higher the number, the greater the SES.

Comparison of Health and Climate Variables

Alpha coefficients of reliabilities and intercorrelations for all the variables used in this study are reported in Table 6.7. As can be seen from the table, three of the health variables—institutional integrity ($r = -.34$, $p < .01$); resource allocation ($r = .33$, $p < .01$); and academic emphasis ($r = .63$, $p < .01$)—were correlated with academic achievement, but only one of the climate variables, teacher frustration ($r = -.31$, $p < .01$), was related to academic achievement. All of the health variables were correlated with organizational commitment, and only teacher intimacy of the five climate variables failed to predict the teachers' commitment to the school; the remaining four variables were significantly associated with commitment. Both health and climate variables were significant predictors of faculty trust, but different patterns of variables emerged for the two types of trust. Not surprisingly, socioeconomic status was related both to academic achievement ($r = .82$, $p < .01$) and organizational commitment ($r = .26$, $p < .05$), but neither faculty trust in the principal nor colleagues was related to socioeconomic status.

The negative correlation between institutional integrity and academic achievement suggests that teachers perceive more pressure and intrusion from the community in schools where students achieve at higher levels. That is, the higher the academic achieve-

Table 6.7 Descriptive Statistics, Reliabilities, and Correlations Among Variables (*N* = 72)

Variables	1	2	3	4	5	6	7	8	9	10	11	12	13	14	15	16
Health																
1. Institutional Integrity	(.91)@															
2. Resource Allocation	.19	(.95)														
3. Principal Influence	.40**	.47**	(.87)													
4. Initiating Structure	.33*	.23*	.58**	(.89)												
5. Consideration	.35**	.25**	.30*	.39**	(.90)											
6. Academic Emphasis	.11	.41**	.45**	.46**	.36**	(.93)										
7. Morale	.44**	.39**	.33**	.34**	.42**	.45**	(.92)									
Climate																
8. Directive Behavior	.01	–.02	.14	–.06	.38**	–.32**	–.03	(.86)								
9. Supportive Behavior	–.29**	–.01	–.20*	.35**	.64**	.15	.16	–.09	(.94)							
10. Engagement	.29**	.30**	.39**	.16	.36**	.35**	.35**	–.21*	.39**	(.86)						
11. Frustration	–.26*	–.41**	–.38**	–.16	–.38**	–.39**	–.38**	.41**	–.31**	–.52**	(.85)					
12. Intimacy	–.11	–.04	–.07	–.15	.02	–.04	.11	–.04	.05	.22*	.01	(.71)				
Effectiveness																
13. Academic Achievement	–.34**	.33**	.18	.10	.11	.63**	.21	–.11	.01	.21	–.31**	.02	(.92)			
14. Commitment	.28**	.31**	.44**	.30**	.36**	.44**	.40**	–.22*	.29**	.45**	–.36**	.13	.20	(.91)		
15. Trust in Principal	.39**	.12	.18	.27*	.51**	.09	.28*	–.17	.56**	.27*	–.24*	.10	–.08	.66**	(.89)	
16. Trust in Colleagues	.31**	.11	.32**	.27*	.36**	.30*	.52**	–.03	.24*	.47**	–.31**	.27*	.07	.65**	.44**	(.92)
SES																
District Factor Group	–.28**	.13	.15	–.04	.17	.53**	.13	–.20*	.03	.17	–.17	.03	.82**	.26*	–.02	–.08

*p < .05; **p < .01; @ Alpha coefficients of reliability are in parentheses.

133

ment of the high school, the more likely teachers view the parents as a source of trouble. Parents in wealthier school districts may be more aggressive and, perhaps, more involved than parents in districts of lesser means—an interpretation supported by the significant negative correlation between SES and institutional integrity. This explanation is supported further by the strong, positive correlation between academic emphasis and SES, as well as by the moderate, negative correlation between principal directiveness and SES.

All of the health variables and four of the five climate variables were significantly correlated with organizational commitment. Healthy schools have committed teachers. Open schools have committed teachers. But intimate schools—those with strong, cohesive social relations—do not necessarily generate teacher commitment. The relatively weak relationship of commitment to SES suggests that commitment is more a consequence of the inner workings of the school rather than the community setting. Theoretically, SES should have a stronger relationship to achievement than to commitment because achievement is more a function of SES, while commitment is a function of the social integration of school personnel (Parsons, 1961).

Both health and climate variables were related to faculty trust in the principal and in colleagues. Only resource allocation from the health inventory and directive principal behavior from the climate battery failed to correlate with a trust measure. In general, healthy schools and open schools are imbued with faculty trust.

The zero-order correlations are instructive, but they may be misleading. The relationship between variables such as academic emphasis and student achievement may well be the accidental consequence of their relationships with yet another variable, such as SES. Therefore, a series of multiple regression analyses was performed to examine the independent effects of health and climate on effectiveness as well as to determine the net effect of all the independent variables on the dependent variables of effectiveness.

We begin our multiple regression analyses by examining the health variables in their explanation of the variance in each of the dependent variables. When academic achievement was regressed on the health variables, a multiple R of .77 ($p < .01$) explained approximately 59% of the variance. Only institutional integrity (beta = −.44, $p < .01$) and academic emphasis (beta = .62, $p < .01$), however, had unique and independent effects on achievement of students. Because SES was related strongly to achievement, an important question is, "Do these aspects of health make a unique contribution to achievement independently of SES?" To answer this question, SES was added to the health measures as a predictor variable. All of the independent variables then explained 75% ($R = .87$, $p < .01$) of the student achievement variance, but only SES (beta = .57, $p < .01$) and academic emphasis (beta = .31, $p < .01$) made separate and significant contributions to the explanation (see Table 6.8). When all of the independent variables (including SES) were used to predict organizational commitment, 35% of the variance was explained ($R = .59$, $p < .01$). None of the variables made a unique and significant contribution to commitment. When all the independent variables were regressed on faculty trust in the principal, the variables combined to explain 32.5% of the variance ($R = .57$, $p < .01$), but only consideration (beta = .44, $p < .01$) made a unique and significant contribution to the explanation of trust in the principal. Similarly, all the independent variables combined to predict faculty trust in colleagues ($R = .55$, $p < .05$), but only morale had a significant, independent relationship with trust in colleagues (beta = .42, $p < .05$). The results are summarized in Table 6.8.

When academic achievement, commitment, and trust were regressed on the climate variables, the multiple R for achievement was not significant; however, the climate variables combined did explain 26% of the variance in commitment ($R = .51$, $p < .01$); 32.5% of variance in trust in the principal ($R = .57$, $p < .01$); and 27% of the variance of trust in colleagues ($R = .52$, $p < .01$). Adding SES to the equations only confirmed the strong independent effect of SES on achievement but had little effect on teacher commitment and faculty trust (see Table 6.9).

Our final analysis considered the influence of all the independent variables, that is, SES, health, and climate properties, on the measures of effectiveness—student achievement, teacher commitment, and faculty trust. In the explanation of student achievement, all of the variables combined to explain 75% of the variance ($R = .87$, $p < .01$). Forty-two percent of the teacher commitment variance was explained by the final regression equation ($R = .65$,

Table 6.8 Regression of Achievement, Commitment, and Trust on Dimensions of School Health and SES ($N = 58$)

	Achievement		Commitment		Faculty Trust in Principal		Faculty Trust in Colleagues	
	r	beta	r	beta	r	beta	r	beta
Health Variables Only Regression #1								
Institutional Integrity	−.34**	−.44**	.32**	.16	.39**	.25	.31**	.05
Initiating Structure	.10	−.17	.28*	−.15	.27*	.04	.27*	−.07
Consideration	.11	−.02	.41**	.21	.51**	.47**	.36**	.14
Principal Influence	.18	.14	.41**	.21	.18	−.02	.32**	.25
Resource Allocation	.33**	.04	.35**	.06	.12	−.01	.11	−.20
Academic Emphasis	.63**	.62**	.41**	.25	.09	−.07	.30*	.11
Morale	.21	.13	.41**	.09	.28*	−.03	.52**	.38*
	$R = .77**$		$R = .58**$		$R = .57**$		$R = .57**$	
Health Variables with SES Regression #2								
SES	.82**	.57**	.26*	.15	−.02	.07	.07	−.03
Institutional Integrity	−.34**	−.16	.32**	.24	.39**	.26	.31**	.06
Initiating Structure	.10	−.07	.28*	−.14	.27*	.14	.27*	−.09
Consideration	.11	−.03	.41**	.17	.51**	.44**	.36**	.16
Principal Influence	.18	.02	.41**	.20	.18	−.05	.32**	.10
Resource Allocation	.33**	.07	.35**	.04	.12	−.12	.11	−.12
Academic Emphasis	.63**	.31**	.41**	.23	.09	−.05	.30*	.06
Morale	.21	.07	.41**	.04	.28*	−.06	.52**	.42*
	$R = .87**$		$R = .59**$		$R = .56*$		$R = .55*$	

*$p < .05$; **$p < .01$

$p < .05$) and 44% of the faculty trust in the principal ($R = .66$, $p < .06$). It was still the case that only SES and academic emphasis made significant and unique contributions to student achievement. None of the independent variables (including SES) made a significant and unique contribution to teacher commitment or to faculty trust in the principal; it is the overall health and climate of a school that determined the commitment teachers have to their school and the trust they have in their principal. Although the independent variables combined to explain about 45% of the vari-

Table 6.9 Regression of Achievement, Commitment, and Trust on Dimensions of School Climate and SES (*N* = 58)

	Achievement		Commitment		Faculty Trust in Principal		Faculty Trust in Colleagues	
	r	beta	r	beta	r	beta	r	beta
Climate Variables Only **Regression #1**								
Supportive Behavior	.01	−.11	.35**	.19	.56**	.54**	.24*	.06
Directive Behavior	−.11	.04	−.21	−.06	−.17	−.09	−.03	.12
Teacher Engagement	.21	−.06	.45**	.28	.27*	−.04	.47**	.36*
Teacher Frustration	−.31**	−.32	−.39**	−.14	−.24*	−.06	−.31**	−.12
Teacher Intimacy	.02	.01	.05	−.02	.10	.07	.27*	.19
		R = .32(ns)		*R* = .51**		*R* = .57**		*R* = .52**
Climate Variables with SES **Regression #2**								
SES	.82**	.80**	.26*	.17	−.02	.02	−.08	−.02
Supportive Behavior	.01	−.06	.35**	.16	.56**	.57**	.24*	.09
Directive Behavior	−.11	.02	−.21	−.05	−.17	−.05	−.03	.06
Teacher Engagement	.21	.02	.45**	.31	.27*	.04	.47**	.33
Teacher Frustration	−.31**	−.14	−.39**	−.12	−.24*	−.03	−.31**	−.07
Teacher Intimacy	.02	.07	.05	−.01	.10	.07	.27*	.28*
		R = .84**		*R* = .57**		*R* = .61**		*R* =.55**

*$p < .05$; **$p < .01$

ance in trust in colleagues, only teacher intimacy made a significant and independent contribution to the variance (beta = .30, $p <$ .05). These results are summarized in Table 6.10.

Discussion

Does the OHI provide a better instrument than the OCDQ-RS for the prediction of school effectiveness? The answer is a qualified yes. In predicting student achievement, we found that the dimensions of the OHI were strongly related to student achievement, and the climate measures were not. Even after controlling for SES, the acknowledged major predictor of student performance,

Table 6.10 Regression of Achievement and Commitment on Dimensions of School Health, Climate, and SES

Health Variables (N = 58)	Achievement		Commitment		Faculty Trust in Principal		Faculty Trust in Colleagues	
	r	beta	r	beta	r	beta	r	beta
SES	.82**	.57**	.26*	.15	−.02	.06	−.08	.01
Institutional Integrity	−.34**	−.16	.32**	.21	.39**	.20	.31**	.10
Initiating Structure	.10	−.06	.28*	.02	.27*	.21	.27*	.04
Consideration	.11	−.04	.41**	−.14	.51**	.03	.36**	.17
Principal Influence	.18	.01	.41**	.18	.18	−.04	.32**	−.02
Resource Allocation	.33**	.06	.35**	.06	.12	−.08	.11	−.21
Academic Emphasis	.63**	.29*	.41**	.20	.09	−.04	.30*	.08
Morale	.21	.06	.41**	.05	.28*	−.02	.52**	.26
Supportive Behavior	.01	.01	.35**	.21	.56**	.42	.24*	−.09
Directive Behavior	−.11	.01	−.21	−.25	−.17	−.14	−.03	.04
Teacher Engagement	.21	−.03	.45**	.16	.27**	.05	.47**	.27
Teacher Frustration	−.31**	−.08	−.39**	.11	−.24*	.01	−.31**	.01
Teacher Intimacy	.02	.04	.05	.06	.10	.13	.27*	.30*
	R = .87**		R = .65*		R = .66*		R = .67*	

*p < .05; **p < .01

the dimensions of health provided a substantial increase in the explanation of student achievement. In fact, the OCDQ-RS adds nothing to the explanation of student achievement that is not already explained by SES and the OHI. In predicting teacher commitment, once again OHI was a slightly better predictor than the OCDQ-RS; however, there was virtually no difference between the two measures for predicting faculty trust.

These comparative findings come as no surprise. As we explained earlier, the development of the OCDQ was not guided by a theoretical perspective, while the OHI was grounded in the theoretical work of Talcott Parsons. Recall that the dimensions of health were developed to measure aspects of Parsonian functional imperatives for the survival and growth of organizations. Healthy schools should have high scores on both instrumental and expressive activities. The combined influence of all the health variables in explaining student achievement was substantial; 59% of the variance was explained. In contrast, the climate variables explained an insignificant 10% of the variance.

It was also the case that SES was related strongly to both student achievement and organizational health. There is little doubt that wealthier school districts have higher levels of student achievement as well as healthier school environments. Our data reflect, however, that academic emphasis of the school makes a significant contribution to the explanation of student achievement that goes beyond the influence of SES. A careful examination of the construct of academic emphasis reveals that it embodies at least three of the six school effectiveness characteristics cited by Edmonds (1979). High student expectations, an orderly work environment, and a strong emphasis on academics are captured in this single health variable—academic emphasis. What is also clear from the analysis is that the positive or assertive leadership that Edmonds and others claim to be instrumental in effective student performance simply is not supported in the current sample. Not one of the six health and climate variables describing assertive leadership—initiating structure, consideration, influence, resource allocation, directiveness, supportiveness—made a unique and significant contribution to the explanation of student achievement. These aspects of the leadership of the principal did not have a direct impact on student performance.

This research finding, that the behavior of the principal is not directly related to instructional effectiveness, has been anticipated by theoretical developments in the field. Bossert and his colleagues (1982) argued that the principal's role is one of affecting the climate and instructional organization available to the teaching staff. The links between administrative behavior and student achievement are complex. It may be that some principals can directly affect student learning by manipulating the instructional organization. Our findings, however, support the notion that the principal's influence is indirect, provided his or her actions lead to the development of a climate with a strong academic emphasis. Thus we hypothesize that one important way a principal influences student learning is by nurturing a climate of academic achievement—that is, by developing a serious and orderly learning environment, strong academic press, and high student expectations. Our data support this hypothesis, even controlling for SES.

Both the health and climate measures explained a significant amount of the variance in organizational commitment, but again the health measure proved a more robust measure than climate. It is theoretically provocative that in the regressions no single subtest of either health or climate makes a significant, independent contribution to teacher commitment. Rather, it is the overall atmosphere or ethos (Good & Weinstein, 1986), whether measured as health or climate, that is associated with commitment. Thus we hypothesize that the patterns of principal and teacher behavior work together to ensure commitment; leadership patterns of the principal must complement the interaction patterns of teachers. The findings also suggest that teacher commitment may be vulnerable to misuses of administrative power (Blase, 1988).

The health and climate variables also explain a significant amount of the variance in faculty trust, both as individual sets of measures and when combined. Using both sets of measures— health and climate—provides a more powerful prediction of faculty trust. Like teacher commitment, in general, it is the overall ethos and climate that is associated with faculty trust; however, intimacy and, to a lesser extent, supportive principal behavior themselves are likely to produce trust.

We also hypothesize, based on the current results, that institutional integrity is an important component or side effect of SES. We recognize that this interpretation lends credence to the criticism that climate is a tautological duplication of context (James & Jones, 1974). We suspect that the negative relationship between institutional integrity and achievement identified in both the correlation and regression analysis may be a function of vigorous parental involvement that can affect the school's program by inducing high expectations. The term integrity has certain obvious connotations that may lead to confusion here. In Parsonian terms institutional integrity clearly is a virtue. As suggested at the outset, however, different measures often get in the way of each other. The concept of institutional integrity is one that needs refinement both conceptually and operationally.

These preliminary findings suggest that if practitioners or researchers are to use only one measure to map the domain of the climate of secondary schools, the OHI may be a more useful vehicle than the OCDQ-RS. But it seems premature to bury the OCDQ-RS. There are so few studies using either measure that important relationships might well be overlooked if researchers were to rely on one at the expense of the other. We suggest that health or climate measures be used where theoretically appropriate. For example, health is likely to be a better predictor of goal achievement, innovativeness, loyalty, and cohesiveness—variables directly linked to the functional necessities described by Parsons (1961). On the other hand, climate is likely to be a better predictor of openness in communication, authenticity, motivation, and participation—variables associated with openness in interaction patterns as described by Halpin (1966).

Healthy schools and open climates are desirable ends in themselves. Even if unrelated to other outcome variables, these constructs are important in their own right. They signify organizational configurations that are good working environments, places where people feel comfortable with the purposes of the organization and their capacity to function as professionals. These are places that promote good mental health because of the cooperative and supportive relations, the low levels of frustration, high levels of morale, and the expression of real engagement in the task at hand. Another important direction of research is to identify those personal and organizational variables that promote healthy schools and open climates.

Summary

It is appropriate at this point to summarize the basic findings of the school climate and health studies.

(1) School health and climate are useful constructs for analyzing the school workplace, and the OHI and OCDQ-RS are practical and useful tools for measuring these constructs.

(2) Although the OHI and the OCDQ-RS are alternate measures of school climate, they complement each other and provide different vantage points. Which measure to use depends on the question. Health is likely a better predictor of variables linked to such functional imperatives as innovation, goal achievement, loyalty, and cohesiveness. Climate is likely the better predictor of variables linked to such measures of interaction as open communication, principal authenticity, and teacher participation in decision making.

(3) Healthy schools and open organizational climates are related to effective schools. Both healthy and open school climates have committed teachers who trust each other and the principal. In addition to the strong explanatory power of socioeconomic status, school health in general and academic emphasis in particular are related to student achievement.

(4) In high schools, health variables that predict trust in the principal are different than those that predict trust in colleagues. Consideration and institutional integrity are the best predictors of trust in the principal, and morale and principal influence are the best predictors of trust in colleagues. Similarly, the climate variables that predict trust follow the same pattern. Supportive principal behavior is the best predictor of trust in the principal, and teacher engagement is the best predictor of trust in colleagues. Principals who protect their teachers from outside forces, who are considerate, and who respect and support teachers as professional colleagues generate trust. It appears, however, that it is the teachers, not the principal, who develop an atmosphere of colleague trust.

(5) Principal influence, the ability of the principal to influence superiors on behalf of teachers, is a critical element in the development of teacher commitment to the school. Only teacher engagement rivals the principal's influence in building faculty commitment.

Thus far, all the reported research has been at the secondary level. We now turn to the elementary school where there has been little research. Our analyses of elementary schools is confined to the OCDQ-RE; the OHI-E is so new that little research is available.

Faculty Trust, Effectiveness, and
School Climate: OCDQ-RE

Just as we anticipated that the OCDQ-RS would be related to faculty trust in the principal and in colleagues, we expected that the OCDQ-RE would predict faculty trust in elementary schools. Openness in interpersonal relations should promote a sense of confidence and trust in others regardless of school level.

Elementary principal behavior is examined along three dimensions—the extent to which it is supportive, directive, or restrictive. Supportive behavior is marked by genuine concern and support of teachers. In contrast, directive behavior is starkly task-oriented with little concern for the needs of the teachers, and restrictive behavior produces impediments for teachers as they try to do their work. Elementary teacher interactions are measured in terms of collegial, intimate, and disengaged behavior. Supportive and professional interaction among teacher colleagues is collegial behavior; intimate behavior involves close relations among teachers not only in but outside school; and disengaged behavior depicts a general sense of alienation and separation among teachers.

In addition to these six dimensions, two underlying aspects of school climate can be delineated. *Openness in principal behavior* is marked by concern for the ideas of teachers (high supportiveness); freedom and encouragement for teachers to experiment and act independently (low directiveness); and structuring the routine aspects of the job so that they do not interfere with teaching (low restrictiveness). *Openness in teacher behavior* refers to teachers' interactions that are meaningful and tolerant (low disengagement); that are friendly, close, and supportive (high intimacy); and that are enthusiastic, accepting, and mutually respectful (high collegial relations).

Remember that trust is associated with a general confidence and overall optimism in occurring events. Faculty trust in the principal is confidence that the principal will keep his or her word and will act in the best interests of the teachers. Faculty trust in colleagues is the belief that teachers can depend on one another in difficult situations.

Although the concepts of organizational climate and trust are not identical, they are complementary, and one would logically expect them to be related in elementary schools. Trust is an intrinsic element of pattern-maintenance (Parsons, 1961). Thus it is reasonable to expect that those elements of organizational climate that are inherently expressive in character will likely be associated with trust. Similarly, those instrumental elements of the organization that hinder expressive development should be negatively related to trust. Moreover, research in the secondary school suggests that principal behavior influences faculty trust in the principal, but does not promote faculty trust in one's colleagues (see Tarter, Bliss, & Hoy, 1989). Similarly, it is teacher behavior that fosters trust in colleagues, not principal leadership. Therefore, we hypothesized the following:

(H.1.) The more supportive the leadership behavior of the principal, the greater the degree of faculty trust in the principal.

(H.2.) The less directive the leadership behavior of the principal, the greater the degree of faculty trust in the principal.

(H.3.) The less restrictive the leadership behavior of the principal, the greater the degree of faculty trust in the principal.

(H.4.) The more collegial the teacher behavior in a school, the greater the degree of faculty trust in colleagues.

(H.5.) The less disengaged the teacher behavior in a school, the greater the degree of faculty trust in colleagues.

(H.6.) The more intimate the teacher behavior in a school, the greater the degree of faculty trust in colleagues.

The two openness measures of climate are reflections of harmony in the instrumental and expressive activities in school life. Consequently, two more hypotheses were proposed:

(H.7.) The more open the principal's behavior, the greater the degree of faculty trust in the principal.

(H.8.) The more open the faculty behavior, the greater the degree of faculty trust in colleagues.

Although the hypotheses imply that climate promotes trust, it is also likely that trust facilitates openness. The relationships are ones of mutual dependence (Homans, 1950).

The theoretical link of climate to effectiveness is not direct. The characteristics of teachers, instructional programs, and students clearly are more direct forces on school effectiveness, especially when measured in terms of student outcomes. Nonetheless, it seems reasonable to expect that the general climate of a school will contribute to its success. Therefore, we explored the relationship of school climate with perceived effectiveness of the schools. Mott (1972) combined several important outcomes to formulate a model of organizational effectiveness; he developed an index to measure the extent to which an organization is efficient, flexible, adaptable, and productive. The Mott index was adapted by Miskel and his colleagues (Miskel, McDonald, & Bloom, 1983) for use in schools, and Hoy and Ferguson (1985) linked this subjective index with more objective measures of school outcomes. The eight-item index had an internal reliability of .88 in the current study.

Using this measure of subjective effectiveness, in which the teachers describe the quantity and quality of services as well as the efficiency and flexibility of the school responses to continuities and interruptions in school life, we examined the relationships between school climate characteristics and perceived school effectiveness. Thus, two final hypotheses are proposed:

(H.9.) Each school climate variable is related to perceived school effectiveness.

(H.10.) Together the six climate variables make contributions to a linear composite that is significantly related to perceived school effectiveness.

The hypotheses were tested using a diverse sample of 44 elementary schools in New Jersey (Witkoskie, 1990). Once again the school was the unit of analysis; that is, all data were aggregated at the school level. Random sets of teachers in each school responded to the instruments while their colleagues were busy responding to another battery of measures. We used school mean scores to test the hypotheses.

Faculty Trust and School Climate

The first three hypotheses argued that faculty trust in the principal would be correlated with the principal's leadership. However, only supportive behavior was related to faculty trust in the principal ($r = .58$, $p < .01$). Neither restrictive nor directive principal behavior was related to this dimension of trust.

The second three hypotheses anticipated that faculty trust in colleagues would be related to the faculty's behavior. Indeed, that was the case. The more collegial the faculty, the more intimate the faculty, and the less disengaged the faculty, the greater the trust of teachers in others ($r = .67$, $r = .43$, $r = -.60$; $p < .01$).

The next two hypotheses expected to find significant relationships between the openness of the principal and faculty trust in the principal, and openness of the teachers and collegial trust. These hypotheses were supported; openness in principal behavior was related to trust in the principal ($r = .49$, $p < .01$); openness in teacher behavior was related to trust in other teachers ($r = .72$, $p < .01$).

Faculty trust in colleagues was significantly correlated with faculty trust in the principal ($r = .43$, $p < .05$). Although there is some relationship between faculty trust in colleagues and principal, the two aspects of trust are different from each other.

Next, we turn our attention to the relative importance of each dimension of climate and the combined influence of all the variables in predicting both aspects of trust. As predicted, the climate variables combine to explain a significant portion of the variance in faculty trust in the principal ($R = .66$, $p < .01$), but only supportive principal behavior (beta = .68, $p < .01$) makes a unique and significant contribution to the variance. Similarly, climate variables combine to predict faculty trust in colleagues ($R = .75$, $p < .01$), but only collegial (beta = .40, $p < .01$) and disengaged (beta = –.30, $p < .05$) made significant and unique contributions to the variance. For a summary of the statistical analyses, see Table 6.11.

Effectiveness and School Climate

Finally, the analysis explores the relationship between school climate and perceived organizational effectiveness. As expected, dimensions of climate were related to teachers' perceptions of school effectiveness. In particular, supportive principal behavior ($r = .29$, $p < .05$); and collegial ($r = .54$, $p < .01$); intimate ($r = .36$, $p < .01$); and disengaged teacher behaviors ($r = –.54$, $p < .01$) were associated with effectiveness. Together the climate variables explained a significant portion of the variance in school effectiveness ($R = .64$, $p < .05$), but only disengaged teacher behavior (beta = –.34, $p < .05$) made a unique and significant contribution to the variance. Interestingly, openness in principal behavior is unrelated to perceived effectiveness ($r = .21$, $n.s.$); it is the openness in teacher behavior that is linked with school effectiveness ($r = .60$, $p < .01$). See Table 6.11.

Table 6.11 Regression of Trust and Effectiveness on Dimensions of
Elementary School Climate

Climate Variables (N = 44)	Principal Trust		Faculty Trust		Perceived Effectiveness	
	r	beta	r	beta	r	beta
Principal Behavior						
Supportive	.58**	.68**	.43**	.11	.29*	−.02
Directive	−.15	−.03	−.06	.04	.06	.16
Restrictive	−.13	.10	−.22	.10	−.23	−.03
Teacher Behavior						
Collegial	.13	−.33	.67**	.40**	.54**	.28
Intimate	.25*	.26	.43**	.20	.36**	.18
Disengaged	−.28*	−.11	−.60**	−.30*	−.54**	−.34*
	R = .66**		R = .75**		R = .64**	
Openness in Principal	.49**		.37**		.21	
Openness in Teachers	.25*		.72**		.60**	

*p < .05; **p < .01

Discussion

The results of this study replicate what we found in the secondary schools. That is, elements of organizational climate that are
inherently expressive are associated with trust. Openness in the
climate of a school and trust in interpersonal relationships complement each other. The measures of trust are distinct from the
dimensions of openness in climate, as is demonstrated in both the
moderate correlations and the variability of the correlations. Although they are related, trust and openness in climate are different concepts, and they operate in different ways within the school.

As we expected, different dimensions of climate are associated
with each aspect of faculty trust. Leadership behavior of the
principal, rather than the interrelationships of the teachers, is the
best predictor of trust in the administration. Likewise, interrelationships among teachers, not the leadership of the principal, are
the best predictors of trust in colleagues. Only supportive behavior makes a unique and significant explanation of trust in the
principal. Principals who are helpful and genuinely concerned
about the professional and personal welfare of their teachers are
likely to have the trust of their teachers. Only collegial and

engaged teacher behavior make unique and significant contributions to trust in colleagues.

Teachers who are engaged in their work also trust their colleagues. It is the teachers who initiate collegiality, and collegiality and trust go hand in hand. One would think that the principal would be a major figure in the creation of such feelings among the faculty, but the data do not demonstrate this. One again is struck by the importance of the teacher group in developing a climate of trust in elementary schools in much the same way as it was in secondary schools. The principal cannot do for teachers what they cannot do for themselves.

Perceived effectiveness is related to elementary school climate. Moreover, it would appear that the critical immediate relationship to effectiveness is openness within the teacher subculture. The principal's role in fostering effective school practices may well be in developing a context or open climate in which engaged teachers are able to function effectively. We would recommend caution in the interpretation of the effectiveness finding. The measure of effectiveness is subjective; it rests on teachers' general perceptions of the operation of the school. The results of this study may underestimate the role of the principal in affecting classroom practices. Clearly, this is fertile ground for further study.

Summary

(1) The OCDQ-RE seems to be a reliable and useful instrument in the measurement of critical school elements. The leadership and teacher properties are related to such important outcome variables as trust and perceived school effectiveness.

(2) Openness in principal behavior seems crucial to generating faculty trust in the principal; however, openness in teacher behavior is the key factor in generating trust in colleagues.

(3) Different patterns of climate variables predict faculty trust in the principal and trust in colleagues. Supportive principal behavior is the best predictor of trust in the principal. Collegial and engaged teacher behaviors are the best predictors of the trust teachers have in one another; behavior of the principal has no apparent direct effect on this relationship.

(4) Openness in the interaction patterns of teachers is most directly related to the perceived effectiveness of the school; principal behavior has little relationship to perceived school effectiveness.

Implications

The research reported here has many implications for both practitioners and scholars of administration. We sketch only three broad possibilities for each.

Implications for Practice

(1) **Assess school health and climate before beginning change efforts.**

We agree with Miles (1969) that the state of organizational health will predict the probable success of most change efforts: "Economy of effort would suggest that we look at the state of an organization's health, as such, and try to improve it—in preference to struggling with a series of more or less inspired short-run change efforts as ends in themselves" (p. 376).

Both the OHI and the OCDQ can provide a snapshot of the state of the school and, thus, either or both measures yield a diagnosis as well as a baseline from which to judge the effect of change strategies. Our experience demonstrates that a principal's perceptions of the health or climate of the school frequently is at variance with the perceptions of teachers. To discover such a discrepancy is not to uncover a problem but rather a symptom. The issue is not to determine in some objective sense whether the climate is open or closed, or healthy or unhealthy, but to find the root causes for the discrepancy in perceptions. For example, the finding of high scores on teacher frustration would indicate that the teachers felt that current administrative practice was carried out with too heavy a hand. This is useful information, but it is more useful if the principal can determine the cause of the feeling of frustration. In short, the measures provide a conceptual basis for the diagnosis of and solution to many organizational problems.

We recommend that working school administrators use the health and climate instruments as a continuing assessment of their own administrative practice. The application of either the OHI or the OCDQ for formative evaluation is not an unqualified recommendation. The essence of formative evaluation is that it is a continuous guide to the improvement of practice. For a principal, the subtests of the OHI and the OCDQ-RS seem to be more appropriate criteria for the evaluation of principal behavior than many of the current standards that masquerade as measures of administrative effectiveness. It is important, however, that there exists a climate of collegiality and trust among administrators if the constructive use of these evaluative tools is to take place. We strongly caution against using any instrument of this kind as summative evaluation.

(2) **The role of the principal may well be to improve instructional effectiveness indirectly through the development of an open, healthy, and trustful climate.**

The debate between "institutional manager" and "instructional leader" obscures both the leadership and managerial characteristics of the administrative role; that is, no principal is totally an instructional leader, nor is any completely a manager. No principal can afford to be ignorant of the instructional process, yet, ultimately, the principal's role is in the creation of conditions in which teachers operate as autonomous professionals.

To argue that the principal should develop an open and healthy climate is one thing; to do it is another. The interrelationships are complex. For example, the practical difference between supportiveness and directiveness may not be clear. The distinction between principal supportiveness and directiveness depends largely on the extent of teachers' freedom either to accept or to reject the principal's suggestions. This much seems clear: simply because the principal intends to be supportive by encouraging teachers' freedom does not mean that teachers will interpret these actions as supportive. Further, the principal's avoidance of directive behavior probably is insufficient to generate a sense of support.

Much of the recent discussion about restructuring schools and school-based management is predicated on the assumption that teachers are professionals and, given the appropriate working conditions and authority, they will make wise decisions in the best interest of the students. Hoy and Forsyth (1986) propose a model of supervision that captures the essence of the independent, yet cooperative, nature of improving instruction in schools; the model is based on the assumption that a basic role of the principal is to establish a healthy, open climate. The measurement tools we have developed in this book can be used by perceptive principals to improve their administrative practice.

(3) **The health and openness of school climates may be necessary conditions for long-term school effectiveness.**

Although the research evidence to date is not abundant, there are connections between health, climate, and effectiveness. When such narrow effectiveness measures as standardized achievement test scores are used, there are predictable relationships between climate and effectiveness. For example, directive principal behavior may lead to the short-term improvement of test scores (Bliss & Pavignano, 1990). Long-term improvements in academic achievement, however, are more likely linked to a school with strong academic emphasis within the context of a healthy and open environment (Hoy, Tarter, & Bliss, 1990). When the effectiveness criteria are more broadly construed to include such variables as teacher commitment or faculty trust, climate and health seem to have strong explanatory power. One may, of course, consider climate and health as dependent variables as well, that is, the realization of healthy and open schools may be a welcome end in itself. Thus a principal might assess the condition of health or climate in a given school and attempt to better the social context. While such outcomes as improved climate are not usually considered a mark of school effectiveness, they probably are indicative of effective administration.

Implications for Research

(1) **To what extent are the OCDQ and OHI useful tools in the prediction of school effectiveness?**

We have developed four parsimonious, reliable, and reasonably valid research tools for measuring organizational climate (OCDQ-RE and OCDQ-RS) and school health (OHI and OHI-E). We have just begun to draw the complex relationships between these measures and effectiveness. We invite replication and refinement of each instrument. All the instruments need to be tested in large samples of schools throughout the country to check the factor stability of each battery and its predictive utility.

In testing these instruments, the dependent measure of effectiveness should not solely be student achievement. Instrumental and expressive outcomes describing events for all participants in the school, that is, students, teachers, principals, and the community, also are appropriate. For students, absenteeism, drop-out rates, self-concept, identification with the school, attitude toward the school and teachers, and good citizenship are a few of the criterion variables that might be measures of school effectiveness. For teachers, absenteeism, trust, commitment, morale, teaching efficacy, satisfaction, self-concept, and attitudes towards students in school are examples of important teacher outcomes. For principals, teacher loyalty, satisfaction, school identification, conflict, burnout, stress, efficacy, and overall student and faculty support are candidates for indices of principal effectiveness. For the community, support for schools, parent participation, community satisfaction, pride in schools, and community conflict about schools are possible effectiveness measures.

Climate and health are indicators of the internal functioning of the organization. They are limited to specific interaction patterns among principals, teachers, and students. There are other important internal functions that should be related to healthy and open schools. For example, we recommend the study of relationships between climate or health and such internal variables as participation in decision making, goal consensus, openness in communication, cooperative teamwork, motivational systems, and control functions.

(2) What conditions promote healthy and open schools?

We have argued elsewhere in this chapter that health and climate are important ends in themselves. If this is the case, then researchers should be interested in the antecedents of productive school climates. Such concepts as community support, parental participation, shared decision making, teachers' professionalism, teacher militancy, union activity, political orientation of the board, succession patterns of principals and superintendents, school structure, school level, and type of community (urban, suburban, and rural) seem likely to be constraining influences on the health and climate of the schools. It should be obvious that many of the relationships between health or climate and other variables typically are not one-way; they are relations of mutual dependence. For example, the professional orientation of teachers can be both a cause of healthy climate and a result of such a climate. We raise these research possibilities because we are committed to the view that healthy and open schools are worthy ends in themselves.

(3) **What are the elements that combine or intervene in the relationship of climate or health to effectiveness?**

The relationship between measures of climate or health and school outcomes is, in all likelihood, not direct. The characteristics of teachers, class size, and teaching practices exert an influence on student achievement (Bridge, Judd, & Moock, 1979; Good & Brophy, 1986). The skills and attitudes that students bring with them to the school influences outcomes as well (Mergendoller & Marchman, 1987). Climate and health probably join with other variables in contributing to school outcomes.

Schools are systems of interacting personalities. Teachers bring with them past experience, work-group traditions, job expectations, attitudes, and individual goals, all of which influence their perceptions of school life. Their role expectations and individual attitudes combine with perceptions to motivate behavior. Moreover, these same variables produce educators' cognitive orientations toward their job, that is, their intellectual understanding of what their jobs are. The expectations, cognitive orientations, and motivational forces produce behavior in the schools that has consequences for effective operation. It should be clear that it will not be easy to untangle this seamless web of intervening variables, but it is an important research task. One research agenda should include path-goal models that seek to explain this complex system of intervening variables.

These practical and research implications merely are illustrative of the heuristic potential of the four instruments that we have developed in this book. We see this work as a beginning, not an end, and we are keenly aware of the limitations of the work. It is for that reason that we urge further research and refinement of both the conceptual underpinnings and the empirical measures.

7 Using the Health and Climate Instruments: A Guide to Action

There is little point in general models if they do not give rise to specific conceptual derivations and empirical applications which illuminate, in however modest degree, significant day-to-day practice.

—Jacob W. Getzels et al.
Educational Administration as a Social Process

The final chapter is written primarily for practitioners who want to use our instruments for organizational analysis and for organizational and professional development. To that end, for each instrument we will (a) briefly review the conceptual foundations; (b) present the form of the instrument to be administered; (c) define the subscales; (d) describe the scoring procedures; and (e) discuss norms and the interpretation of the results. In short, we will provide all the information that principals and teachers—and researchers, for that matter—need to administer, score, and interpret the health and climate scales. We believe that these scales, either alone or in combination, can be used systematically to analyze the school workplace and to develop strategies to improve the climate and health of schools.

The Organizational Climate Description
Questionnaire for Elementary Schools: The OCDQ-RE

Organizational climate is a broad term that refers to teachers' *perceptions* of their general work environment; it is influenced by the formal and informal structures of the school as well as by the personalities of the teachers and the leadership behavior of the principal. Put simply, the set of internal characteristics that distinguishes one school from another and influences the behavior of teachers is its organizational climate. The climate roughly may be perceived as the personality of the school; that is, personality is to individual as climate is to organization.

The OCDQ-RE measures the basic dimensions of elementary school climate. The principal's behavior is examined along three dimensions: the extent to which it is supportive, directive, and restrictive. Supportive behavior is genuine concern for and support of teachers. In contrast, directive behavior is starkly task-oriented with little concern for the needs of the teachers, and restrictive behavior produces impediments for teachers as they try to do their work. Likewise, three critical aspects of teacher behavior—collegial, intimate, and disengaged—are identified.

Collegial behavior supports open and professional interaction among teacher colleagues, and intimate behavior describes the quality of the personal relations among teachers. In comparison, disengaged behavior depicts a general sense of alienation and separation among teachers in school. These fundamental features of principal and teacher behavior are elaborated and summarized in Table 7.1.

In addition to these six specific dimensions, two underlying general aspects of school climate have been identified. The three specific characteristics of principal behavior define a general feature of leader behavior, which is termed openness. *Openness in principal behavior* is marked by an openness and concern for the ideas of teachers (high supportiveness); freedom and encouragement for teachers to experiment and act independently (low directiveness); and structuring the routine aspects of the job so that they do not interfere with teaching (low restrictiveness).

Similarly, three specific dimensions of teacher behavior define *openness in teacher behavior,* which refers to teachers' interactions that are meaningful and tolerant (low disengagement); that are

Table 7.1 Dimensions of Organizational Climate (OCDQ-RE)

PRINCIPAL'S BEHAVIOR

Supportive Behavior reflects a basic concern for teachers. The principal listens and is open to teacher suggestions. Praise is given genuinely and frequently, and criticism is handled constructively. Supportive principals respect the professional competence of their staffs and exhibit both a professional and personal interest in each teacher.

Directive Behavior is rigid monitoring of teacher behavior. Principals maintain close and constant control over all teacher and school activities, down to the smallest details.

Restrictive Behavior hinders, rather than facilitates, teacher work. The principal burdens teachers with paperwork, committee requirements, and other demands that interfere with their teaching responsibilities.

TEACHERS' BEHAVIOR

Collegial Behavior supports open and professional interactions among teachers. Teachers are proud of their school, enjoy working with their colleagues, and are enthusiastic, accepting, and mutually respectful of the professional competence of their colleagues.

Intimate Behavior reflects a cohesive and strong network of social support among the faculty. Teachers know each other well, are close personal friends, socialize together regularly, and provide strong support for each other.

Disengaged Behavior refers to a lack of meaning and focus to professional activities. Teachers are simply putting in time and are non-productive in group efforts or team building; they have no common goals. Their behavior is often negative and critical of their colleagues and the organization.

---

friendly, close, and supportive (high intimacy); and that are enthusiastic, accepting, and mutually respectful (high collegial relations). Thus the OCDQ-RE provides a description of the school climate in terms of six specific and two general dimensions. That is, each school can be described by mapping its profile along the

PRINCIPAL BEHAVIOR

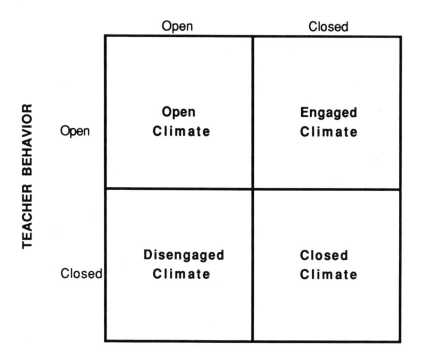

Figure 7.1. Typology of School Climates

six dimensions and by computing the openness of the principal and the openness of the faculty.

These two general dimensions are relatively independent; consequently, they can be used to develop a typology of school climates. If the two openness dimensions are cross-partitioned, four categories of school climate are defined (see Figure 7.1).

Open Climate

The distinctive characteristics of the open climate are cooperation, respect, and openness within the faculty and between the faculty and principal. The principal listens and is receptive to teacher ideas, gives genuine and frequent praise, and respects the competence of faculty (high supportiveness). Principals also give their teachers independence to perform without close scrutiny (low directiveness) and provide facilitating leadership devoid of bureaucratic trivia (low restrictiveness). Likewise, the faculty supports open and professional behavior (high collegial relations) among teachers. Teachers know each other well and are typically close personal friends (high intimacy). They cooperate and are committed to teaching and their jobs (low disengagement). In brief, the behavior of both the principal and teachers is genuine and open.

Engaged Climate

The engaged climate is marked, on the one hand, by ineffective attempts of the principal to lead, and on the other, by high professional performance of the teachers. The principal is rigid and authoritarian (high directiveness) and respects neither the professional expertise nor personal needs of the faculty (low supportiveness). In addition, the principal is seen as burdening faculty with unnecessary busywork (high restrictiveness). Surprisingly, however, the teachers simply ignore the principal's unsuccessful attempts to control, and conduct themselves as productive professionals. They respect and support each other, are proud of their school, and enjoy their work (high collegiality). They not only respect each others' professional competence but also like each other as friends (high intimacy). The teachers come together as a cooperative unit engaged and committed to the teaching-learning task (high engagement). In brief, the teachers are productive in spite of weak principal leadership; the faculty is cohesive, committed, supportive, and engaged.

Disengaged Climate

The disengaged climate stands in stark contrast to the engaged. The principal's leadership behavior is strong, supportive, and concerned. The principal listens to and is open to teachers' views (high supportiveness); gives teachers the freedom to act on the basis of their professional knowledge (low directiveness); and relieves teachers of most of the burdens of paperwork and bureaucratic trivia (low restrictiveness). Nevertheless, the faculty reacts badly; teachers are unwilling to accept responsibility. At best, the faculty simply ignores the initiatives of the principal; at worst, the faculty actively works to immobilize and sabotage the principal's leadership attempts. Teachers not only dislike the principal, they do not like each other as friends (low intimacy) or respect each other as colleagues (low collegiality). The faculty is clearly disengaged from their work. Although the principal is supportive, flexible, and noncontrolling (i.e., open), the faculty is divided, intolerant, and uncommitted (i.e., closed).

Closed Climate

The closed climate is the antithesis of the open. The principal and teachers simply go through the motions, with the principal stressing routine trivia and unnecessary busywork (high restrictiveness) and teachers responding minimally and exhibiting little commitment to the tasks at hand (high disengagement). The principal's leadership is seen as controlling and rigid (high directiveness) as well as unsympathetic and unresponsive (low supportiveness). These misguided tactics are accompanied not only by teacher frustration and apathy, but also by suspicion and a lack of faculty respect for colleagues as well as for administrators (low intimacy and noncollegiality). In sum, closed climates have principals who are nonsupportive, inflexible, hindering, and controlling, and a faculty that is divided, apathetic, intolerant, and disingenuous.

The OCDQ-RE Form

The OCDQ-RE is a 42-item questionnaire. Teachers describe their school behavior. They respond along a four-point scale defined by the categories "rarely occurs," "sometimes occurs," "often occurs," and "very frequently occurs." The entire instrument as it is administered to teachers is presented in Table 7.2.

Administering the Instrument

The OCDQ-RE is best administered as part of a faculty meeting. It is important to guarantee the anonymity of the teacher; they are not asked to sign the questionnaire and no identifying

Table 7.2 OCDQ-RE

OCDQ-RE

DIRECTIONS: THE FOLLOWING ARE STATEMENTS ABOUT YOUR SCHOOL. PLEASE INDICATE THE EXTENT TO WHICH EACH STATEMENT CHARACTERIZES YOUR SCHOOL BY CIRCLING THE APPROPRIATE RESPONSE.

RO=RARELY OCCURS SO=SOMETIMES OCCURS O=OFTEN OCCURS VFO=VERY FREQUENTLY OCCURS

1. The teachers accomplish their work with vim, vigor, and pleasure...................... RO SO O VFO

2. Teachers' closest friends are other faculty members at this school....................... RO SO O VFO

3. Faculty meetings are useless... RO SO O VFO

4. The principal goes out of his/her way to help teachers... RO SO O VFO

5. The principal rules with an iron fist....................................... RO SO O VFO

6. Teachers leave school immediately after school is over... RO SO O VFO

7. Teachers invite faculty members to visit them at home... RO SO O VFO

8. There is a minority group of teachers who always oppose the majority................ RO SO O VFO

9. The principal uses constructive criticism... RO SO O VFO

10. The principal checks the sign-in sheet every morning.. RO SO O VFO

11. Routine duties interfere with the job of teaching................................ RO SO O VFO

12. Most of the teachers here accept the faults of their colleagues............................ RO SO O VFO

13. Teachers know the family background of other faculty members........................ RO SO O VFO

14. Teachers exert group pressure on non-conforming faculty members................ RO SO O VFO

15. The principal explains his/her reasons for criticism to teachers........................ RO SO O VFO

16. The principal listens to and accepts teachers' suggestions................................... RO SO O VFO

17. The principal schedules the work for the teachers.. RO SO O VFO

18. Teachers have too many committee requirements.. RO SO O VFO

19. Teachers help and support each other.. RO SO O VFO

20. Teachers have fun socializing together during school time................................ RO SO O VFO

21. Teachers ramble when they talk at faculty meetings.. RO SO O VFO

(continues)

Table 7.2 (continued)

22. The principal looks out for the personal welfare of teachers............................. RO SO O VFO

23. The principal treats teachers as equals... RO SO O VFO

24. The principal corrects teachers' mistakes... RO SO O VFO

25. Administrative paperwork is burdensome at this school...................................... RO SO O VFO

26. Teachers are proud of their school... RO SO O VFO

27. Teachers have parties for each other.. RO SO O VFO

28. The principal compliments teachers... RO SO O VFO

29. The principal is easy to understand... RO SO O VFO

30. The principal closely checks classroom (teacher) activities............................... RO SO O VFO

31. Clerical support reduces teachers' paperwork... RO SO O VFO

32. New teachers are readily accepted by colleagues... RO SO O VFO

33. Teachers socialize with each other on a regular basis.. RO SO O VFO

34. The principal supervises teachers closely... RO SO O VFO

35. The principal checks lesson plans... RO SO O VFO

36. Teachers are burdened with busy work.. RO SO O VFO

37. Teachers socialize together in small, select groups.. RO SO O VFO

38. Teachers provide strong social support for colleagues.. RO SO O VFO

39. The principal is autocratic.. RO SO O VFO

40. Teachers respect the professional competence of their colleagues..................... RO SO O VFO

41. The principal monitors everything teachers do... RO SO O VFO

42. The principal goes out of his/her way to show appreciation to teachers............. RO SO O VFO

Table 7.3 The Items that Compose the Six Subtests of the OCDQ-RE

Principal's Behavior

Supportive behavior items   *Questionnaire #*

  1. The principal goes out of his/her way to help teachers.   (4)

  2. The principal uses constructive criticism.   (9)

  3. The principal explains his/her reasons for criticism to teachers. (1 5)

  4. The principal looks out for the personal welfare of teachers.   (2 2)

  5. The principal compliments teachers.   (2 8)

  6. The principal listens to and accepts teachers' suggestions.   (1 6)

  7. The principal treats teachers as equals.   (2 3)

  8. The principal is easy to understand.   (2 9)

  9. The principal goes out of his/her way to show appreciation to teachers.   (4 2)

Directive behavior items

  1. The principal rules with an iron fist.   (5)

  2. The principal checks the sign-in sheet every morning.   (1 0)

  3. The principal schedules the work for the teachers.   (1 7)

  4. The principal corrects teachers' mistakes.   (24)

  5. The principal closely checks classroom (teacher) activities.   (3 0)

  6. The principal checks lesson plans.   (3 5)

(continues)

code is placed on the form. Few object to responding to the instrument, which takes less than 10 minutes to complete. Someone other than the principal should collect the data. It is important to create a nonthreatening atmosphere where teachers can be honest. All of the health and climate instruments follow the same pattern of administration.

Table 7.3 (continued)

---

7. The principal is autocratic. (39)

8. The principal monitors everything teachers do. (41)

9. The principal supervises teachers closely. (34)

Restrictive behavior items

1. Routine duties interfere with the job of teaching. (11)

2. Teachers have too many committee requirements. (18)

3. Administrative paperwork is burdensome at this school. (25)

* 4. Clerical work reduces teachers' paperwork. (31)

5. Teachers are burdened with busywork. (36)

Teachers' Behavior

Collegial behavior items

1. The teachers accomplish their work with vim, vigor, and pleasure. (1)

* 2. Teachers leave school immediately after school is over. (6)

3. Most of the teachers here accept the faults of their colleagues. (12)

4. Teachers help and support each other. (19)

5. Teachers are proud of their school. (26)

6. New teachers are readily accepted by their colleagues. (32)

* 7. Teachers socialize together in small, select groups. (37)

8. Teachers respect the professional competence of their colleagues. (40)

(continues)

The Subscales

The 42 items of the instrument define the six dimensions of the OCDQ-RE. The items are presented in Table 7.3. Each item is scored by assigning 1 to "rarely occurs," 2 to "sometimes occurs," 3

Table 7.3 (continued)

Intimate behavior items

1. Teachers' closest friends are other faculty members at this school. (2)

2. Teachers invite faculty members to visit them at home. (7)

3. Teachers know the family background of other faculty members. (13)

4. Teachers have fun socializing together during school time. (20)

5. Teachers have parties for each other. (27)

6. Teachers socialize with each other on a regular basis. (33)

7. Teachers provide strong social support for colleagues. (38)

Disengaged behavior items

1. Faculty meetings are useless. (3)

2. There is a minority group of teachers who always oppose the majority. (8)

3. Teachers exert group pressure on non-conforming members. (14)

4. Teachers ramble when they talk at faculty meetings. (21)

*Score is reversed

to "often occurs," and 4 to "very frequently occurs." When an item is reverse scored (indicated by an asterisk in Table 7.3), "rarely occurs" receives a 4, "sometimes occurs" receives a 3, and so on. Each item is scored for each teacher. Then an average school score for *each item* is computed because the school is the unit of analysis. For example, if school A has 15 teachers responding to the OCDQ-RE, each individual questionnaire is scored and then an average score for all teachers is computed for each item. Thus the average score for the 15 teachers is calculated for item 1 and then item 2 and so on. The average school scores for the items comprising each subtest are added to yield school subtest scores. The six subtest scores represent the climate profile for the school.

Scoring the OCDQ-RE

Step 1: Score each item for each teacher with the appropriate number (1, 2, 3, or 4). Be sure to reverse score items 6, 31, 37.

Step 2: Calculate an average school score for each item. In the example above, one would add all 15 scores on each item and then divide by 15. Round the scores to the nearest hundredth. This score represents the average school item score. You should have 42 average school item scores before proceeding.

Step 3: Sum the average school item scores as follows:

Supportive Behavior (*S*) = 4 + 9 + 15 + 16 + 22 + 23 + 28 + 29 + 42

Directive Behavior (*D*) = 5 + 10 + 17 + 24 + 30 + 34 + 35 + 39 + 41

Restrictive Behavior (*R*) = 11 + 18 + 25 + 31 + 36

Collegial Behavior (*C*) = 1 + 6 + 12 + 19 + 26 + 32 + 37 + 40

Intimate Behavior (*Int*) = 2 + 7 + 13 + 20 + 27 + 33 + 38

Disengaged Behavior (*Dis*) = 3 + 8 + 14 + 21

These six scores represent the climate profile of the school. How does your school compare with others? We have supplied information on a large and diverse sample of New Jersey elementary schools, which gives a rough basis for comparing your school with others. The average scores and standard deviations for each climate dimension are summarized below. Standard deviations tell us how close most schools are to the average; the smaller the standard deviation, the closer most schools are to the typical school.

	Mean (M)	Standard Deviation (SD)
Supportive Behavior (S)	23.34	4.85
Directive Behavior (D)	19.34	3.20
Restrictive Behavior (R)	12.98	1.55
Collegial Behavior (C)	23.11	2.69
Intimate Behavior (Int)	17.23	2.14
Disengaged Behavior (Dis)	6.98	1.26

To make the comparisons easy, we recommend that you standardize each of your subtest scores. Standardizing the scores gives them a "common denominator" that allows direct comparison among all schools.

Computing Standardized Scores of the OCDQ-RE

Step 1: Convert the school subtest scores to standardized scores with a mean of 500 and a standard deviation of 100, which we call SdS scores. Use the following formula:

SdS for S = 100 × (S – 23.34) / 4.85 + 500

First compute the difference between your school score on S and the mean of 23.84 for the normative sample (S – 23.84). Then multiply the difference by 100 [100 × (S – 23.84)]. Next divide the product by standard deviation of the normative sample (4.85). Then add 500 to the result. You have computed a standardized score (SdS) for the supportive behavior subscale (S). Repeat the process for each dimension as follows:

SdS for D = 100 × (D – 19.34)/3.20 + 500
SdS for R = 100 × (R – 12.98)/1.55 + 500
SdS for C = 100 × (C – 23.11)/2.69 + 500
SdS for Int = 100 × (Int – 17.23)/2.14 + 500
SdS for Dis = 100 × (Dis – 6.98)/1.26 + 500

You have standardized your school scores against the normative data provided in the New Jersey sample. For example, if your school score is 600 on supportive behavior, it is one standard deviation above the average score on supportive behavior of all schools in the sample; that is, the principal is more supportive than 84% of the other principals. A score of 300 represents a school that is two standard deviations below the mean on the subtest. You may recognize this system as the one used in reporting individual scores on the SAT, CEEB, and GRE. The range of these scores is presented below.

If the score is 200, it is lower than 99% of the schools.
If the score is 300, it is lower than 97% of the schools.
If the score is 400, it is lower than 84% of the schools.
If the score is 500, it is average.
If the score is 600, it is higher than 84% of the schools.
If the score is 700, it is higher than 97% of the schools.

If the score is 800, it is higher than 99% of the schools.

There are two other scores that easily can be computed and are usually of interest to teachers and principals. Recall that two openness dimensions were determined in the second-order factor analysis of the OCDQ-RE. Accordingly, the two openness measures can be computed as follows:

$$\text{Principal Openness} = \frac{(\text{SdS for } S) + (1000 - \text{SdS for } D) + (1000 - \text{SdS for } R)}{3}$$

$$\text{Teacher Openness} = \frac{(\text{SdS for } C) + (\text{SdS for } Int) + (1000 - \text{SdS for } Dis)}{3}$$

These openness indices are interpreted the same way as the subtest scores, that is, the mean of the "average" school is 500. Thus a score of 650 on teacher openness represents a highly open faculty.

Prototypic profiles of climates have been constructed using the normative data from the New Jersey sample of elementary schools (see Table 7.4). Therefore, you can compare the fit of your own school climate to the four prototypes. Compare the standardized scores of your school with each of the prototypes in Table 7.4 to determine which of the four climate types your school most closely resembles. Note that a given school can be described by

Table 7.4 Prototypic Profiles of Elementary School Climate Types

Climate Dimension	Open Climate	Engaged Climate	Disengaged Climate	Closed Climate
Supportive	574(H)	423(L)	553(H)	381(L)
Directive	436(L)	555(H)	445(L)	610(H)
Restrictive	433(L)	551(H)	448(L)	555(H)
Collegial	615(H)	584(H)	423(L)	395(L)
Intimate	602(H)	561(H)	446(L)	447(L)
Disengaged	446(L)	430(L)	610(H)	590(H)
Principal Openness	571(H)	439(L)	553(H)	439(L)
Teacher Openness	590(H)	572(H)	420(L)	417(L)
Total	**1,161**	**1,011**	**973**	**856**

NOTE: H = High; L = Low

one or two indices. A total score of 1,150 or more is almost certain to be the mark of a school with an open climate. By the same token, a school with a score below 850 will have a closed climate. Most school scores, however, fall between these extremes and can be diagnosed only by carefully comparing all elements of the climate with the four prototypes. We have changed the numbers into categories ranging from high to low by using the following conversion table:

Above 600	Very high
551-600	High
525-550	Above average
511-524	Slightly above average
490-510	Average
476-489	Slightly below average
450-475	Below average
400-449	Low
Below 400	Very low

We recommend using all six dimensions of OCDQ-RE to gain a finely tuned picture of school climate.

An Example

We were recently asked by a local school district to examine the climates of its elementary schools. The OCDQ-RE was administered to the teachers at faculty meetings. The data then were returned to us and, using the procedures described above, we scored and analyzed the climate of the schools. School data can be scored by our computer program, which includes a comparison of your school with the normative sample and classifies the climate.[1] Two of the schools, Adams and Jefferson, serve as our examples.

The scores have been standardized so that the average score for an elementary school in the sample is 500 and the standard deviation is 100. We have done this for two reasons. First, the scores are easily compared with others in the sample; and second, their interpretation is not unlike that of SAT scores, scores with which most teachers and administrators are familiar. For example, a score of 600 on the Supportive Principal Behavior scale is a relatively high score. Similarly, a score of 500 represents a school that is average in comparison to others, while a 400 is a low score.

The climate profiles for Adams and Jefferson and a brief sketch of the climate of each school are given below.

CLIMATE PROFILE FOR ADAMS ELEMENTARY SCHOOL

PRINCIPAL'S BEHAVIOR

Supportive Behavior	575 (High)
Directive Behavior	495 (Average)
Restrictive Behavior	428 (Low)

TEACHERS' BEHAVIOR

Collegial Behavior	586 (High)
Intimate Behavior	563 (High)
Disengaged Behavior	460 (Below average)

Openness of Principal Behavior	551 (High)
Openness of Teacher Behavior	563 (High)

TOTAL   1,114

The climate of Adams Elementary School is quite open. Teachers are highly open and professional in their interactions with each other (high collegiality). They also demonstrate a strongly cohesive and substantial network of social support (high intimacy), and they are typically tolerant and engaged in meaningful professional activities (average disengagement). There also is substantial openness of the principal's behavior (high). The principal is more supportive of teachers than most elementary principals (high on supportive behavior). Moreover, the principal is neither restrictive (low) nor especially directive in behavior (average); in fact, the principal facilitates teacher activity by not burdening them with busywork.

CLIMATE PROFILE FOR JEFFERSON ELEMENTARY SCHOOL

PRINCIPAL'S BEHAVIOR

Supportive Behavior	471 (Below average)
Directive Behavior	528 (Above average)
Restrictive Behavior	522 (Slightly above average)

TEACHERS' BEHAVIOR

Collegial Behavior	468 (Below average)
Intimate Behavior	478 (Slightly below average)
Disengaged Behavior	571 (High)

Openness of Principal Behavior	474 (Below average)

Openness of Teacher Behavior   458 (Below average)

Total   932

The most distinctive features of Jefferson Elementary School are the high disengagement of the teachers and the lack of principal support. Teachers are not engaged in productive group efforts with either the principal or other faculty members (high disengagement), and they do not respond well to the principal's directive leadership. They are irritated by the restrictive behavior of the principal (slightly above average). They feel burdened with paperwork and other demands that interfere with their teaching responsibilities. Moreover, they do not believe that the principal is particularly open to their ideas and suggestions (below average on supportive behavior). Similarly, the teachers neither are supportive of each other (below average on collegiality) nor particularly friendly with each other (below average in intimacy). The school climate of Jefferson is relatively closed.

The contrast between these two schools is arresting. Adams is a good place to work. The principal's leadership is enlightened, and the faculty respond as professionals; they are committed to the task at hand and supportive of each other as well as the principal. The interpersonal relationships are genuine. When the principal does criticize, it is for a constructive purpose and the teachers accept that. This is not a school to be tinkered with; the work environment complements the teaching-learning task.

Jefferson, by comparison, is not a good place to teach or to practice administration. Suspicion and turmoil pervade the halls and classrooms of this school. There is a leadership void. The principal is not there to be supportive. Rules, regulations, and busywork are substitutes for active educational leadership. Teachers respond by disengaging from the collective task. They are not friendly with each other, and they do not support each other. In brief, these teachers do not enjoy teaching at Jefferson. There is no quick fix here, but it is in everyone's best interest to change the climate of the school.

The principal has created an almost intolerable situation. The Board of Education and superintendent have charged this third-year principal with the personal challenge of raising the test scores of his underachieving school. The principal has responded by instituting a machine-like system of control that specifies what and how teachers must teach and he monitors their compliance with close supervision and burdensome forms. The faculty response has been disintegration; teachers no longer support each other and friendships have been lost. Teachers complain of pointless busywork. In all likelihood, a new principal will soon be found to restructure the professional relationships at Jefferson.

The Organizational Climate Description
Questionnaire for Secondary Schools: The OCDQ-RS

The OCDQ-RS is a 34-item climate instrument with five dimensions describing the behavior of secondary teachers and principals. The instrument, unlike the original OCDQ, was designed for *secondary* schools. It measures two aspects of principal leadership—supportive and directive behavior. Supportive principal behavior meets both the social needs and task achievement of the faculty. The principal is helpful, genuinely concerned with teachers, and attempts to motivate them by using constructive criticism and by setting an example through hard work. In contrast, directive behavior is rigid and domineering control.

Similarly, three dimensions of teacher behavior are described—engaged, frustrated, and intimate. Engaged teacher behavior reflects a faculty in which teachers are proud of their school, enjoy working with each other, are supportive of their colleagues, and are committed to the success of their students. On the other hand, frustrated teacher behavior depicts a faculty burdened with routine duties, administrative paperwork, and excessive assignments unrelated to teaching. Finally, intimate teacher behavior reflects a strong and cohesive network of social relations among the faculty. The five basic dimensions of principal and teacher behavior are summarized in Table 7.5.

Four of the five aspects of school interaction also form a general dimension of school climate—openness. Open principal behavior is reflected in genuine relationships with teachers in which the principal creates a supportive environment, encourages teacher participation and contribution, and frees teachers from routine busywork so they can concentrate on teaching. In contrast, closed principal behavior is rigid and nonsupportive. Open teacher behavior is characterized by sincere, positive, and supportive

Table 7.5 Dimensions of Organizational Climate (OCDQ-RS)

PRINCIPAL'S BEHAVIOR

Supportive Principal Behavior is characterized by efforts to motivate teachers by using constructive criticism and setting an example through hard work. At the same time, the principal is helpful and genuinely concerned with the personal and professional welfare of teachers. Supportive behavior is directed toward both the social needs and task achievement of the faculty.

Directive Principal Behavior is rigid and domineering supervision. The principal maintains close and constant control over all teachers and school activities down to the smallest details.

TEACHERS' BEHAVIOR

Engaged Teacher Behavior is reflected by high faculty morale. Teachers are proud of their school, enjoy working with each other, and are supportive of their colleagues. Teachers are not only concerned about each other, they are committed to the success of their students. They are friendly with students, trust students, and are optimistic about the ability of students to succeed.

Frustrated Teacher Behavior refers to a general pattern of interference from both administration and colleagues that distracts from the basic task of teaching. Routine duties, administrative paperwork, and assigned nonteaching duties are excessive; moreover, teachers irritate, annoy, and interrupt each other.

Intimate Teacher Behavior reflects a strong and cohesive network of social relationships among the faculty. Teachers know each other well, are close personal friends, and regularly socialize together.

---

relationships with students, administrators, and colleagues; teachers are committed to their school and the success of their students; moreover, they find the work environment facilitating rather than frustrating. In brief, *openness* refers to a school climate where both the teachers' and principal's behaviors are authentic, energetic, goal-directed, and supportive, and in which satisfaction is derived both from task accomplishment and social interaction.

Intimacy is a facet of secondary school climate that stands alone; unlike elementary school climate, intimacy is not part of the openness construct. Intimate teacher behavior builds a strong and cohesive network of social relationships among the faculty. Teachers know each other well, have close personal friends among the faculty, and socialize together regularly. The friendly social interactions that are the essence of this construct are limited, however, to social needs; in fact, task accomplishment is not germane to this dimension.

Thus the OCDQ-RS provides a description of school climate in terms of five specific and two general dimensions. Each school can be described by mapping its profile along the five dimensions.

The OCDQ-RS Form

The OCDQ-RS is a 34-item questionnaire on which educators are asked to describe the extent to which specific behavior patterns occur in the school. The responses vary along a four-point scale defined by the categories "rarely occurs," "sometimes occurs," "often occurs," and "very frequently occurs." The entire instrument as it is administered to teachers is presented in Table 7.6.

The Subscales

After the OCDQ-RS is administered, the subtests are scored. Each subtest is presented in Table 7.7. Recall that the items are scored by assigning 1 to "rarely occurs," 2 to "sometimes occurs," 3 to "often occurs," and 4 to "very frequently occurs." Each item is scored for each teacher. Then an average school score for *each item* is computed. The average school scores for the items comprising each subtest are added to yield school subtest scores.

Scoring the OCDQ-RS

Step 1: Score each item for each teacher with the appropriate number (1, 2, 3, or 4).

Step 2: Calculate an average school score for each item. Round the scores to the nearest hundredth. This score represents the average school item score. You should have 34 average school item scores before proceeding.

Table 7.6 OCDQ-RS

OCDQ-RS

DIRECTIONS: THE FOLLOWING ARE STATEMENTS ABOUT YOUR SCHOOL. PLEASE INDICATE THE EXTENT TO WHICH EACH STATEMENT CHARACTERIZES YOUR SCHOOL BY CIRCLING THE APPROPRIATE RESPONSE.

RO=RARELY OCCURS SO=SOMETIMES OCCURS O=OFTEN OCCURS VFO=VERY FREQUENTLY OCCURS

1. The mannerisms of teachers at this school are annoying... RO SO O VFO

2. Teachers have too many committee requirements... RO SO O VFO

3. Teachers spend time after school with students who have individual problems..... RO SO O VFO

4. Teachers are proud of their school.. RO SO O VFO

5. The principal sets an example by working hard himself/herself........................... RO SO O VFO

6. The principal compliments teachers... RO SO O VFO

7. Teacher-principal conferences are dominated by the principal............................ RO SO O VFO

8. Routine duties interfere with the job of teaching... RO SO O VFO

9. Teachers interrupt other faculty members who are talking in faculty meetings... RO SO O VFO

10. Student government has an influence on school policy... RO SO O VFO

11. Teachers are friendly with students... RO SO O VFO

12. The principal rules with an iron fist.. RO SO O VFO

13. The principal monitors everything teachers do... RO SO O VFO

14. Teachers' closest friends are other faculty members at this school.................... RO SO O VFO

15. Administrative paper work is burdensome at this school..................................... RO SO O VFO

16. Teachers help and support each other.. RO SO O VFO

17. Pupils solve their problems through logical reasoning.. RO SO O VFO

18. The principal closely checks teacher activities.. RO SO O VFO

19. The principal is autocratic... RO SO O VFO

20. The morale of teachers is high.. RO SO O VFO

21. Teachers know the family background of other faculty members........................ RO SO O VFO

(continues)

Table 7.6 (continued)

22. Assigned non-teaching duties are excessive.. RO SO O VFO

23. The principal goes out of his/her way to help teachers.. RO SO O VFO

24. The principal explains his/her reason for criticism to teachers........................ RO SO O VFO

25. The principal is available after school to help teachers when
     assistance is needed.. RO SO O VFO

26. Teachers invite other faculty members to visit them at home............................ RO SO O VFO

27. Teachers socialize with each other on a regular basis.. RO SO O VFO

28. Teachers really enjoy working here.. RO SO O VFO

29. The principal uses constructive criticism... RO SO O VFO

30. The principal looks out for the personal welfare of the faculty........................... RO SO O VFO

31. The principal supervises teachers closely... RO SO O VFO

32. The principal talks more than listens.. RO SO O VFO

33. Pupils are trusted to work together without supervision..................................... RO SO O VFO

34. Teachers respect the personal competence of their colleagues........................... RO SO O VFO

Table 7.7　The Items that Compose the Five Subtests of the OCDQ-RS

Principal's Behavior	
Supportive behavior items	*Questionnaire #*

1. The principal sets an example by working hard himself/herself. (5)

2. The principal compliments teachers. (6)

3. The principal goes out of his/her way to help teachers. (23)

4. The principal explains his/her reasons for criticism to teachers. (24)

5. The principal is available after school when assistance is needed. (25)

6. The principal uses constructive criticism. (29)

7. The principal looks out for the personal welfare of faculty. (30)

Directive behavior items

1. Teacher-principal conferences are dominated by the principal. (7)

2. The principal rules with an iron fist. (12)

3. The principal monitors everything teachers do. (13)

4. The principal closely checks teacher activities. (18)

5. The principal is autocratic. (19)

6. The principal supervises teachers closely. (31)

7. The principal talks more than listens. (32)

(continues)

Step 3: Sum the average school item scores as follows:

Supportive Behavior (S) = 5 + 6 + 23 + 24 + 25 + 29 + 30
Directive Behavior (D) = 7 + 12 + 13 + 18 + 19 + 31 + 32
Engaged Behavior (E) = 3 + 4 + 10 + 11 + 16 + 17 + 20 + 28 + 33 + 34
Frustrated Behavior (F) = 1 + 2 + 8 + 9 + 15 + 22
Intimate Behavior (Int) = 14 + 21 + 26 + 27

Table 7.7 (continued)

Teachers' Behavior

Engaged behavior items

1. The teachers spend time after school with students who have individual problems. (3)

2. Teachers are proud of their school. (4)

3. Student government has an influence on school policy. (1 0)

4. Teachers are friendly with students. (1 1)

5. Teachers help and support each other. (1 6)

6. The pupils solve their problems through logical reasoning. (1 7)

7. The morale of teachers is high. (2 0)

8. Teachers really enjoy working here. (2 8)

9. Pupils are trusted to work together without supervision. (3 3)

10. Teachers respect the personal competence of their colleagues. (3 4)

Frustrated behavior items

1. The mannerisms of teachers in this school are annoying. (1)

2. Teachers have too many committee requirements. (2)

3. Routine duties interfere with the job of teaching. (8)

4. Teachers interrupt other faculty members who are talking in faculty meetings. (9)

5. Administrative paper work is burdensome in this school. (1 5)

6. Assigned non-teaching duties are excessive. (2 2)

(continues)

You may wish to compare your school profile with other schools. To make the comparison easy, we recommend that you convert each school score to a standardized score. The current data base on secondary schools is drawn from a large, diverse sample of schools in New Jersey. The average scores and standard deviations for each climate dimension are summarized below.

Table 7.7 (continued)

Intimate behavior items

1. Teachers' closest friends are other faculty members at this school.   (14)

2. Teachers know the family background of other faculty members.   (21)

3. Teachers invite other faculty members to visit them at home.   (26)

4. Teachers socialize with each other on a regular basis.   (27)

	Mean (M)	Standard Deviation (SD)
Supportive Behavior (S)	18.19	2.66
Directive Behavior (D)	13.96	2.49
Engaged Behavior (E)	26.45	1.32
Frustrated Behavior (F)	12.33	1.98
Intimate Behavior (Int)	8.80	.92

Computing the Standardized Scores for the OCDQ-RS

Step 1: Convert the school subtest scores to standardized scores with a mean of 500 and a standard deviation of 100, which we call SdS scores. Use the following formula:

$$\text{SdS for } S = 100 \times (S - 18.19)/2.66 + 500$$

First compute the difference between your school score on S and the mean for the normative sample ($S - 18.19$). Then multiply the difference by 100 [$100 \times (S - 18.19)$]. Next divide the product by the standard deviation of the normative sample (2.66). Then add 500 to the result. You have computed a standardized score (SdS) for the supportive behavior subscale (S). Repeat the process for each dimension as follows:

$$\text{SdS for } D = 100 \times (D - 13.96)/2.49 + 500$$
$$\text{SdS for } E = 100 \times (E - 26.45)/1.32 + 500$$
$$\text{SdS for } F = 100 \times (F - 12.33)/1.98 + 500$$
$$\text{SdS for } Int = 100 \times (Int - 8.80)/.92 + 500$$

There is one other score that easily can be computed and is often of interest, the general openness index for the school climate.

$$\text{Openness} = \frac{(\text{SdS for } S) + (1000 - \text{SdS for } D) + (\text{SdS for } E) + (1000 - \text{SdS for } F)}{4}$$

This openness index is interpreted the same way as the subtest scores, that is, the mean of the "average" school is 500. Thus a score of 600 on openness represents a highly open school climate, one that is one standard deviation above the average school; this means that the school is more open than 84% of the schools in the normative sample.

Prototypic profiles for the climate of schools have been constructed using the normative data from the New Jersey sample of secondary schools (see Table 7.8). Thus one can examine the fit of one's own school and compare it to the contrasting prototypes. An overall openness score of 620 or more, for instance, is almost certain to be the mark of an open school. We recommend using all five dimensions of the OCDQ-RS, however, to gain a finely tuned picture of school climate.

An Example

Harding High School is a school that we were not invited to assess; however, it is an actual school from our data set. We scored

Table 7.8 Prototypic Profiles of Open and Closed Secondary School Climates

Climate Dimension	Open Climate	Closed Climate
Supportive Behavior	629(H)	398(L)
Directive Behavior	414(L)	642(H)
Engaged Behavior	627(H)	383(L)
Frustrated Behavior	346(L)	641(H)
Intimate Behavior	465(L)	463(L)
School Openness*	599(H)	375(L)

NOTE: H = High; L = Low

$$*\text{Openness} = \frac{(\text{SdS for } S) + (1000 - \text{SdS for } D) + (\text{SdS for } E) + (1000 - \text{SdS for } F)}{4}$$

the school as described above. The climate profile at Harding High School and a brief sketch of its climate follow.

CLIMATE PROFILE FOR HARDING HIGH SCHOOL

PRINCIPAL'S BEHAVIOR
Supportive Behavior	530 (Above average)
Directive Behavior	558 (High)

TEACHERS' BEHAVIOR
Engaged Behavior	340 (Very low)
Frustrated Behavior	761 (Very high)
Intimate Behavior	449 (Low)

Openness of the School	413 (Low)

Harding High School has a closed organizational climate. Here is a principal who is trying hard but to little avail. He sets an example of commitment and industriousness for his teachers. At the same time, he shows concern and support for his faculty and asks them to do nothing that he is not already doing (above-average support). But as much as he is concerned about the welfare of the teachers, he does not give them the freedom to act on their own initiative; he is directive. Teacher behavior at Harding is about as closed as you will find in any high school. Morale is extremely low. Teachers do not like each other, the school, or the students. They are frustrated by the close monitoring of the administration and what they consider to be excessive paperwork and meaningless routine (high frustration). There is no cohesiveness among the faculty in this school (low intimacy); they neither work together nor socialize together.

We cannot comment on why the school has this pattern because we have no data other than this snapshot of the climate of the school. The climate profile is the beginning of a process of diagnosis and eventual change, not an end in itself. We received no invitation to suggest change strategies for Harding High. Until the administration and teachers decide that *they* want to change, we suspect that the school will muddle through with teachers and administrators playing games with each other, with all participants frustrated, and the students the ultimate losers—not a good place to work, not a good place to learn.

The Organizational Health Inventory
for Secondary Schools: OHI

Organizational health is another broad term that refers to teachers' perceptions of their work environment. Our framework for conceiving the health of the school is based upon the theoretical analysis of Parsons, Bales, and Shils (1953). All social systems must solve four basic problems if they are to survive, grow, and develop. Parsons and his colleagues refer to these as the imperative functions of adaptation, goal attainment, integration, and latency. In other words, schools must solve the problems of accommodating to their environments, attaining goals, maintaining the solidarity of the work force, and developing a value system. Parsons (1967) also noted that schools have three distinct levels of control over these activities—the technical, managerial, and institutional.

The *technical level* of the school is concerned with the teaching-learning process. The primary function of the school is to produce educated students. Moreover, teachers and supervisors have immediate responsibility for solving the problems associated with effective learning and teaching.

The *managerial level* controls the internal administrative function of the organization. Principals are the administrative officers of the school. They allocate resources and coordinate the work effort. They must find ways to develop teacher loyalty, trust, and commitment as well as to motivate teachers and to influence their own superiors.

The *institutional level* connects the school with its environment. Schools need legitimacy and support in the community. Both administration and teachers need backing if they are to perform their respective functions in a harmonious fashion without undue pressure from individuals and groups from outside the school.

This broad Parsonian perspective provided the theoretical underpinnings for defining and operationalizing school health. Specifically, *a healthy school is one in which the technical, managerial, and institutional levels are in harmony; and the school is meeting both its instrumental and expressive needs as it successfully copes with disruptive external forces and directs its energies toward its mission.*

Seven aspects of school health were conceptualized and measured using the Parsonian framework. Dimensions were selected to represent each of the basic needs of all social systems as well as the three levels of organizational control. At the institutional level, a dimension called institutional integrity was conceived as the ability of the school to remain relatively independent from its environment. Four managerial dimensions were conceptualized. Initiating structure (principal behavior that is starkly task- and achievement-oriented) and consideration (principal behavior that supports harmonious interpersonal relationships) were viewed as basic leadership dimensions. Resource support (principal behavior that ensures the availability of necessary classroom supplies) and principal influence (the ability to influence superiors) were conceived as essential managerial activities. Finally, two critical aspects of the technical level were identified. Morale is a key integrative property of teacher life, and academic emphasis was conceptualized as a basic feature of effective schools that linked productive teacher and student interactions. The elements of organizational health are summarized in Table 7.9 and brief vignettes of the healthy and unhealthy school are given below.

Healthy School

A healthy school is protected from unreasonable community and parental pressures. The board successfully resists all narrow efforts of vested interest groups to influence policy (high institutional integrity). The principal of a healthy school is a dynamic leader, integrating both task-oriented and relations-oriented leader behavior. Such behavior is supportive of teachers, yet provides high standards for performance (high consideration and initiating structure). Moreover, the principal has influence with her or his superiors, which is demonstrated by the ability to get what is needed for the effective operation of the school (high influence). Teachers in a healthy school are committed to teaching and learning. They set high but achievable goals for students, maintain high standards of performance, and promote a serious and orderly learning environment. Furthermore, students work hard on their school work, are highly motivated, and respect other students who achieve academically (high academic influence). Classroom supplies, instructional materials, and supplementary

Table 7.9 Dimensions of Organizational Health of Secondary Schools (OHI)

INSTITUTIONAL LEVEL

Institutional Integrity describes a school that has integrity in its educational program. The school is not vulnerable to narrow, vested interests of community groups; indeed, teachers are protected from unreasonable community and parental demands. The school is able to cope successfully with destructive outside forces.

MANAGERIAL LEVEL

Initiating Structure is task- and achievement-oriented behavior. The principal makes his or her attitudes and expectations clear to the faculty and maintains definite standards of performance.

Consideration is principal behavior that is friendly, supportive, and collegial. The principal looks out for the welfare of faculty members and is open to their suggestions.

Principal Influence is the principal's ability to affect the actions of superiors. The influential principal is persuasive, works effectively with the superintendent, simultaneously demonstrates independence in thought and action.

Resource Support refers to a school where adequate classroom supplies and instructional materials are available and extra materials are easily obtained.

TECHNICAL LEVEL

Morale is the sense of trust, confidence, enthusiasm, and friendliness among teachers. Teachers feel good about each other and, at the same time, feel a sense of accomplishment from their jobs.

Academic Emphasis refers to the school's press for achievement. High but achievable goals are set for students; the learning environment is orderly and serious; teachers believe students can achieve; and students work hard and respect those who do well academically.

---

materials always are available (high resource support). Finally, in healthy schools, teachers like each other, trust each other, are enthusiastic about their work, and identify positively with the school. They are proud of their school (high morale).

Unhealthy School

The unhealthy school is vulnerable to destructive outside forces. Teachers and administrators are bombarded by unreasonable parental demands, and the school is buffeted by the whims of the public (low institutional integrity). The school is without an effective principal. The principal provides little direction or structure (low initiating structure); exhibits little encouragement and support for teachers (low consideration); and has little clout with superiors (low influence). Teachers do not feel good about their colleagues or their jobs. They act aloof, suspicious, and defensive (low morale). Instructional materials, supplies, and supplementary materials are not available when needed (low resource support). Finally, there is little press for academic excellence. Neither teachers nor students take academic life seriously; in fact, academically oriented students are ridiculed by their peers and viewed by their teachers as threats (low academic emphasis).

The OHI Form

The OHI is a 44-item questionnaire on which educators are asked to describe their behavior. The responses vary along a four-point scale defined by the categories "rarely occurs," "sometimes occurs," "often occurs," and "very frequently occurs." The entire instrument as it is administered to teachers is presented in Table 7.10.

Administering the Instrument

The OHI is best administered as part of a faculty meeting. It is important to guarantee the anonymity of the respondents; teachers are not asked to sign the questionnaire and no identifying code is placed on the form. Most teachers do not object to responding to the instrument, which takes less than 10 minutes to complete. We recommend that someone other than an administrator collect the data. What is important is to create an atmosphere where teachers give candid responses. All of the health instruments follow the same pattern of administration.

The Subscales

The items that define each subtest are presented in Table 7.11. The items are scored by assigning 1 to "rarely occurs," 2 to "sometimes occurs," 3 to "often occurs," and 4 to "very frequently occurs." When an item is reverse scored (noted by an asterisk in Table 7.11), "rarely occurs" receives a 4, "sometimes occurs" receives a 3, and so on. Each item is scored for each teacher. Then *each item* is averaged for the school. For example, if school A has 60 teachers responding to the OHI, each individual questionnaire is scored and then an average score for all teachers is computed for each item. Thus the average score for the 60 teachers is calculated by adding all teacher scores for item 1 and dividing by 60 (number of teachers), then the same for item 2, and so on. The average school scores for the items comprising each subtest are then added to yield school subtest scores. The seven subtest scores represent the health profile for the school.

Scoring the OHI

Step 1: Score each item for each respondent with the appropriate number (1, 2, 3, or 4). Be sure to reverse score items 8, 15, 20, 22, 29, 30, 34, 36, 39.

Step 2: Calculate an average school score for each item. In the example above, one would add all 60 scores on each item and then divide the sum by 60. Round the scores to the nearest hundredth. This score represents the average school item score. You should have 44 school item scores before proceeding.

Step 3: Sum the average school item scores as follows:

Institutional Integrity (*II*) = 1 + 8 + 15 + 22 + 29 + 36 + 39

Initiating Structure (*IS*) = 4 + 11 + 18 + 25 + 32

Consideration (*C*) = 3 + 10 + 17 + 24 + 31

Principal Influence (*PI*) = 2 + 9 + 16 + 23 + 30

Resource Support (*RS*) = 5 + 12 + 19 + 26 + 33

Morale (*M*) = 6 + 13 + 20 + 27 + 34 + 37 + 40 + 42 + 44

Academic Emphasis (*AE*) = 7 + 14 + 21 + 28 + 35 + 38 + 41 + 43

Table 7.10 OHI

OHI

DIRECTIONS: THE FOLLOWING ARE STATEMENTS ABOUT YOUR SCHOOL.
PLEASE INDICATE THE EXTENT TO WHICH EACH STATEMENT
CHARACTERIZES YOUR SCHOOL BY CIRCLING THE APPROPRIATE RESPONSE.

RO=RARELY OCCURS SO=SOMETIMES OCCURS O=OFTEN OCCURS VFO=VERY FREQUENTLY OCCURS

1. Teachers are protected from unreasonable community and parental demands........ RO SO O VFO

2. The principal gets what he or she asks for from superiors.................................. RO SO O VFO

3. The principal is friendly and approachable... RO SO O VFO

4. The principal asks that faculty members follow standard rules and regulations.... RO SO O VFO

5. Extra materials are available if requested.. RO SO O VFO

6. Teachers do favors for each other.. RO SO O VFO

7. The students in this school can achieve the goals that have been set for them........ RO SO O VFO

8. The school is vulnerable to outside pressures... RO SO O VFO

9. The principal is able to influence the actions of his or her superiors.................... RO SO O VFO

10. The principal treats all faculty members as his or her equal............................... RO SO O VFO

11. The principal makes his or her attitudes clear to the school............................... RO SO O VFO

12. Teachers are provided with adequate materials for their classrooms................... RO SO O VFO

13. Teachers in this school like each other... RO SO O VFO

14. The school sets high standards for academic performance................................... RO SO O VFO

15. Community demands are accepted even when they are not
     consistent with the educational program.. RO SO O VFO

16. The principal is able to work well with the superintendent................................ RO SO O VFO

17. The principal puts suggestions made by the faculty into operation...................... RO SO O VFO

18. The principal lets faculty know what is expected of them................................... RO SO O VFO

19. Teachers receive necessary classroom supplies.. RO SO O VFO

20. Teachers are indifferent to each other.. RO SO O VFO

21. Students respect others who get good grades.. RO SO O VFO

(continues)

Table 7.10 (continued)

22. Teachers feel pressure from the community...............................	RO SO O VFO
23. The principal's recommendations are given serious consideration by his or her superiors..	RO SO O VFO
24. The principal is willing to make changes..............................	RO SO O VFO
25. The principal maintains definite standards of performance..............................	RO SO O VFO
26. Supplementary materials are available for classroom use...............................	RO SO O VFO
27. Teachers exhibit friendliness to each other...........................	RO SO O VFO
28. Students seek extra work so they can get good grades............................	RO SO O VFO
29. Select citizen groups are influential with the board............................	RO SO O VFO
30. The principal is impeded by the superiors.............................	RO SO O VFO
31. The principal looks out for the personal welfare of faculty members..................	RO SO O VFO
32. The principal schedules the work to be done.........................	RO SO O VFO
33. Teachers have access to needed instructional materials..	RO SO O VFO
34. Teachers in this school are cool and aloof to each other..	RO SO O VFO
35. Teachers in this school believe that their students have the ability to achieve academically..	RO SO O VFO
36. The school is open to the whims of the public..	RO SO O VFO
37. The morale of the teachers is high........................	RO SO O VFO
38. Academic achievement is recognized and acknowledged by the school....................	RO SO O VFO
39. A few vocal parents can change school policy..	RO SO O VFO
40. There is a feeling of trust and confidence among the staff....................................	RO SO O VFO
41. Students try hard to improve on previous work....................................	RO SO O VFO
42. Teachers accomplish their jobs with enthusiasm..............................	RO SO O VFO
43. The learning environment is orderly and serious................................	RO SO O VFO
44. Teachers identify with the school................................	RO SO O VFO

Table 7.11   The Items that Compose the Seven Subtests of the OHI

INSTITUTIONAL LEVEL

Institutional Integrity items   *Questionnaire #*

  1. Teachers are protected from unreasonable community and parental demands.   (1)

* 2. The school is vulnerable to outside pressures.   (8)

* 3. Community demands are accepted even when they are not consistent
    the educational program.   (1 5)

* 4. Teachers feel pressure from the community.   (2 2)

* 5. Select citizen groups are influential with the board.   (2 9)

* 6. The school is open to the whims of the public.   (3 6)

* 7. A few vocal parents can change school policy.   (3 9)

MANAGERIAL LEVEL

Consideration items

1. The principal is friendly and approachable.   (3)

2. The principal treats all faculty members as his or her equal.   (1 0)

3. The principal puts suggestions made by the faculty into operation.   (1 7)

4. The principal is willing to make changes.   (24)

5. The principal looks out for the personal welfare of faculty members.   (3 1)

(continues)

These seven scores represent the health profile of the school. You may wish to compare your school profile with other schools. To do so, we recommend that you standardize each school score so that you can easily compare the different tests. The current data base on secondary schools is drawn from a large, diverse sample of schools from New Jersey. The average scores and standard deviations for each health dimension are summarized below.

Table 7.11 (continued)

Initiating Structure items   *Questionnaire #*

1. The principal asks that faculty members follow standard rules and regulations.   (4)

2. The principal makes his or her attitudes clear to the school.   (1 1)

3. The principal lets faculty know what is expected of them.   (1 8)

4. The principal maintains definite standards of performance.   (2 5)

5. The principal schedules the work to be done.   (3 2)

Resource Support items

1. Extra materials are available if requested.   (5)

2. Teachers are provided with adequate materials for their classrooms.   (1 2)

3. Teachers receive necessary classroom supplies.   (1 9)

4. Supplementary materials are available for classroom use.   (2 6)

5. Teachers have access to needed instructional material.   (3 3)

Principal Influence items

1. The principal gets what he or she asks for from superiors.   (2)

2. The principal is able to influence the actions of his or her superiors.   (9)

3. The principal is able to work well with the superintendent.   (1 6)

4. The principal recommendations are given serious consideration by his or her superiors.   (2 3)

* 5. The principal is impeded by superiors.   (3 0)

(continues)

	Mean (M)	Standard Deviation (SD)
Institutional Integrity (*II*)	18.61	2.66
Initiating Structure (*IS*)	14.36	1.83
Consideration (*C*)	12.83	2.03
Principal Influence (*PI*)	12.93	1.79
Resource Allocation (*RA*)	13.52	1.89
Morale (*M*)	25.05	2.64
Academic Emphasis (*AE*)	21.33	2.76

Table 7.11 (continued)

TECHNICAL LEVEL

Morale items   *Questionnaire #*

  1. Teachers do favors for each other.   (6)

  2. Teachers in the school like each other.   (13)

* 3. Teachers are indifferent to each other.   (20)

  4. Teachers exhibit friendliness to each other.   (27)

* 5. Teachers in this school are cool and aloof to each other.   (34)

  6. The morale of teachers is high.   (37)

  7. Teachers accomplish their jobs with enthusiasm.   (42)

  8. There is a feeling of trust and confidence among the staff.   (40)

  9. Teachers identify with the school.   (44)

Academic Emphasis items

  1. Students in this school can achieve the goals that have been set for them.   (7)

  2. The school sets high standards for academic performance.   (14)

  3. Students respect others who get good grades.   (21)

  4. Students seek extra work so they can get good grades.   (28)

  5. Teachers in this school believe that their students have the ability to achieve academically.   (35)

  6. Academic achievement is recognized and acknowledged by the school.   (38)

  7. Students try hard to improve on previous work.   (41)

  8. The learning environment is orderly and serious.   (43)

*Score is reversed

Computing the Standardized Scores for the OHI

Step 1: Convert the school subtest scores to standardized scores with a mean of 500 and a standard deviation of 100, which we call the SdS score. Use the following formula:

SdS for II = 100 × (II − 18.61)/2.66 + 500

First compute the difference between your school score on II and the mean for the normative sample (II − 18.61). Then multiply the difference by 100 [100 × (II − 18.61)]. Next divide the product by the standard deviation of the normative sample (2.66). Then add 500 to the result. You have computed a standardized score (SdS) for the institutional integrity subscale. Repeat the process for each dimension as follows:

SdS for IS = 100 × (IS − 14.36)/1.83 + 500
SdS for C = 100 × (C − 12.83)/2.03 + 500
SdS for PI = 100 × (PI − 12.93)/1.79 + 500
SdS for RA = 100 × (RA − 13.52)/1.89 + 500
SdS for M = 100 × (M − 25.05)/2.64 + 500
SdS for AE = 100 × (AE − 21.33)/2.76 + 500

You have standardized your school scores against the normative data provided in the New Jersey sample. For example, if your school score is 700 on institutional integrity, it has more institutional integrity than 97% of the schools in the sample.

An overall index of school health can be computed as follows:

Health = [(SdS for II) + (SdS for IS) + (SdS for C) + (SdS for PI)
+ (SdS for RS) + (SdS for M) + (SdS for AE)]/7

This health index is interpreted the same way as the subtest scores, that is, the mean of the "average" school is 500. Thus a score of 650 on the health index represents a very healthy school, one that is healthier than 93% of the schools.

Prototypic profiles for healthy and unhealthy schools have been constructed using the normative data from the New Jersey sample of secondary schools (see Table 7.12). Here one can compare the fit of one's own school to the contrasting prototypes. An overall health index of 650 or more is almost certain to be the mark of a healthy school.

Table 7.12 Prototypic Profiles of Contrasting Health Types for Secondary Schools

Health Dimension	Healthy School	Unhealthy School
Institutional Integrity	605(H)	443(L)
Initiating Structure	659(H)	404(L)
Consideration	604(H)	390(L)
Principal Influence	634(H)	360(L)
Resource Support	598(H)	404(L)
Morale	603(H)	402(L)
Academic Emphasis	603(H)	383(L)
Overall Health	615(H)	398(L)

NOTE: H = High; L = Low

An Example

We assessed the climate of Harding High School in the preceding example using the OCDQ-RS. We decided to look at Harding High from another vantage point, the health of the organization.

HEALTH PROFILE FOR HARDING HIGH SCHOOL

INSTITUTIONAL LEVEL
   Institutional Integrity   420 (Low)

MANAGERIAL LEVEL
   Initiating Structure   455 (Below average)
   Consideration   514 (Slightly above average)
   Principal Influence   266 (Very low)
   Resource Support   370 (Very low)

TECHNICAL LEVEL
   Morale   308 (Very low)
   Academic Emphasis   379 (Very low)

   Health Index for Harding High   387 (Very low)

Harding is a sick school. This is a real school; only the name has been changed. Not surprisingly, this closed climate is an unhealthy school. The OHI, however, provides additional data and a different perspective of what is wrong with Harding than did the OCDQ-RS. Harding is a school in which outside groups are attempting to influence educational decisions within the school (low institutional integrity). Instructional materials and supplies are difficult to obtain (very low resource support); and the principal, although seen as friendly, supportive, and collegial (average consideration), has no apparent influence with superiors, who do not take him seriously (very low principal influence). The principal's attempts to maintain structure within the school are below the average of other high schools. Teachers do not get much of a sense of accomplishment from their jobs, nor are they confident in their fellow teachers or even friendly with them (very low morale). The press for academic achievement in Harding is abysmal; teachers have no confidence in the students to achieve.

These new data about Harding supply new hints about its problems. This may well be a school that is being starved. The principal seems in an untenable position. He is reasonably well-liked by the teachers, but he has no influence with his superiors in the central administration. He has been unable to get what the teachers feel are the necessary instructional materials to do a good job. His faculty is demoralized; in fact, it seems as though they have given up. The problems of Harding may not merely be school problems; they appear to be part of a district pattern of neglect.

It would be tempting to suggest changes that ought to be made at Harding, but such suggestions would not be productive. The teachers and administrators at Harding are the best people to explain why this pattern of unhealthy dynamics exists; and, they are critically placed to suggest and implement possibilities for change. Any program of successful change must involve the teachers at Harding. Climate and health profiles are only means toward effective change, not ends in themselves.

The Organizational Health Inventory
for Elementary Schools: OHI-E

The OHI-E is a 37-item health measure. Five aspects of school health are conceptualized and measured using the Parsonian framework. Dimensions were selected to represent each of the basic needs of all social systems as well as the three levels of organizational control. At the institutional level, a dimension called institutional integrity was conceived as the ability of the school to remain relatively independent from its environment. The managerial activities of collegial leadership and resource influence were viewed as basic leadership dimensions. Collegial leadership combines social support of teachers with the initiation of structure to accomplish school goals. Resource influence is the ability of the principal to obtain the material resources requested by teachers. Two critical aspects of the technical level were also identified. Teacher affiliation, a key mechanism for integrating school life, is the friendliness and commitment of the teachers to the school, colleagues, and students that make the school a community. Academic emphasis, the school's press for achievement, is the setting of high but achievable student goals and the commitment of both students and teachers to academic excellence. The fundamental features of school health are defined in Table 7.13.

A healthy school is one in which the technical, managerial, and institutional levels are in harmony; and the school is meeting its needs as it successfully copes with disruptive external forces and directs its energies toward its mission. School health captures the positive contribution of all five dimensions. Brief vignettes of the healthy and unhealthy schools can be drawn.

Healthy School

The healthy elementary school is a pleasant place. It is protected from unwarranted intrusion (high institutional integrity). Teachers like the school, the students, and each other (high teacher affiliation). They see the students as diligent in their learning (high academic emphasis). They see the principal as their ally in the improvement of instruction; the principal is approachable, supportive, and considerate, yet establishes high standards of teacher performance (high collegial leadership). Teachers rely upon the principal to foster a structure in which learning can take place and, at the same time, to be a leader sensitive to the social and emotional needs of the group. The principal has influence with organizational superiors and is seen by the teachers as someone who can deliver the teaching resources they need (high resource influence). The healthy school has no need to coerce cooperation; it is given freely by professionals who are in basic agreement about the task at hand.

Table 7.13 Dimensions of Organizational Health of Elementary Schools (OHI-E)

INSTITUTIONAL LEVEL

Institutional Integrity describes a school that has integrity in its educational program. The school is not vulnerable to narrow, vested interests of community groups; indeed, teachers are protected from unreasonable community and parental demands. The school is able to cope successfully with destructive outside forces.

MANAGERIAL LEVEL

Collegial Leadership refers to behavior by the principal that is friendly, supportive, open, and guided by norms of equality. At the same time, however, the principal sets the tone for high performance by letting people know what is expected of them.

Resource Influence describes principal's ability to affect the action of superiors to the benefit of teachers. Teachers are given adequate classroom supplies, and extra instructional materials and supplies are easily obtained.

TECHNICAL LEVEL

Teacher Affiliation refers to a sense of friendliness and strong affiliation with the school. Teachers feel good about each other and, at the same time, have a sense of accomplishment from their jobs. They are committed to both their students and their colleagues. They find ways to accommodate to the routine, accomplishing their jobs with enthusiasm.

Academic Emphasis refers to the school's press for achievement. The expectation of high achievement is met by students who work hard, are cooperative, seek extra work, and respect other students who get good grades.

Unhealthy School

An unhealthy school, by way of contrast, is a sad place. The school is an arena for various pressure groups to work out their own agendas (low institutional integrity). The principal is inactive and ineffective in moving the school towards its goals or in building a sense of community among the teachers (low collegial leadership). The principal has no influence with superiors, and teachers see themselves on the short end of supplies (low resource influence). They feel they do not have what they need to teach. The teachers do not like one another, the school, or the youngsters (low teacher affiliation). They see the students as academically unworthy; in the view of the teachers, these children do not work hard, do not do their homework, are difficult to work with in class, and are not serious about learning (low academic emphasis).

In all likelihood, the unhealthy school is not capable of adapting to the environment because there is no central leadership. The school is turned into a political arena as it loses its institutional integrity. The principal abdicates, in effect, and goals are compromised. The teachers lose a sense of integration with the school and its mission and see the students as unwilling learners.

The OHI-E Form

The OHI-E is a 37-item questionnaire on which educators describe their behavior. The responses vary along a four-point scale defined by the categories "rarely occurs," "sometimes occurs," "often occurs," and "very frequently occurs." The entire instrument, ready to be administered to teachers, is presented in Table 7.14.

The Subscales

After the OHI-E is administered to the faculty, the items for each scale are scored (see Table 7.15). The items are scored by assigning 1 to "rarely occurs," 2 to "sometimes occurs," 3 to "often occurs," and 4 to "very frequently occurs." When an item is reverse scored, "rarely occurs" receives a 4, "sometimes occurs" a 3, and so on. Each item is scored for each teacher. Then *each item* is averaged for the school because the school is the unit of analysis and, finally, school subtest scores are calculated.

Scoring the OHI

> *Step 1:* Score each item for each teacher with the appropriate number (1, 2, 3, or 4). Be sure to reverse score items 6, 8, 14, 19, 25, 29, 30, 37.

Step 2: Calculate an average school score for each item. For example, if the school has 20 teachers, add all 20 teacher scores on each item and then divide the sum by 20. Round the scores to the nearest hundredth. This score represents the average school item score. You should have 37 school item scores before proceeding.

Step 3: Sum the average school item scores as follows:

Institutional Integrity (II) = 8 + 14 + 19 + 25 + 29 + 30

Collegial Leadership (CL) = 1 + 3 + 4 + 10 + 11 + 15 + 17 + 21 + 26 + 34

Resource Influence (RI) = 2 + 5 + 9 + 12 + 16 + 20 + 22

Teacher Affiliation (TA) = 13 + 23 + 27 + 28 + 32 + 33 + 35 + 36 + 37

Academic Emphasis (AE) = 6 + 7 + 18 + 24 + 31

These five scores represent the health profile of the school. You may wish to compare your school profile with other schools to see how you are doing. Elementary schools drawn from a large, diverse sample of schools in New Jersey provide a rough base of comparison. The average scores and standard deviations for each health dimension are summarized below.

	Mean (M)	Standard Deviation (SD)
Institutional Integrity (*II*)	16.06	2.77
Collegial Leadership (*CL*)	24.43	3.81
Resource Influence (*RI*)	20.18	2.48
Teacher Affiliation (*TA*)	26.32	2.98
Academic Emphasis (*AE*)	14.66	1.59

To make the comparison more meaningful, we recommend that you standardize each school score so the different scales can be compared easily.

Computing the Standardized Scores for the OHI-E

Step 1: Convert the school subtest scores to standardized scores with a mean of 500 and a standard deviation of 100, which we call the SdS score. Use the following formula:

SdS for II = 100 × (II – 16.06)/2.77 + 500

Table 7.14   OHI-E

OHI-E

DIRECTIONS: THE FOLLOWING ARE STATEMENTS ABOUT YOUR SCHOOL.
PLEASE INDICATE THE EXTENT TO WHICH EACH STATEMENT
CHARACTERIZES YOUR SCHOOL BY CIRCLING THE APPROPRIATE RESPONSE.

RO=RARELY OCCURS SO=SOMETIMES OCCURS O=OFTEN OCCURS V=VERY FREQUENTLY OCCURS

1. The principal explores all sides of topics and admits that other opinions exist.....	RO SO O VFO
2. The principal gets what he or she asks for from superiors..................................	RO SO O VFO
3. The principal discusses classroom issues with teachers...	RO SO O VFO
4. The principal accepts questions without appearing to snub or quash the teacher...	RO SO O VFO
5. Extra materials are available if requested..	RO SO O VFO
6. Students neglect to complete homework..	RO SO O VFO
7. Students are cooperative during classroom instruction...	RO SO O VFO
8. The school is vulnerable to outside pressures..	RO SO O VFO
9. The principal is able to influence the actions of his or her superiors...................	RO SO O VFO
10. The principal treats all faculty members as his or her equal...............................	RO SO O VFO
11. The principal goes out of his or her way to show appreciation to teachers........	RO SO O VFO
12. Teachers are provided with adequate materials for their classrooms...................	RO SO O VFO
13. Teachers in this school like each other..	RO SO O VFO
14. Community demands are accepted even when they are not consistent with the educational program..	RO SO O VFO
15. The principal lets faculty know what is expected of them...................................	RO SO O VFO
16. Teachers receive necessary classroom supplies...	RO SO O VFO
17. The principal conducts meaningful evaluations...	RO SO O VFO
18. Students respect others who get good grades..	RO SO O VFO
19. Teachers feel pressure from the community..	RO SO O VFO
20. The principal's recommendations are given serious consideration by his or her superiors..	RO SO O VFO

(continues)

Table 7.14 (continued)

21. The principal maintains definite standards of performance................................	RO SO O VFO
22. Supplementary materials are available for classroom use................................	RO SO O VFO
23. Teachers exhibit friendliness to each other..	RO SO O VFO
24. Students seek extra work so they can get good grades............................	RO SO O VFO
25. Select citizen groups are influential with the board............................	RO SO O VFO
26. The principal looks out for the personal welfare of faculty members.................	RO SO O VFO
27. Teachers express pride in their school..	RO SO O VFO
28. Teachers identify with the school..	RO SO O VFO
29. The school is open to the whims of the public......................................	RO SO O VFO
30. A few vocal parents can change school policy..	RO SO O VFO
31. Students try hard to improve on previous work..................................	RO SO O VFO
32. Teachers accomplish their jobs with enthusiasm..............................	RO SO O VFO
33. The learning environment is orderly and serious...............................	RO SO O VFO
34. The principal is friendly and approachable......................................	RO SO O VFO
35. There is a feeling of trust and confidence among the staff................................	RO SO O VFO
36. Teachers show commitment to their students....................................	RO SO O VFO
37. Teachers are indifferent to each other..............................	RO SO O VFO

Table 7.15   The Items that Compose the Five Subtests of the OHI-E

Institutional Level

Institutional integrity items   *Questionnaire #*

1. The school is vulnerable to outside pressures.*   (8)

2. Teachers feel pressure from the community.*   (1 9)

3. A few vocal parents can change school policy.*   (3 0)

4. The school is open to the whims of the public.*   (2 9)

5. Community demands are accepted even when they are not consistent with the
   educational program.*   (1 4)

6. Select citizen groups are influential with the board.*   (2 5)

Managerial Level

Collegial leadership

1. The principal treats faculty as his or her equal.   (1 0)

2. The principal explores all sides of topics and admits that other opinions exist. (1)

3. The principal goes out of his/her way to show appreciation to teachers.   (1 1)

4. The principal is friendly and approachable.   (3 4)

5. The principal accepts questions without appearing to snub or quash the teacher.   (4)

6. The principal looks out for the personal welfare of faculty members.   (2 6)

7. The principal discusses classroom issues with teachers.   (3)

8. The principal conducts meaningful evaluations.   (1 7)

(continues)

First compute the difference between your school score on II and the mean for the normative sample ($II -$ 16.06). Then multiply the difference by 100 [$100 \times (II -$ 16.06)]. Next divide the product by the standard deviation of the normative sample (2.77). Then add 500 to

Table 7.15 (continued)

---

9. The principal lets faculty know what is expected of them. (15)

10. The principal maintains definite standards of performance. (21)

Resource influence

1. Extra materials are available if requested. (5)

2. Supplementary materials are available for classroom use. (22)

3. Teachers receive necessary classroom supplies. (16)

4. The principal gets what he or she asks for from superiors. (2)

5. Teachers are provided with adequate materials for their classrooms. (12)

6. The principal is able to influence the actions of his or her superiors. (9)

7. The principal's recommendations are given serious consideration by his or her superiors. (20)

Technical level

Teacher affiliation items

1. Teachers exhibit friendliness to each other. (23)

2. Teachers express pride in this school. (27)

3. Teachers in this school like each other. (13)

4. Teachers are indifferent to each other.* (37)

5. Teachers accomplish their jobs with enthusiasm. (32)

6. Teachers identify with the school. (28)

(continues)

the result. You have computed a standardized score (SdS) for the institutional integrity subscale.
Repeat the process for each dimension as follows:

$$\text{SdS for } CL = 100 \times (CL - 24.43)/3.81 + 500$$
$$\text{SdS for } RI = 100 \times (RI - 20.18)/2.48 + 500$$

Table 7.15   (continued)

7. Teachers show commitment to their students.	(36)
8. There is a feeling of trust and confidence among the staff.	(35)
9. The learning environment is orderly and serious.	(33)

Academic emphasis items

1. Students respect others who get good grades.	(18)
2. Students try hard to improve on previous work.	(31)
3. Students seek extra work so they can get good grades.	(24)
4. Students neglect to complete homework.*	(6)
5. Students are cooperative during classroom instruction.	(7)

*Score is reversed

$$\text{SdS for } TA = 100 \times (TA - 26.32)/2.98 + 500$$
$$\text{SdS for } AE = 100 \times (AE - 14.66)/1.59 + 500$$

You have standardized your school scores against the normative data provided in the New Jersey sample. For example, if your school score is 400 on institutional integrity, your school has less institutional integrity than about 84% of the other schools.

An overall index of school health can be computed as follows:

$$\text{Health} = \frac{(\text{SdS for } II) + (\text{SdS for } CL) + (\text{SdS for } RI) + (\text{SdS for } TA) + (\text{SdS for } AE)}{5}$$

This health index is interpreted the same way as the subtest scores, that is, the mean of the "average" school is 500. Thus a score of 700 on the health index represents a very healthy school, one that is healthier than 97% of all the schools.

Prototypic profiles for healthy and unhealthy schools have been constructed using the normative data from the New Jersey sample of elementary schools (see Table 7.16). One can examine the fit of one's own school to the contrasting prototypes. An overall health index of 650 or more is almost certain to be the mark of a

Table 7.16 Prototypic Profiles of Contrasting Health Types for Elementary Schools

Health Dimension	Healthy School	Unhealthy School
Institutional Integrity	583(H)	438(L)
Collegial Leadership	617(H)	363(L)
Resource Influence	595(H)	389(L)
Teacher Affiliation	609(H)	342(L)
Academic Emphasis	578(H)	359(L)
Overall Health	596(H)	378(L)

NOTE: H = High; L = Low

healthy school. We recommend using all five dimensions of OHI-E to gain a finely tuned picture of school health.

An Example

Kennedy Elementary School, a healthy school, is one of the schools in a continuing study of school health and effectiveness. Kennedy is also an effective school in terms of student achievement. Basic skill scores for students rank among the highest in the state. Let us examine the health profile of this school.

HEALTH PROFILE FOR KENNEDY ELEMENTARY SCHOOL

INSTITUTIONAL LEVEL
    Institutional Integrity   649 (Very high)

MANAGERIAL LEVEL
    Collegial Leadership   594 (High)
    Resource Influence   670 (Very high)

TECHNICAL LEVEL
    Teacher Affiliation   549 (Above average)
    Academic Emphasis   634 (Very high)

    Health Index for Kennedy Elementary   619 (Very high)

Kennedy Elementary School is a good place to work and a great place to go to school. The expectation of high student achievement is met by students who work hard, are cooperative, and respect each other (high academic emphasis). Teachers are committed to their students and colleagues. Although teachers are friendly with each other (above average affiliation), their primary orientation is to their students. The principal at Kennedy is respected by her superiors, influences them, and obtains all instructional materials that are needed by her teachers (high resource influence). The principal also is respected by her subordinates who describe her as friendly, open, and supportive. At the same time, she sets the tone for high performance (high collegial leadership). Kennedy is a healthy school not to be tampered with.

A Conclusion and a Caution

Why use the climate and health inventories? Will they make schools better? There are no guarantees or quick fixes. But we believe that open and healthy schools are better schools. Teachers are more productive, administrators are more reflective, and students achieve at higher levels. Academic emphasis is an integral part of an open, healthy school. True, the climate of a school can be open and student achievement not high, but when openness is linked with a press for achievement—that is, high but achievable student goals are set, the learning environment is orderly and serious, teachers believe students can achieve, and students are committed to doing well—schools are successful. Students achieve at high levels.

We return to Harding High School by presenting the comprehensive health and climate picture of the school. Figure 7.2 compares Harding's profile with the prototype of the open and healthy school. Harding is a school that must change if teachers and students are to be productive. Unfortunately, administrators at Harding act as if they are unaware of the problems or unwilling to engage in the task of change. They hunker down in the hope that their problems will go away.

Not all administrators react this way. In fact, most are curious about the character of the workplace and welcome a systematic look at what is happening in their school. The health and climate instruments are simple devices that do the job easily. There is an initial phase of enthusiasm with the measures as administrators see both a way to capture the tone of their school and a direction for improvement. In larger districts, the instruments have even

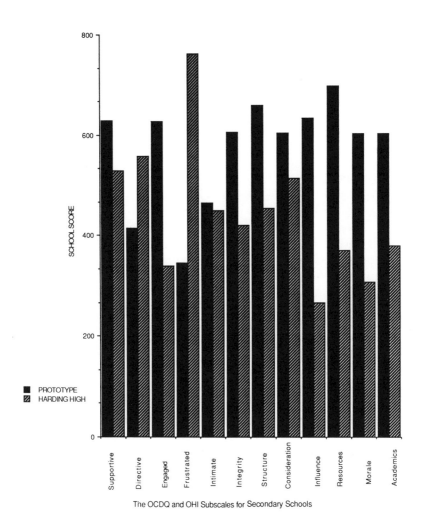

Figure 7.2. A Comparison of Harding High with the Prototype of Open and Healthy Schools

been adapted for use at the department level. The optimism certainly arises from the usefulness of the instrument, but not solely. Some department chairs and principals confide that the climate and health results allow them to bring some order to the relatively chaotic state of the literature on change. There is no end to injunctions for school administrators; some have suggested there are more solutions than problems. In any event, administrators who have used the OHI rave about its usefulness. They claim they are better able to sort out how they are truly received by their teachers. For most of them, the news is mixed. Often the message is blunt. The principal burdens teachers with trivia and busywork and does not go to bat for them.

The typical principal response is "I disagree" or "that's wrong." But the issue here is not who is right and who is wrong. The feelings of the teachers are real and based on something. The principal may indeed behave as described or may be misperceived as behaving that way. It really does not matter. Teachers act on their beliefs and perceptions. Principals need to come to understand the basis of the beliefs of the teachers so that they can respond directly and adroitly. The instruments neither lie nor explain, they simply describe. They are tools for reflection and action.

We believe in the efficacy of the OHI and OCDQ, but we would not want to overpromise their benefits or see them used inappropriately. They mirror the interaction patterns in a school. They are the foundations for self-analysis and organizational improvement. We believe—and there is research evidence (see Chapter 6)—that the instruments measure important sets of variables that are related to positive teacher and student performance. Open and healthy schools are good places. People like each other and they like their schools. Trust, commitment, cooperation, loyalty, and teamwork are the hallmarks of such schools. Schools are transformed into educational communities where individuals come to respect each other and help each other. We caution against using either battery of tests for summative evaluation. To do so would be to weaken their utility as tools for organizational development and improvement.

Rather than an impression of school atmosphere, the instruments provide reasonably valid and reliable descriptions of health and climate. The measures are relatively unobtrusive, simple to administer, and easy to score. If teachers are guaranteed anonymity, there is no problem in getting them to respond. In fact, teachers enjoy the opportunity to express honest opinions without fear of retaliation. None of the instruments requires more than 10 minutes to complete. The test batteries should be given to teachers as part of a regular faculty meeting. If half the teachers respond to the OCDQ and the other half to the OHI, a complete profile can be obtained in 10 minutes or less. It is a good idea to have periodic assessments of health and climate.

We encourage the use of the instruments. Simply reproduce them and use them. Share your results with us so that we can refine the measures and develop comprehensive norms. Many administrators learned to use such instruments when they were in graduate school, but their skills have grown rusty. If we can help you, let us know.

Note

1. For information on computer scoring and analysis of your school climate (OCDQ-RE or OCDQ-RS) or school health (OHI-E or OHI), contact Professor Wayne K. Hoy, Graduate School of Education, Rutgers University, New Brunswick, NJ 08903.

References

Anderson, C. S. (1982). The search for school climate: A review of the research. *Review of Educational Research, 52,* 368-420.

Andrews, J.H.M. (1965). School organizational climate: Some validity studies. *Canadian Education and Research Digest, 5,* 317-334.

Appleberry, J. B., & Hoy, W. K. (1969). The pupil control ideology of professional personnel in open and closed elementary schools. *Educational Administration Quarterly, 5,* 74-85.

Argyris, C. (1964). *Integrating the individual and the organization.* New York: John Wiley.

Ashforth, S. J. (1985). Climate formations: Issues and extensions. *Academy of Management Review, 25,* 837-847.

Ashton, P. T. (1985). Motivation and the teacher's sense of efficacy. In C. Ames & R. Ames (Eds.), *Research on motivation in education: Vol. 2. The classroom milieu* (pp. 141-174). Orlando, FL: Academic Press.

Ashton, P. T., & Webb, R. B. (1986). *Making a difference: Teacher's sense of efficacy and student achievement.* New York: Longman.

Barnard, C. L. (1938). *Functions of the executive.* Cambridge, MA: Harvard University Press.

Bass, B. N. (1981). *Stogdill's handbook of leadership.* New York: Free Press.

Blase, J. J. (1988). The politics of favoritism: A qualitative analysis of the teachers' perspective. *Educational Administration Quarterly, 24,* 152-177.

Bliss, J., & Pavignano, D. (1990). *Notes on authenticity and climate.* Unpublished paper, Rutgers University, New Brunswick, NJ.

Bossert, S. T., Dwyer, D. C., Rowan, B., & Lee, G. V. (1982). The instructional management role of the principal. *Educational Administration Quarterly, 18,* 34-64.

Bridge, R. G., Judd, C. M., & Moock, P. R. (1979). *The determinants of educational outcomes.* Cambridge, MA: Ballinger.

Brown, R. J. (1964). *Identifying and classifying organizational climates in Twin City area elementary schools.* Unpublished doctoral dissertation, University of Minnesota.

Carlson, R. O. (1964). Environmental constraints and organizational consequences: The public school and its clients. In D. E. Griffiths (Ed.), *Behavioral Science and Educational Administration* (pp. 262-272). Chicago: University of Chicago Press.

Carver, F., & Sergiovanni, T. (1969). Notes on the OCDQ. *Journal of Educational Administration, 7,* 71-81.

Cattell, R. B. (1952). *Factor analysis.* New York: Harper.

Childers, J. H., & Fairman, M. (1985). Organizational health: School counselor as facilitator. *Planning and Changing, 16,* 161-166.

Clark, E., & Fairman, M. (1983). Organizational health: A significant force in planned change. *NASSP Bulletin, 67,* 108-113.

Clover, S.I.R. (1984). *Organizational climates of elementary schools in New Jersey: A revision and expansion of the organizational climate description questionnaire.* Unpublished doctoral dissertation, Rutgers University, New Brunswick, NJ.

Conway, J. A. (1976). Test of linearity between teachers' participation in decision making and their perceptions of schools as organizations. *Administrative Science Quarterly, 21,* 130-139.

Corwin, R. G. (1965). Professional persons in public organizations. *Educational Administration Quarterly, 1,* 1-22.

Deal, T., & Kennedy, A. (1982). *Corporate cultures.* Reading, MA: Addison-Wesley.

DeCotiis, T. A., & Summers, T. P. (1987). A path analysis of a model of the antecedents and consequences of organizational commitment. *Human Relations, 40,* 445-470.

Doyle, W. (1983). Academic work. *Review of Educational Research, 53,* 159-199.

Dyer, W. G. (1985). The cycle of cultural evolution in organizations. In R. H. Kilmann, M. J. Saxton, R. Serpa, & Associates (Eds.), *Gaining control of the corporate culture* (pp. 200-230). San Francisco: Jossey-Bass.

Edmonds, R. R. (1979). Effective schools for the urban poor. *Educational Leadership, 37,* 15-24.

Etzioni, A. (1975). *A comparative analysis of complex organizations* (2nd ed.). New York: Free Press.

Fairman, M., Holmes, M., Hardage, J., & Lucas, C. S. (1979). *Manual for the organizational health instrument.* Fayetteville, AR: Diagnostic and Development Corporation.

Fiedler, F. E. (1972). The effects of leadership training and experience: A contingency model interpretation. *Administrative Science Quarterly, 17,* 453-470.

Firestone, W. A., & Wilson, B. L. (1985). Using bureaucratic and cultural linkages to improve instruction: The principal's contribution. *Educational Administration Quarterly, 21,* 7-31.

Forehand, G. A., & Gilmer, B. (1964). Environmental variation in studies of organizational behavior. *Psychological Bulletin, 62,* 361-381.

Frost, P. J., Moore, L. F., Louis, M. R., Lundberg, C. C., & Martin, J. (1985). *Organizational culture.* Beverly Hills, CA: Sage.

Geertz, C. (1973). *The interpretation of cultures.* New York: Basic Books.

Gellerman, S. (1959). The company personality. *Management Review, 48,* 69-76.

Gilmer, B. (1966). *Industrial psychology* (2nd ed.). New York: McGraw-Hill.

Golembiewski, T. T., & McConkie, M. (1975). The centrality of interpersonal trust in group processes. In C. L. Cooper (Ed.), *Theories of group processes* (pp. 131-185). New York: John Wiley.

Good, T. L., & Brophy, J. E. (1986). School effects. In M. Wittrock (Ed.), *Handbook of research on teaching* (3rd ed., pp. 570-602), New York: Macmillan.

Good, T. L., & Weinstein, R. S. (1986). Schools make a difference: Evidence, criticisms, and new directions. *American Psychologist, 41,* 1090-1092.

Goodenough, W. (1971). *Culture, language, and society.* Reading, MA: Addison-Wesley.

Hall, D. T., Schneider, B., & Nygren, H. T. (1970). Personal factors in organizational identification. *Administrative Science Quarterly, 15,* 176-189.

Hall, J. W. (1972). A comparison of Halpin and Croft's organizational climates and Likert and Likert's system. *Administrative Science Quarterly, 17,* 586-590.

Halpin, A. W. (1966). *Theory and research in administration.* New York: Macmillan.

Halpin, A., & Croft, D. (1962, August). *The organizational climate of schools* (Contract No. SAE 543-8639). Washington, DC: U.S. Office of Education.

Halpin, A. W., & Croft, D. B. (1963). *The organizational climate of schools.* Chicago: Midwest Administration Center of the University of Chicago.

Hayes, A. W. (1973). *A reappraisal of the Halpin-Croft model of the organizational climate of schools.* Paper presented at the American Educational Research Association, New Orleans.

Herriott, R. E., & Firestone, W. A. (1984). Two images of schools as organizations: A refinement and an elaboration. *Educational Administration Quarterly, 20,* 41-58.

Hersey, P., & Blanchard, K. H. (1982). *Management of organization behavior: Utilizing human resources* (4th ed.). Englewood Cliffs, NJ: Prentice-Hall.

Homans, G. C. (1950). *The human group.* New York: Harcourt, Brace & World.

Hoy, W. K. (1968). Pupil control and organizational socialization: The influence of experience on the beginning teacher. *School Review, 76,* 312-323.

Hoy, W. K. (1969). Pupil control ideology and organizational socialization: A further examination of the influence of experience on the beginning teacher. *School Review, 77,* 257-265.

Hoy, W. K. (1972a). Dimensions of student alienation and characteristics of public high schools. *Interchange, 3,* 36-52.

Hoy, W. K. (1990). Organizational climate and culture: A conceptual analysis of the school workplace. *Journal of Educational and Psychological Consultation, 2,* 146-168.

Hoy, W. K., & Clover, S.I.R. (1986). Elementary school climate: A revision of the OCDQ. *Educational Administration Quarterly, 22,* 93-110.

Hoy, W. K., & Feldman, J. A. (1987). Organizational health: The concept and its measure. *Journal of Research and Development in Education, 20,* 30-38.

Hoy, W. K., & Ferguson, J. (1985). A theoretical framework and exploration of organizational effectiveness in schools. *Educational Administration Quarterly, 21,* 117-134.

Hoy, W. K., & Forsyth, P. B. (1986). *Supervision of instruction: Theory into practice.* New York: Random House.

Hoy, W. K., & Kupersmith, W. J. (1985). The meaning and measure of faculty trust. *Educational and Psychological Research, 5,* 1-10.

Hoy, W. K., & Miskel, C. G. (1987). *Educational administration: Theory, research, and practice* (3rd ed.). New York: Random House.

Hoy, W. K., & Rees, R. (1977). The bureaucratic socialization of student teachers. *Journal of Teacher Education, 28,* 23-26.

Hoy, W. K., Tarter, C. J., & Bliss, J. (1990). Organizational climate, school health, and effectiveness: A comparative analysis. *Educational Administration Quarterly, 26,* 260-279.

James, L. R., & Jones, A. P. (1974). Organizational climate: A review of the theory and research. *Psychological Bulletin, 81,* 1096-1112.

Kaiser, H. F. (1960). The application of electronic computers to factor analysis. *Educational and Psychological Measurement, 20,* 141-151.

Kerlinger, F. (1986). *Foundations of behavioral research* (3rd ed.). New York: Holt, Rinehart and Winston.

Kilmann, R. H., Saxton, M. J., Serpa, R., & Associates (1985). *Gaining control of the corporate culture.* San Francisco: Jossey-Bass.

Kimpston, R. D., & Sonnabend, L. C. (1975). Public schools: The interrelationships between organizational health and innovativeness and between organizational health and staff characteristics. *Urban Education, 10,* 27-48.

Knapp, T. R. (1977). The unit-of-analysis problem in applications of simple correlational analysis in educational research. *Journal of Educational Statistics, 2,* 171-186.

Knapp, T. R. (1982). The unit and the context of analysis for research in educational administration. *Educational Administration Quarterly, 18,* 1-13.

Kottkamp, R. B., & Mulhern, J. A. (1987). Teacher expectancy, motivation, open to closed climate, and pupil control ideology in high schools. *Journal of Research and Development in Education, 20,* 9-18.

Kottkamp, R. B., Mulhern, J. A., & Hoy, W. K. (1987). Secondary school climate: A revision of the OCDQ. *Educational Administration Quarterly, 23,* 31-48.

Lanier, J., & Little, J. W. (1985). Research on teacher education. In M. Wittrock (Ed.), *Handbook of research on teaching* (3rd ed., pp. 527-569). New York: Macmillan.

Lieberman, A., & Rosenholtz, S. (1987). The road to school improvement: Barriers and bridges. In J. I. Goodlad (Ed.), *The ecology of school renewal: NSSE yearbook,* (pp. 79-98). Chicago: University of Chicago Press.

Little, J. M. (1982). Norms of collegiality and experimentation. *American Educational Research Journal, 19,* 325-340.

Litwin, G. H., & Stringer, R. A. (1968). *Motivational and organizational climate.* Boston, MA: Graduate School of Business Administration, Harvard University.

Lorsch, J. W. (1985). Strategic myopia: Culture as an invisible barrier to change. In R. H. Kilmann, M. J. Saxton, R. Serpa, & Associates (Eds.), *Gaining control of the corporate culture* (pp. 84-102). San Francisco: Jossey-Bass.

Lortie, D. (1975). *Schoolteacher: A sociological study.* Chicago: University of Chicago Press.

Malinowski, B. (1961). *Argonauts of the Western Pacific.* London: Routledge & Kegan Paul.

March, J., & Simon, H. (1958). *Organizations.* New York: John Wiley.

Martin, J. (1985). Can organizational culture be managed? In P. J. Frost, L. F. Moore, M. R. Louis, C. C. Lundberg, & J. Martin, *Organizational Culture,* (p. 95), Beverly Hills, CA: Sage.

Mayo, E. (1945). *The social problems of industrial civilization.* Boston, MA: Graduate School of Business Administration, Harvard University.

McGregor, D. (1960). *The human side of enterprise.* New York: McGraw-Hill.

Mergendoller, J. R., & Marchman, V. A. (1987). Friends and associates. In V. Richardson-Koehler (Ed.), *Educators' handbook: A research perspective* (pp. 297-328). New York: Longman.

Miles, M. B. (1965). Education and innovation: The organization in context. In M. Abbott & J. Lovell (Eds.), *Changing perspectives in educational administration* (pp. 54-72). Auburn, AL: Auburn University.

Miles, M. B. (1969). Planned change and organizational health: Figure and ground. In F. D. Carver & T. J. Sergiovanni (Eds.), *Organizations and human behavior* (pp. 375-391). New York: McGraw-Hill.

Miles, M. B. (1975). Comment from Miles. *Urban Education, 10,* 46-48.

Mintzberg, H. (1979). *The structuring of organizations.* Englewood Cliffs, NJ: Prentice-Hall.

Mintzberg, H. (1983). *Power in and around organizations.* Englewood Cliffs, NJ: Prentice-Hall.

Mintzberg, H. (1989). *Mintzberg on management.* New York: Free Press.

Miskel, C., DeFrain, F., & Wilcox, K. (1980). A test of expectancy work motivation theory in educational organizations. *Educational Administration Quarterly, 16,* 70-92.

Miskel, C., McDonald, D., & Bloom, S. (1983). Structural and expectancy linkages within schools and organizational effectiveness. *Educational Administration Quarterly, 19,* 49-82.

Miskel, C., & Ogawa, R. (1988). Work motivation, job satisfaction, and climate. In N. J. Boyan (Ed.), *Handbook of research on educational administration* (pp. 279-304). New York: Longman.

Mott, P. E. (1972). *The characteristics of effective organizations.* New York: Harper & Row.

Mowday, R. T., Steers, R. M., & Porter, L. W. (1979). The measure of organizational commitment. *Journal of Vocational Behavior, 14,* 224-247.

Mullins, J. (1976). *Analysis and synthesis of research utilizing the organizational climate descriptive questionnaire: Organizations other than elementary schools.* Doctoral dissertation, University of Georgia.

New Jersey Department of Education (1984). *New Jersey statewide testing system high school proficiency test: 1983-1984 technical report.* Trenton, NJ: New Jersey State Department of Education.

Ouchi, W. (1981). *Theory Z.* Reading, MA: Addison-Wesley.

Ouchi, W., & Wilkins, A. L. (1985). Organizational culture. *Annual Review of Sociology, 11,* 457-483.

Pace, C. R., & Stern, G. C. (1958). An approach to the measure of psychological characteristics of college environments. *Journal of Educational Psychology, 49,* 269-277.

Packard, J. S. (1988). The pupil control studies. In N. J. Boyan (Ed.), *Handbook of research on educational administration* (pp. 185-208). New York: Longman.

Parsons, T. (1951). *The social system.* Glencoe, IL: Free Press.

Parsons, T. (1961). An outline of the social system. In T. Parsons, E. Shils, K. D. Naegele, & J. R. Pitts (Eds.), *Theories of society: Foundations of modern sociological theory* (Vol. 1, pp. 30-79). New York: Free Press.

Parsons, T. (1967). Some ingredients of a general theory of formal organization. In A. W. Halpin (Ed.), *Administrative theory in education* (pp. 40-72). New York: Macmillan.

Parsons, T., Bales, R. F., & Shils, E. A. (1953). *Working papers in the theory of action.* Glencoe, IL: Free Press.

Pascale, R. T., & Athos, A. (1981). *The art of Japanese management.* New York: Simon & Schuster.

Pelz, D. C. (1952). Influence: A key to effective leadership in the firstline supervisor. *Personnel, 29,* 209-217.

Peters, T., & Waterman, R. (1982). *In search of excellence: Lessons from America's best-run companies.* New York: Harper & Row.

Pettigrew, A. W. (1979). On studying organizational culture. *Administrative Science Quarterly, 24,* 570-581.

Podgurski, T. P. (1990). *School effectiveness as it relates to group consensus and organizational health of elementary schools.* Unpublished doctoral dissertation, Rutgers University, New Brunswick, NJ.

Porter, L. W., Steers, R. M., Mowday, R. T., & Boulian, P. V. (1974). Organizational commitment, job satisfaction, and turnover among psychiatric technicians. *Journal of Applied Psychology, 59,* 603-609.

Purkey, S. C., & Smith, M. S. (1983). Effective schools: A review. *The Elementary School Journal, 83,* 427-452.

Radcliffe-Brown, A. (1952). *Structure and function in primitive society.* London: Oxford University Press.

Ralph, J. H., & Fennessey, J. J. (1983). Science or reform: Some questions about the effective schools model. *Phi Delta Kappan, 64,* 689-694.

Rokeach, M. (1960). *The open and closed mind.* New York: Basic Books.

Rossman, G. B., Corbett, H. D., & Firestone, W. A. (1988). *Change and effectiveness in schools.* Albany, NY: State University of New York Press.

Rotter, J. B. (1967). A new scale for the measurement of interpersonal trust. *Journal of Personality, 35,* 651-655.

Rowan, B., Bossert, S. T., & Dwyer, D. C. (1983). Research on schools: A cautionary note. *Educational Researcher, 12,* 24-31.

Rummel, R. J. (1970). *Applied factor analysis.* Evanston, IL: Northwestern University Press.

Rutter, M., Maugham, B., Ouston, J., & Smith, A. (1979). *Fifteen thousand hours: Secondary schools and their effects on children.* Cambridge, MA: Harvard University Press.

Sarason, S. (1971). *The culture of the school and the problem of change.* Boston: Allyn & Bacon.

Schein, E. H. (1985). *Organizational culture and leadership.* San Francisco: Jossey-Bass.

Schwandt, D. R. (1978). *Analysis of school organizational climate research 1962-1977: Toward construct clarification.* Unpublished doctoral dissertation, Wayne State University, Detroit, MI.

Schwartz, H. M., & Davis, S. M. (1981). Matching corporate culture and business strategy. *Organizational Dynamics, 59,* 30-48.

Sebastian, S., Thom, C., & Muth, R. (1989, August). *Power, conflict, and school climate in India*. Paper presented at the Annual Meeting of the American Educational Research Association, San Francisco.

Selznick, P. (1957). *Leadership in administration*. New York: Harper & Row.

Sheldon, M. E. (1971). Investments and involvements as mechanisms. *Administrative Science Quarterly, 16*, 142-150.

Silver, P. (1983). *Educational administration: Theoretical perspectives on practice and research*. New York: Harper & Row.

Sirotnik, K. A. (1980). Psychometric implications of the unit-of-analysis problem (with examples from the measurement of organizational climate). *Journal of Educational Measurement, 17*, 248-284.

Slavin, R. E. (1984). *Research methods in education: A practical guide*. Englewood Cliffs, NJ: Prentice-Hall.

Steers, R. M. (1977). *Organizational effectiveness: A behavioral view*. Santa Monica, CA: Goodyear.

Tagiuri, R. (1968). The concept of organizational climate. In R. Tagiuri & G. W. Litwin (Eds.), *Organizational climate: Explorations of a concept* (pp. 1-32). Boston, MA: Division of Research, Graduate School of Business Administration, Harvard University.

Tangri, S., & Moles, O. (1987). Parents and the community. In V. Richardson-Koehler (Ed.), *Educator's handbook: A research perspective* (pp. 519-551). New York: Longman.

Tarter, C. J., Bliss, J., & Hoy, W. K. (1989). School characteristics and faculty trust in secondary schools. *Educational Administration Quarterly, 25*, 294-308.

Tarter, C. J., & Hoy, W. K. (1988). The context of trust: Teachers and the principal. *The High School Journal, 72*, 17-24.

Tarter, C.J., Hoy, W.K., & Kottkamp, R. (1990). School climate and organizational commitment. *Journal of Research and Development in Education, 23*, 236-242.

Vroom, V. (1964). *Work and motivation*. New York: John Wiley.

Waldman, B. (1971). *Organizational climate and pupil control ideology of secondary schools*. Unpublished doctoral dissertation, Rutgers University, New Brunswick, NJ.

Waller, W. (1932). *The sociology of teaching*. New York: John Wiley.

Watkins, J. F. (1968). The OCDQ—An application and some implications. *Educational Administration Quarterly, 4*, 46-61.

Wilkins, A. L., & Patterson, K. J. (1985). You can't get there from here: What will make culture-change projects fail. In R. H. Kilmann, M. J. Saxton, R. Serpa, & Associates (Eds.), *Gaining control of the corporate culture* (pp. 262-291). San Francisco: Jossey-Bass.

Willower, D. J., Eidell, T. L., & Hoy, W. K. (1967). *The school and pupil control ideology* (Monograph No. 24). University Park: Pennsylvania State University.

Witkoskie, L. (1990). *Organizational climate in elementary schools*. Unpublished paper, Rutgers University, New Brunswick, NJ.

Index

Administration of instruments,
 159-160, 184, 206-207
Anderson, Carolyn, 8, 10, 130
Andrews, John, 18
Appleberry, James, 18
Argyris, Chris, 21
Ashforth, Blake, 7
Ashton, Patricia, 105
Athos, Anthony, 3
Authenticity, 82

Bales, Robert, 67, 181
Barnard, Chester, 4
 commitment and, 126
Bass, Bernard, 125
Blanchard, Kenneth, 44
Blase, Joseph, 140
Bliss, James, viii, 115, 131, 144, 151
Bloom, Susan, 145
Bossert, Steven, 2, 27
 principal's role and, 139
Boulian, Paul, 121, 122
Bridge, Gary, 153
Brophy, Jere, 153
Brown, Robert, 18

Carlson, Richard, 101
Carver, Donald, 18, 48
Cattel, Raymond, 29
Clark, Elizabeth, 23
Clover, Sharon, viii, 44
Commitment, 121-142
 OCDQ-RS and, 127-130
 OHI and, 121-127
 OHI, OCDQ-RS and, 130-142
 See also OCQ

Conway, James, 105
Corwin, Ronald, 105
Croft, Donald, 3-4, 10-19, 26, 46, 48
 development of OCDQ, 10-19
 unit of analysis problem, 29
 standards for subtest, 36
 See also OCDQ

Davis, Stanley, 5
Deal, Terrance, 3
DeCotiis, T. A., 131
DeFrain, JoAnn, 59
DFG. See District Factor Group
District Factor Group (DFG)
 socioeconomic status measure
 (SES) measure, 132
 See also Socioeconomic status
Doyle, Walter, 27
Dwyer, David, 2, 27
Dyer, W. Gibb, 5

Edmonds, Ronald, 2, 27
 leadership, achievement, and, 139
Effectiveness, 89, 130-141. See also
 Mott, Paul
Eidell, Terry, 27
Etzioni, Amitai, 67

Fahy, Frank, viii
Fairman, Marvin, 23, 65, 67
Feldman, John, viii, 72
 final version of OHI, 72
Fennessey, James, 2
Ferguson, Judith, 145
Fiedler, Fred, 85
Firestone, William, 85, 98

Forehand, Garlie, 4
Forsyth, Patrick, 120, 121, 150
Frost, Peter, 3

Geertz, Clifford, 8
Gellerman, Saul, 3
Getzels, Jacob, 154
Gilmer, Beverly, 3, 4
Golembiewski, Robert, 108
Golhar, Madhu, viii
Good, Thomas, 140, 153
Goodenough, Ward, 8

Hall, Douglas, 122
Hall, Richard, 130
Halpin, Andrew, 3, 4, 10-19, 26, 27,
    48, 50, 125, 141
  "feel" of schools, 25
  development of OCDQ, 10-19
  unit of analysis problem, 29
  standards for subtests, 36
  climate and effectiveness, 46
  See also OCDQ
Hardage, James, 65, 67
Hartley, Carolyn, viii
Hayes, Andrew, 19, 27
  aloofness (OCDQ), 30
Herriott, Robert, 85, 98
Hersey, Paul, 44
High School Proficiency Test (HSPT),
    131. See also Effectiveness
Holmes, Morris, 65, 67
Homans, George, 115, 144
Hoy, Wayne, 10, 18, 27, 42, 48,
    108-109, 115, 120, 123, 125, 131,
    144, 145, 150-151, 207
HSPT. See High School Proficiency
    Test

James, Lawrence, 139
Jones, Allan, 139
Judd, Charles, 153

Kaiser, H., 77
Kennedy, Allan, 3
Kilman, Ralph, 3, 5, 6
Kimpston, R. D., 23, 65, 67.
    See also OHDQ

Knapp, Thomas, 50
Kottkamnp, Robert, 48, 59-60, 85, 123
Kupersmith, William, 82, 108-109

Lanier, Judith, 105
Lee, Ginny, 27
Lieberman, Ann, 105
Little, Judity, 105
Litwin, George, 3
Lorsch, Jay, 4
Lortie, Dan, 59, 85
Louis, Meryl, 3
Loyalty, 125-127
Lucas, Connie, 65, 67
Lundberg, Craig, 3

Malinowski, Bronislaw, 8
March, James, 122
Martin, JoAnne, 3, 5
Mayo, Elton, 4
McConkie, M., 108
McDonald, David, 145
McGregor, Douglas, 1
Miles, Matthew, 19, 21-24, 124
  dimensions of health, 22(table)
  health and change, 83, 149
  healthy organization, 65-66
  organizational health and school
    system, 64
Mintzberg, Henry, 4, 98, 105
Miskel, Cecil, 5, 8, 10, 18, 130, 145
Moles, Oliver, 105
Moock, Peter, 153
Moore, Larry, 3
Motivation and OCDQ-RS, 59-61
Mott, Paul, 144-145.
    See also Effectiveness
Mowday, Richard, 121, 122
Mulhaire, Carol, viii
Mulhern, John, viii, 48, 53, 85
  OCDQ-RS and motivation, 59-61
Mullins, John, 18
Muth, Rodney, 60

New Jersey Department of Education.
    See Distract Factor Group; High
    School Proficiency Test
Nygren, Harold, 122

OCDQ, 10-19
  criticisms, 18-19
  research strategy, 12-15
  open and closed climates, 15-17
  overview, 11
OCDQ-RE, 25-46, 155-171
  academic press and, 44
  administration of, 159-162
  climate types, 38-40, 157-159
  dimensions, 156(table)
  effectiveness and, 142-149
  factor analysis, 37-39
  final form, 31(table), 160-161(table)
  item generation, 26-28
  openness index, 41-42
  reliabilities, 33-34
  scoring, 165-168
  subtests, 32-33, 162-164(table)
  trust and, 142-149
  See also Parsons, Talcott
OCDQ-RS, 46-63, 171-180
  commitment and, 121-127
  dimensions, 52-54, 172(table)
  effectiveness and, 130-132
  final form, 53(table), 174-175(table)
  item generation, 48-50
  OCDQ, compared with, 61
  OHI, compared with, 130-141
  personal view, 47
  pilot study, 50-52
  practice implications, 63, 149-151
  reliabilities, 54, 57
  research implications, 63, 151-153
  scoring, 173-179
  subtests, 52-57, 176-178(table)
  trust and, 114-121
  unit of analysis, 50-51
OCQ, 131. *See also* Commitment
Ogawa, Rodney, 8, 10, 18, 130
OHI, 64-84, 181-193
  administration, 184
  commitment and, 137-141
  dimensions, 73-74, 183(table)
  effectiveness, 130-141, 136(table)
  final version, 72(table),
    186-187(table)
  health index, 79-81
  healthy school, 68, 181-182

OCDQ-RS and, 130-141
  parsonian theory, 67-70, 181-182
  reliabilities, 75
  scoring, 185-192
  subtests, 75-76, 188-190(table)
  trust and, 107-114, 135-136
OHI-E, 65-106, 193-204
  dimensions, 93-96, 96(table),
    195(table)
  final form, 198-199(table)
  health index, 103
  parsonian framework, 96-100,
    97(table), 193-194
  practice implications, 105-106
  reliabilities, 93
  research implications, 103-105
  scoring, 196-204
  subtests, 200-202(table)
Organizational climate
  culture, compared with, 4-5, 7-9,
    9(table)
  defined, 10
  history, 3-4, 10
  personality metaphor, 4, 9-10
Organizational Climate Description
  Questionnaire. *See* OCDQ;
    OCDQ-RS
Organizational Climate Description
  Questionnaire for Elementary
  Schools. *See* OCDQ-RE
Organizational culture, 4-9
  assumptions, 5
  climate and, 9(table)
  defined, 5
  norms and values, 6-7
Organizational health, 19-24
  climate and, 19-22
  early measures, 23-24
  See also Miles, Matthew; OHI;
    OHI-E
Organizational Health Description
  Questionnaire. *See* OHDQ
Organizational Health Inventory for
  Elementary Schools. *See* OHI-E
Organizational Health Inventory for
  Secondary Schools. *See* OHI
Ouchi, William, 3, 6, 8
  productivity and trust, 82

Pace, Charles, 3
Packard, John, 27
Parsons, Talcott
  commitment and integration, 134
  OHI and, 67-70
  parsonian framework, 69(table),
    96-100, 97(table), 114,
    130-131, 138, 181-182,
    193-194
Pascale, Richard, 3
Patterson, Kerry, 5
Pavignano, Deborah, viii, 151
Pelz, Donald, 125
Peters, Thomas, 3, 6, 82
Pettigrew, Andrew, 3
Podgurski, Thomas, viii, 86
Porter, Lyman, 121, 122
Purkey, Stewart, 2, 27

Radcliffe-Brown, Alfred, 8
Ralph, John, 2
Rees, Richard, 125
Rimmer, Robert, viii
Rokeach, Milton, 10
Rosenholtz, Susan, 105
Rotter, Rudolph, 108
Rowan, Brian, 2, 27
Rummel, R. J., 29, 77
Rutgers Research Group on Organiza-
  tional Behavior, 56

Saxton, Mary, 3
Schein, Edgar, 3, 5
Schneider, Benjamin, 122
Schwandt, D. R., 18
Schwartz, Howard, 5
Sebastian, Soosai, 60
Selznick, Phillip, 4
Sergiovanni, Thomas, 18, 48
Serpa, Roy, 3
SES. See Socioeconomic status
Sheldon, Mary, 122
Shils, Edward, 67, 181

Silver, Paula, 18
Simon, Herbert, 122
Sirotnik, Kenneth, 28, 50
  unit of analysis problem, 28-29,
    50-51
Slavin, Robert, 107
Smith, Marshall, 2, 27
Socioeconomic status (SES), 91
  achievement, commitment, institu-
    tional integrity, trust, and,
    131-142
Sonnabend, Leslie, 23, 65, 67
Stern, George, 3
Stringer, Richard, 3
Summers, T. P., 131

Tagiuri, Renato, 3, 4, 10
Tangri, Susan, 105
Tarter, C. John, 82, 109, 115, 120, 123,
    131, 144, 151
Theory Z, 3
Thom, Carl, 60
Travlos, Arthur, viii
Trust, 82
  OCDQ-RE, 142-146, 147(table)
  OCDQ-RS and, 114-121, 138(table)
  OHI and, 107-114, 138(table)

Unit of analysis problem, 28-29, 50-51

Vroom, Victor, 59

Waldman, Bruce, 48
Waller, Willard, 27
Waterman, Robert, 3, 6, 82
Watkins, James, 18
Webb, Rodman, 105
Weinstein, Rhona S., 140
Wilcox, Kay, 59
Wilkins, Allan, 3, 4, 8
Willower, Donald, 27
Witkowski, Louise, viii, 145
Woolfolk, Anita, viii

About the Authors

Wayne K. Hoy, former Chairman of the Department of Educational Administration and Associate Dean of Academic Affairs at Rutgers University, is now a professor in the Graduate School of Education. Professor Hoy received his B. A. degree from Lock Haven State College in 1959 and his D. Ed. from The Pennsylvania State University in 1965. His primary research interests are theory and research in administration, the sociology of organizations, and the social psychology of administration. In 1973 he received the Lindback Foundation Award for Distinguished Teaching, and in 1987 the Alumni Award for Professional Research. He is past secretary-treasurer of the National Conference of Professors of Educational Administration (NCPEA) and is past president of the University Council for Educational Administration (UCEA). He is a past member of the editorial board of the *Educational Administration Quarterly* and currently serves on the editorial board of the *Journal of Educational Administration*. Professor Hoy is coauthor with Professors D. J. Willower and T. J. Eidell of *The School and Pupil Control Ideology* (1967); with Professor Cecil Miskel of *Educational Administration: Theory, Research, and Practice* (1987); and with Patrick Forsyth of *Effective Supervision: Theory into Practice* (1986). His work has been published extensively in the research and professional literature.

C. John Tarter is an Assistant Professor in the Department of Educational Administration at St. John's University in New York City. He is a former college administrator and public school teacher. He received his B. A. degree from the California State College at San Bernardino in 1966; his M. A. degree from the University of California, Riverside, in 1969; and his Ed. D. from Rutgers University in 1984. He was a recipient of the Phi Delta

Kappa Research Award in 1976. He has published in the *Journal of Educational Administration, Educational Administration Quarterly, High School Journal, Planning and Changing,* and *The Journal of Research and Development in Education.* Professor Tarter's research interests lie in the areas of organizational behavior, organizational structures, and research methodologies.

Robert B. Kottkamp is Associate Professor and directs the doctoral program in Educational Administration and Policy Studies in the School of Education, Hofstra University. His long-term research interests include the study of teaching as an occupation, the principalship, school climate and effectiveness, and the use of reflection as a means for improving teaching and administrative behavior. His studies have appeared in *Phi Delta Kappan, Educational Administration Quarterly, Journal of Research and Development in Education, Alberta Journal of Educational Research,* and *Education in Urban Society.* With several administrators, teachers, and university colleagues, he currently is exploring the relationship between developing more reflective practice and the improvement of school climate and effectiveness.

DATE DUE			

Hoy   238803